**Energy
Decision
Making**

Energy Decision Making

**The Interaction of
Law and Policy**

Joseph P. Tomain
Drake University
Sheila S. Hollis
Butler, Binion, Rice,
Cook & Knapp

LexingtonBooks
D.C. Heath and Company
Lexington, Massachusetts
Toronto

Library of Congress Cataloging in Publication Data
Tomain, Joseph P., 1948–
   Energy decision making.

   Includes index.
   1. Power resources—Law and legislation—United States.
2. Administrative law—United States. 3. Administrative procedure—
United States—Decision making. I. Hollis, Sheila S. II. Title.
KF2120.T65   1982   346.7304'679   81–47747
ISBN 0–669–04800–3   347.3064679

Published simultaneously in Canada

Printed in the United States of America

International Standard Book Number: 0–669–04800–3

Library of Congress Catalog Card Number: 81–47747

*To Windsong, John, and Emily—for
your generous love.*

*To my parents,
Joseph and Bernice Tomain.*

Contents

Acknowledgments

How the federal government makes decisions concerning natural resources used to produce energy is the subject of this book. *Energy* is
defined as the capacity to do work, and, aside from the work of the
authors, the energy of others must be gratefully acknowledged.

Drake University Law School partially supported the research of this
book with a grant to Joseph Tomain for the summer of 1981. He was
very ably assisted in his research efforts by Bryan Rachlin, class of 1980,
and Pamela Greenman, class of 1983. Finally, Professor Tomain sincerely
expresses his gratitude to Ms. Karla Westberg for her excellent and
cheerful secretarial assistance.

The law firm of Butler, Binion, Rice, Cook and Knapp graciously
supported and encouraged this undertaking by Sheila Hollis. A special
note of thanks should go to Anne Siegel, an associate of the firm, who
assisted in research, and to Lori Knoernschild for her aid in typing and
proofreading as well as to Linda Parks and Cheryl Powell who helped
type the book.

Introduction

Energy, and the issues of its availability and price, has been prominent in the public consciousness for less than a decade. Prior to the Arab oil embargo in October 1973 the only publicly discerned or recognized central-government policy regarding energy was to assume the continued supply of cheap abundant resources to feed the needs of the energy-hungry country. About 1970 policymakers awakened to the possibility that domestic supplies of cheap, readily obtainable energy were disappearing. To supplement declining domestic supplies and satisfy increased national demand, the nation became increasingly dependent on foreign-energy sources. That dependence, although reduced, continues today, and our government's energy decisions during the past decade directly reflect perceptions of the magnitude of that dependence.

When supplies of energy were abundant and costs were relatively low, government regulation affecting energy was generally effected through common-law doctrine, that is, judge-made case law. Doctrines such as those of prior appropriation and the rule of capture were created and administered by the states. The primary purpose of these laws was the protection of a particular state's (usually a producing state's) interest in a particular resource. The rules developed to conserve the oil and natural-gas supplies of the state while encouraging proper drainage of hydrocarbon reserves. This disposition of energy resources provided a predictable flow of these fuels into the American economy. The philosophy of conservation through controlled production dominated the 1950s and 1960s. After a tumultuous attempt to reshape totally energy policies by the Carter administration, the simple formula of the past is once again a comfortable port to which the Reagan administration is returning. Prior to the 1970s, the role of the federal government in many areas was relatively pedestrian and had minimal effect on the development of many natural resources. However, energy in the 1970s finally became a power issue—one that engendered public controversy and demanded resolution of conflicts in goals and methods. Although historically the federal government generally had limited its role to the regulation of sales and transportation of some energy resources in interstate commerce, particularly wholesale sales and transport of electricity and natural gas, suddenly the federal government became the focal point of virtually every aspect of decision making in the energy business. From initiation of exploratory activity to the burning of a unit of energy in the consumer's oven, most steps in the process were affected by federal laws and regulations. Exceptions to the laissez-faire noninterventionist approach of the 1950s and 1960s were numerous, however, particularly in times of war or other major emergencies, when regulation reared its controversial head.

Since 1970, the publicly perceived scarcity of domestic supplies, deep concerns about the security of the traditional foreign-energy-supply sources together with severe doubts about the stability of the international energy supply-and-demand pool, have provided the fertile base for the growth of the role of the federal government in the control of energy policy. Although the Reagan administration has attempted to shift attention away from the so-called energy-scarcity mentality and from fear of reliance on foreign-energy sources, the energy issues that precipitated strong regulatory reactions in the Nixon, Ford, and Carter administrations have not suddenly evaporated. Rather, the authors believe that these issues are artificially dormant for the moment. If any major supply interruption from foreign sources were to occur or if demand for energy increased significantly more rapidly than predicted today, the federal government would be forced to respond to chaos. The chaos would revolve around the equitable distribution of diminished oil supply and the economic adjustments necessarily attendant to vast price increases in a supply-constrained environment. A belief that the marketplace can resolve every problem including the critical supply shortage is misplaced. The present administration should not ignore history and rely on the market to ensure even the roughest justice in the distribution of hardship and burden in a supply crisis. Thus, dismantlement of virtually all institutional structures to deal with supply interruption is a simplistic answer to complex issues of governance of the nation in an area of fundamental importance. This observation does not assume that the world has not changed since the embargo of 1973 and the fall of the Shah of Iran in 1979. United States reliance on imported crude has dropped significantly. However, even now 40 percent of our supplies come from foreign sources that, in large part, cannot be considered secure.

It is in this context, then, that this book studies how the federal government makes decisions that affect the allocation and distribution of energy resources in times of scarcity or plenty. At first glance a book on federal regulation of energy may seem outdated before it is published, because laws and regulations change at least with every new administration and major technological advance. Nevertheless, a system and structure by which decisions are made about energy policy, administration, and enforcement of energy-related law is discernible. The purpose of this book is to examine that underlying structure. It is the belief of the authors that the basic energy-decision-making apparatus is in place (even if in exile) and will continue to be called on in the future as the matrix in which decisions will be made. Although it is not a perfect decision-making mechanism, it can work—albeit sometimes in spite of the omnipresent political influences on the process. Furthermore, we believe that energy issues and the government's response to them are reflective of issues in larger society. The topic of this book is an example of how a legal system responds to our society's technological consciousness in the formulation of energy policies. We also examine the long-term implications of that pattern of periodically perceived crises and government's response to them.

Energy policy is the product of complex, overlapping, uncoordinated sets of decisions by all levels and branches of government. It is affected in the most basic sense by factors outside the control of government, including actions of foreign countries, multinational corporations, and marketplace and consumer reaction to political and economic realities. A truly comprehensive energy-policy study, if one were possible, would encompass energy-related decisions made by foreign governments as well as state and local governments. However, this book focuses on the decision-making apparatus of the U.S. federal government.

The book is written by two lawyers. This caveat is given to indicate our particular world view. Our hope is that a larger audience may find our analysis useful. For lawyers, the book will give a political overview of how policies are made in the legal framework we discuss. For the nonlawyer, such as the public official, student of government, industry manager, or layperson we discuss the legal variables that necessarily affect energy decision making.

We look at one public policy area—energy. The energy story as it unfolds in this book has many facets. We take a unique look at it herein— as children of the sixties and as young lawyers of the seventies we have been endeared to a conception that substantive policies of continuity and universal approval are more important than technicalities, more valuable than procedural niceties, and more meaningful than mere processes. Yet, because of the rapidity of change in national and world economics and markets, domestic and international politics, and scientific and techno-logical advances, energy policies cannot be based on universal truths— they are anything but static. For us to make sense of the policymaking process we resorted to comfortable lawyers' territory: looking for struc-tures, not categorical truths, used to decide a universal and critical issue: how to supply the need of our society for energy. Energy has been defined as the capacity to do work. Thus, for our society to work, we must explore the methods by which government encourages or dampens the fulfilling of the need for the catalyst of economic activity—energy. These structures are for the most part fairly static institutions. The energy laws grafted on to the structures change continuously. We, as lawyers, seek solace in the fact that the process by which those laws are formulated, implemented, interpreted, and changed is more predictable.

Thus, our book is about processes of decision making. Part I examines the institutional structures through which energy decisions are made. Within those structures certain methodologies are used to make decisions, and these methodologies are the subject of part II. The final part of the book discusses the types of values inherent in these institutions and methodologies, which are thus reflected in substantive rules and decisions. Lest the reader think that this is a sterile account of legal apparatus we caution that we do not believe that processes are contentless, that institutions are devoid of human failings and aspirations, nor that processes are not often policy determinative. An undercurrent of the book is that the way institutions are structured is reflective of the human values that structured them, and consequently form and process belie the substantive tensions and pulls within any policy. This book describes the energy decision-making process and speculates on the inherent tensions within these processes that have and will affect whatever policies are developed.

Part I
The Institutional Structure of Energy Decision Making

1

Administrative Law

Energy decision making involves all branches of government—the executive, legislative, and judicial. Less visibly but often more importantly, energy decision making occurs in significant part through the less widely known fourth branch of government, the administrative agencies. This latter branch is the primary focus of this book's exploration of the unique way decisions about energy are made in the United States. We have noted the power issue inherent in energy decisions. The natural attraction to power and jurisdiction over major decisions is a raison d'être for government officials' involvement and final actions. This is painfully evident in any study of energy decision making. The undercurrent of desire for power to decide society's major issues is a pervasive theme of our analysis.

Agency Life Cycle

Administrative law has developed in recognizable cycles. How these cycles are revealed in the field of energy law will be explored in part I. The regulation of any industry, in this case a complex system of producers, transporters, distributors, and sellers of energy, starts from the presumption that an industry is best left unregulated and operating in a natural market state. The free market, the hope goes, is the best mechanism for setting prices and allocating resources. If, however, for some reason the free-market mechanism does not run as smoothly as hypothesized, if prices do not respond to demand, if a particular class of consumers is severely injured by the market, or for other policy reasons, then some government policymakers assert the existence of a market failure to justify stepping into the system to correct the apparent market defect. Corrective measures are applied to an industry with the hope and intent of approximating the efficient precision and workings of the free and competitive market, that state where the supposed inexorable laws of Adam Smith fulfill the aspiration that the greatest happiness will be accorded to the greatest number.[1] Once an instance of market failure is found then government policymakers seek a regulatory tool to remedy the ill. These regulatory tools in their broadest classification are (1) those designed for economic regulation, in which case economic efficiency is the goal, and

3

(2) those designed for social regulation, where the goal is fairness or equity.

The effectiveness or efficiency of the regulatory program elected naturally depends on its inherent appropriateness as a tool to remedy the perceived malady. By its very nature the structure of administrative law imposes costs (transaction costs) on the regulated industry and on the government and citizenry in the form of administration, recordkeeping, compliance programs, and studies of government actions. As part of the economic system of society, members of society who use the industry's service or product also share in the transaction costs. These transaction costs can have the anomalous effect of increasing the inefficiency of a market rather than decreasing it if the regulatory device selected is inappropriate for the task or if it is poorly administered. The costs (in efficiency, fairness, or both) of administering a program can outweigh its potential gains. If that is the case then we have an example of regulatory failure—the regulatory device simply does not work—the door has so many locks on it that it falls of its own weight. Basically, two choices are available at this point. The arm of government can choose to deregulate an industry or segment of an industry (as in the case of the decontrol of crude oil) or the government can undertake some type of regulatory reform. In the chapters to come we will discuss the predicate for regulation, the regulatory tools available to correct instances of perceived market failure, the regulatory tools available to deal with the fault in the system, reasons for failure of those regulatory devices, and possible ways to correct the breakdown of the regulatory process.

A Short History of Administrative Law

The most significant, and perhaps intractable, contribution that the United States has made to world legal systems is administrative law. Virtually no citizen, let alone lawyer, can escape dealing with administrative agencies at some level of government on a daily basis. Agencies and their outpouring of paper and politics pervade our legal structure and fashion our lives in the most fundamental respects. In the realm of energy resources, the prices of oil, gas, electricity, coal, and renewable energy are directly and indirectly affected by the actions of such federal agencies as the Department of Energy, Treasury Department, Department of Interior, and departments of Commerce and State. Your electric or gas bill essentially is the product of decisions by your local state public-utility commission. More law is made by administrative agencies and departments than by the courts and Congress combined. The total dollar value of decisions made by administrative bodies outweighs that made by the court system. Thus, it is of absolute importance to understand the function, operation, and rules of the game in these less-than-celebrated bodies.

Although prototypes of regulatory agencies can be found in the late eighteenth century, the first true American federal regulatory agency, the Interstate Commerce Commission (ICC), was born in 1887. The ICC was established primarily to regulate the railroad industry, a paradigmatic example of a monopoly. The size of and entry costs for starting a railroad were and are prohibitive for all except very large and well-endowed financiers. Consequently, few railroad companies were established. Once they were entrenched the market forces that could be manipulated by the few actors in the industry were designed to keep potential competitors out. Once this was accomplished, rates for railroad services could be set without regard to competition. Thus consumers paid higher prices than those that would have prevailed in a true free competitive market. The ICC was authorized by the delegated authority of the Congress to respond to this monopolistic situation by granting licenses to operate railroads along certain routes and by the establishing of just and reasonable rates for the services offered by the railroads. Thus, the first phase of administrative law, as demonstrated in the ICC experience, can be characterized as the federal government (1) perceiving individual instances of market imperfections or market dislocations and (2) responding by creation of the agency to oversee the economic regulation of a specific industry.

The next phase in the evolution of administrative law is the period of the rapid growth and expansion in the number of agencies and their jurisdictional reach. The explosive growth phase occurred during the Roosevelt administration's New Deal era. Instead of individual responses to individual industry problems this period of growth sought to remedy the ills and malfunctions of the whole economy. Basically, these agencies, most of which still exist and function today, were created for purposes of wholesale economic regulation.

The New Deal agencies are said to have been created because of three notable characteristics.[2] First, administrative agencies are theorized to have expertise in the subject area. Agencies are created primarily because Congress as a body cannot effectively cope with the subtleties and complexities that surround the regulation of complicated, monopolistic industries with the necessary degree of sophistication. Agencies are the specialized bodies, creations of Congress, charged with administering certain laws and regulations requiring specialized expertise. The second desired characteristic of the administrative agencies is that they are to be insulated from direct political control. Federal administrative-agency heads are not elected, and this freedom from direct political accountability was thought to allow officials to operate without the threat of decisional compromise because of political pressure. Those bodies known as "independent agencies," which are answerable to but distinct from the legislature, are particularly insulated from political pressure and are designed to function free of direct influence of the executive. Third, the agencies were to be shielded from overburdensome and unnecessarily detailed judicial oversight. Strict limitation on judicial review was a basic precept in the creation of the agency. Courts were not to interfere with agency decisions unless the agency acted in an arbitrary and capricious manner or acted without substantial evidence to support its decision. These three ideals comprise the model of the New Deal agency characteristics.

The Federal Power Commission (FPC) is an example of an agency that grew to follow the precepts of the New Deal agency. Its jurisdiction, at its inception in 1920, was limited to matters involving the hydroelectric resources of the country. However, in the New Deal era it was transformed into an agency with the power to set rates for the wholesale prices of electricity and natural gas sold or transported in interstate commerce. With these powers the FPC could develop intense expertise in the operations of these industries. Thus emerged the first energy regulatory agency.

The second growth of administrative agencies occurred during the Great Society era of the 1960s. These agencies did not grow in response to the political and economic climate of the 1930s, which called primarily for economic relief and protection through regulation. Rather, these agencies were created in an atmosphere of a society with a relatively healthy economy in which wealth and access to the American postwar dream were perceived by many to be unevenly and discriminatorily distributed. These agencies were primarily designed to redress social and environmental ills. They created entitlements and sought, and still seek (albeit in a significantly reduced manner), a proper and just distribution of the wealth as well as the burdens of society. Instead of concentrating on economic regulation, the second crop of agencies promulgated social, health, safety, and environmental regulations. Eventually, however, the goals of these agencies were pursued in a manner that affected at least indirectly the economy of the country. Further, in a declining economy and with the emergence of a psychology of scarcity the goals of these agencies are perceived as threatening. Thus, in the final analysis, socially and environmentally oriented agencies became intertwined with the same issues that led to the creation of the New Deal agencies. In this context, the Reagan administration has eliminated or severely pruned these agencies to free the economy from unnecessary regulation and thus restore economic well-being through the free market.

The structure of the 1960s agency as defined by Congress, was different from the New Deal agency, however. The basic difference was that the agencies were to be principal architects of policymaking rather than Congress. Congress set a broad standard, but the agencies were given more discretion to design and develop policies to achieve congressional goals. The devices agencies used to reach that end, such as greater use of rule making and further attempted restrictions on judicial review, support the thesis that agencies were charged, either explicitly or by default, with the responsibility for designing broad policy alternatives.[3] This structural development to invest agencies with more policymaking responsibility was significant and necessary given the changing agendas and competing interests that agencies faced in the 1960s and continue to face today. Presently, agencies exercise extraordinary power over economic and social issues. Not infrequently, economic issues compete with social issues, and reconciliation between these competing goals becomes necessary. One way of accommodating disparate sets of objectives is to fashion a comprehensive national policy. The natural evolution of administrative law in this century has been set in the grand attempt to set a comprehensive national policy in broad areas of social, economic, and political objectives.

We have thus traveled from pure economic regulation, to social regulation, to policymaking charged to honor both sets of interests and still permit policymakers to survive in the political world. Surviving in the political world has been difficult for some agencies—particularly for the post–New Deal and Great Society agency the Department of Energy (DOE). It was influenced by both the original economic-regulation emphasis of the New Deal agencies and the social and environmental orientations of the Great Society agencies. At this writing it has been dismantled indirectly through a series of crude budget cuts and is threatened with total elimination by the Reagan administration. Many of its functions, should it be eliminated by Congress according to the Reagan plan, will be parceled out to other agencies, specifically the departments of Commerce and Interior. Thus energy decision making will continue despite the absence of a specific cabinet-level department charged with those duties.

Energy decision making may be viewed as predominantly or primarily an issue of economic regulation. Nevertheless, the equity of economic regulation is inevitably questioned. In energy, economic and equity variables explicitly or implicitly require development of a policy to weigh the impact of decisions by government on real people and businesses. This book later explores the two questions of what is the proper balance between economic regulation and the equity of its effects on the citizens of the country and how should that balance be achieved.

The Administrative Procedure Act

Within the last two decades federal administrative agencies have grown in size and number. This trend may now be checked by the policies of the Reagan administration, although even now the number of regulations produced annually are staggering. In a field such as energy, which changes rapidly because of continuing changes in supply, markets, and technology, regulatory responses must respond quickly as well. The economic and technological imperatives coupled with the fact that administrative law is predominantly procedural in nature raises the question of the efficacy and efficiency of a general overarching arrangment of sometimes static administrative laws and procedures.

All administrative agencies are guided by the Administrative Procedure Act (APA).[4] The APA is the framework of the entire administration-agency structure. The APA also bridges agency action to the judicial-review process. This relatively compact law, as its name implies, is essentially procedural in nature and sets the ground rules for administrative law making. Familiarity with the APA is vital because it sets the boundaries within which an agency must operate. The APA is designed to serve as a check against excessive judicial interference with agency decisions by limiting courts' authority to overrrule or set aside only those decisions that are arbitrary or are not supported by substantial evidence.

One issue indirectly examined in this book is whether this general procedural law functions adequately. Should administrative law become more substantive and should that substance relate more to the subject of the regulation? Can the APA serve both the ICC and the DOE satisfactorily? Should, for example, the administrative regulations that govern the Department of Energy uniquely reflect the idiosyncratic policies of that department? If so, how should the agency and agency procedures reflect this linkage?

Scope of Agency Authority

Administrative agencies are described as the fourth branch of government. This description is euphemistic, however, because agencies are not creatures of the Constitution; rather they are creations of Congress. Before a federal administrative agency may exist it must be created by Congress through a statute. Thus, one of the most fundamental challenges to any particular administrative action is one that questions the agency's legitimacy. To put it another way, does the agency have the power to exercise authority in a particular way or does the agency properly act within the scope of powers delegated to it by Congress? An attack on agency action on the ground that the agency exceeded the scope of delegation is often an academic exercise, because congressional delegation tends to be broad. However, the point of such a challenge is that an agency must base its actions on the grant of powers to it by the law creating it. Congress, not the agency, determines the design of the agency and its powers and responsibilities.

Another common challenge to an agency's legitimacy is an attack on the basis that Congress abused its own power by an overly broad delegation of authority to an agency. Congress must first identify a problem area and define the contours of the problem before an issue is committed to an administrative agency. Without sufficient definition the agency cannot proceed to define the contours of its own authority. The truth of the matter is that the U.S. Supreme Court has not overturned a congressional delegation as overly broad since 1935, although there are some signs that the delegation doctrine is resurfacing.[5]

Generally, agencies are created to handle perceived problems in the market that are too complex and chronic to be dealt with effectively by Congress. Because agencies are seen as specialized bodies, focused regulatory entities with specific expertise bound to discharge their duties in the public interest, in a very real sense they perform functions of each of the three branches of government. The basic powers of the agencies can be broadly categorized as adjudicative, legislative, and enforcement. Agencies have the power to make judicial or quasi-judicial decisions by adjudicating disputes in a triallike setting. They are empowered to decide particular controversies endemic to their charge to regulate.

Agencies are also notorious legislators, producing more so-called law through the issuance of regulations than does Congress. The ponderous stuff of agency law making is published in the daily Federal Register and is later codified in the Code of Federal Regulations. These regulations are formulated after public hearings not dissimilar to a congressional hearing.

Finally, agencies are given the authority to enforce their laws. Without the power to enforce the laws the agencies are charged with administering, the powers granted by Congress are hollow. Thus, the enforcement activities of agencies provide an effective barometer of the capacity of the regulatory body to do what its mandate requires.

As will be discussed, agencies perform in a limited arena, each of the functions of government theoretically operating to protect the public interest and to properly apply specialized expertise. Unfortunately, this ideal is seldom realized.

Examples of Market Failure

A formal list of the classic justifications for the exercise of regulatory authority can only take account of rationales based on certain widely held beliefs. Many of the reasons for the focus of regulation in a particular area are based almost exclusively on the failure of a positive economic model to operate properly and are therefore concerned with economic efficiency. Other reasons are concerned less with economic efficiency than with principles and ideals of fairness and equity as these standards are perceived by the law makers creating an administrative body to redress societal injustices. The following sets forth most of the justifications relied on by law makers for imposition of regulation in a particular market.

Control of Monopoly Power

Control of a perceived monopoly is the traditional reason for price and profit regulation.[6] Where economies of scale are so great as to make it inefficient for more than one firm (or a small number of firms in the case of oligarchies) to supply a service or product, or where geographic or economic factors make service or sales by only one entity feasible, the spectre of a natural monopolist appears. It is generally believed that the dreaded natural monopolist will run amok and charge higher rates for its services than would be charged in a free market. To stem abuses of the free-market-pricing system of choice and competition the government steps in, to act in the "public interest," to set prices, or to establish access to markets. This government intervention is designed to approximate the results that would prevail if the free market existed.

Rent Control

Those who own interests in a commodity may earn windfall profits, a kind of economic rent, when prices increase. For example, those who held large stocks of crude oil prior to OPEC price increases earned huge economic rents when prices went up worldwide. The extraordinary increase in value of the same commodity caused controversy and resentment on the part of consumers. Such public sentiment eventually is reflected in the law either through the imposition of price controls or through taxation of the excess economic rents. The Crude Oil Windfall Profits Tax Act of 1980 is a clear example of a device to recapture those windfalls and to redistribute the economic rents to a larger portion of society.[7]

Correcting for Spillovers

Often the price of a product is established in a way that does not reflect costs of the product eventually borne by third parties. A prime example of this problem is the price of electricity. The public at large may suffer air pollution from coal-fired power plants or may be required to incur costs of relocation because of a nuclear-power-plant accident. These costs, instead of being absorbed by the utility and its shareholders who, in the so-called free market, would be charged with responsibility and liability, may be suffered by citizens who may not even consume the utility's electric energy. An agency may attempt to reroute these costs to the utility, its shareholders, its consumers, or in some cases the taxpayer. Correction for the spillover of consequences and costs to the public is widespread and will be discussed in greater detail in chapter 7.

Correcting for Inadequate Information

Before consumers and other affected persons can make reasonably intelligent choices about where to live, what type of service or product to buy, or how to protect themselves from environmental problems they must have certain vital information. The information the individual consumer may require may be as basic as "this product may be hazardous to your health" or as complicated as weighing the price efficiency of converting from a fuel-oil furnace to natural-gas-fired furnace. In other cases, the information required for a decision affecting a large segment of society may be vast, complex, and contradictory. The Nuclear Regulatory Commission (NRC), for example, requires massive quantities of information before a license is granted to build a nuclear-power plant. These plans are available to the public and are subject to scrutiny in licensing proceedings. Even with the inundation of the agency and the public with information, major decisions may be made that are, in retrospect, wrong or inadequate.

Excessive Competition

A fear has existed, in certain industries, that too much competition will drive a large number of firms out of business. Thus, portions of an industry seek the protective mantle of regulation to guard them from the unleashed forces of the free market. This fear constituted the major reason advanced for the regulation of the trucking, railroad, and airline industries in the 1930s. A typical gambit for a firm or industry that seeks the protection of government regulation is to request an agency to set the rates that a firm may charge for its product. The rate-making process, discussed in chapter 6, effectively guarantees that a prudently operated firm will earn a reasonable profit on its regulated product or service. A large capital-intensive industry such as an interstate oil pipeline may well benefit from such economic regulation. Such protectionist measures have been dispensed with by recent administrations, and the full effects of the market are subjecting affected industries to the rigors of real-world tough competition. The bankruptcy of Braniff Airlines is testimony to this, as is the difficulty of oil refiners following crude oil decontrol in 1981.

Rationalization

Rationalization as a justification is based on the belief that an industry would remain too underfinanced, too small, or would lack sufficient organization to produce a product perceived as needed by society. Recently, with the passage of the Energy Security Act of 1980, Congress set up a quasi-governmental corporation, the U.S. Synthetic Fuels Corporation (SFC), to stimulate development of synthetic fuels through purchase guarantees, loans, and loan guarantees. The government initially accepted the responsibility of financing a new high-cost, advanced-technology industry. Such a role for government is clearly the subject of great disagreement and has resulted, in the case of the SFC, in hesitation and uncertainty as to its function and basic viability under the Reagan administration, which has proposed legislation to abolish it. Such disagreement, exemplified by the SFC, becomes more embarrassing and unavoidable in an administration publicly committed to reduce government spending by reducing or eliminating industry subsidies and market interference. As a result, the SFC, the jewel in the crown of the Carter energy strategy, has become a controversial albatross at odds with the goals of the Reagan administration.

Regulatory Tools

Administrative agencies employ various regulatory tools to accomplish their mandate. A central issue is whether those tools work to achieve agency goals. If the chosen tool fails to reach the desired end or, worse, exacerbates the problem it is supposed to remedy, then there is a mismatch or a regulatory failure.[8] Thus an analysis of agency methods fits into a simple analogue: note the problem, for example, a case of market failure; choose a tool to correct that defect; and, finally, evaluate the effectiveness of that tool in this situation.

The array of devices available is substantial. Among them is the power and authority to control who enters certain markets and industries. Through such tools as licenses and certificates of convenience and public necessity an agency can decide who may legitimately market natural gas in interstate commerce or build a power plant. An agency often has jurisdiction to set rates for a product or service. For energy resources the price-setting function directly affects the supply and demand for a resource and may effectively create a market. In the natural-gas industry, prior to the Natural Gas Policy Act of 1978 (NGPA), the FPC under the Natural Gas Act of 1938 (NGA) and state governments under state law both set the price for natural gas depending on whether the sale was interstate or intrastate. The effect was the creation of dual markets, intrastate and interstate, with disparate availability of and prices for natural gas. Because it was widely believed that the lower prices set by the federal government created an artificial shortage, the markets were unified in large part by the NGPA. The rate-setting function as exercised by the FPC under the NGA had worked to segregate markets. When Congress assumed the rate-setting role by creation of statutorily set prices for interstate and intrastate gas sales, it sought to recreate a national market for natural gas.

Agencies also set standards to guide industry activity. The bulk of environmental, health, and safety regulation consists of the imposition of standards on products, services, and activities. Service subject to regulation under the NGA or the Federal Power Act (FPA) must not be unduly discriminatory. Environmental statutes prescribe pollution limits. Coal-fired power plants, among others are precluded from emitting excessive amounts of substances that degrade the quality of the air under the Clean Air Act. Laws also exist that give the Environmental Protection Agency (EPA) the authority to set standards governing water quality, toxic or hazardous wastes, solid waste, and other matters. Extensive regulatory structures exist to set standards for mine, plant, and worker safety, to name a few.

Agencies have numerous ways of directing the flow of capital and encouraging or discouraging investments. The DOE and SFC are charged with administering grant programs to promote the development of alternative energy sources such as biomass, solar energy, geothermal resources, alcohol and synthetic fuels. Financing devices are available to guarantee loans, support prices, and provide seed money for demonstration projects.

A pervasive monetary tool, not usually administered by any regulatory agency, is the tax structure. Tax policy can be molded to achieve desired regulatory goals. For example, electric utilities—over the past decade the scourge of the financial world because of static or diminishing returns on investment—were the beneficiary in the Economic Recovery Tax Act of 1981 (ERTA) of a number of tax breaks to utilities and shareholders designed to strengthen the utilities and hence encourage investment in the electric-utility industry. A system of tax credits, deductions, accelerated depreciation, and the level of the tax rates themselves determine the availability of money for investment.

Agencies also have enforcement powers. They can sue violators of their rules and rulings, seek equitable remedies such as damages or restitution, civil penalties, and, in some instances, through enforcement by the Department of Justice, pursue criminal sanctions for willful and knowing violations of the regulatory statutes.

The extent of the powers that can be wielded by an agency are set out in the laws establishing the agency as eventually realized in the regulations governing agency conduct. Agencies use different combinations of these tools at different times to achieve their objectives, and no one device is a solution to all an agency's problems of administration.

Adjudication and Rule Making

Agencies have two major modes of decision making, adjudication and rule making. The standards for when each is appropriate or required are set out in the APA. Adjudication is generally dispute resolution that attempts to resolve a specific conflict that affects individuals, an entity, or a group of entities. It is either retrospective, in which the main concern is what happened to particular disputants, or prospective, in which the matter decided fixes the future relationship of particular parties. Adjudication involves a trial type of hearing as opposed to a legislative type of hearing. Section 554 of the APA requires a hearing to be provided in every case of adjudication required by statute to be "on the record after opportunity for an agency hearing." Certain limited exceptions to this rule are enumerated in the statute. Persons entitled to a hearing are given notice of it, and all interested parties have the opportunity to submit evidence to the agency. Parties are entitled to counsel, and agencies may issue subpoenas if authorized by law. Evidence presented at adjudicatory hearings required by section 554 is taken under oath, and the hearing officer is authorized to issue subpoenas, rule on offers of proof, receive relevant evidence, allow depositions, and otherwise govern the course of the hearing. A party is entitled to present oral or written evidence and to conduct such cross-examination as may be required for a full disclosure of the facts. A transcript is required and constitutes the exclusive record of the proceeding that may be relied upon in appellate review. When a hearing is required under the act, section 556 establishes the requirements for the particular procedural mode. The decision that results from the hearing must include a statement of findings and conclusions, the basis for the decision on all the material issues of fact and law, and the appropriate relief or denial of the relief. Like judicial decisions, agency adjudications create precedents. However, unique factual circumstances often present themselves in each adjudication and require a new, specifically tailored decision in each case. Like judicial trials, the evidence and issues presented in an adjudication reflect the special characteristics and unique circumstances of each matter.

In contrast to adjudication, agencies also engage in rule making, which is directly analogous to the legislative process. Rule making is usually prospective and affects large numbers of individuals or entities. Rule making is policy oriented rather than a mechanism for individual dispute settlement. A trial type of adjudicatory hearing is generally ill-suited to the establishment of broadly applicable policies, and in circumstances demanding resolution of an issue that affects a large class of entities the administrative agency turns to its legislative powers and undertakes a rule-making proceeding.

Rule making takes place under the designation of "formal" or "informal" under the terms of the APA. Informal rule making, also known as "notice and comment" rule making, consists of the issuance of the notice of the proposed rule and the provision of an opportunity to participate in the rule making through the submission of written data. The opportunity for oral presentation may or may not be provided. This procedure is also known as a "paper hearing."

Formal rule making includes the procedural safeguards applicable to informal rule making as well as those required in an APA section 556 hearing. The necessity for this type of rule making is triggered when a statute requires that rules be made "on the record after an opportunity for an agency hearing."[9]

The fundamental difference between rule making and adjudication is the difference between dispute resolution and policymaking. The implications of this distinction are important for the formulation of energy policy. Indeed, with the creation of the DOE with its consolidation of jurisdiction over many energy-related programs, and with the passage of major legislation including the National Energy Act of 1978 and the Energy Security Act of 1980, the administrative process was called on to resolve more disputes, formulate more policies and standards, and monitor more ongoing problems than ever before. Such an onslaught of jurisdictional responsibility stimulated the use of the rule-making mechanism more often than the adjudicatory method.

It is not an increase in issues needing resolution that pushed energy decision making toward rule making. Rather it was an escalation in the complexity of the issues. Because of uncertainties present in technology, the economy, and in the world and national political climates in which energy agencies operate, the ramifications of a particular energy decision are not easily foreseen. Yet, in response to the demands to prevent another energy crisis there exists a compelling need to reach correct, well-informed and far-reaching decisions. The realities of society make energy policymaking a decision-forcing process—right or wrong. Agencies have been forced to make these long-run decisions, even though serious questions remain open or unresolvable and much of the evidence necessary to make a well-founded decision may be unavailable.

Another inescapable factor in the energy decision-making process is that environmental concerns have spurred sensitivity to the ecological, health, and safety issues of energy development. As a result, more parties seek to be heard in agency hearings. It is common to have hearings in which the agency, the regulatee, its competitors, and consumer and environmental intervenor groups, seek an opportunity to be heard and to test available evidence on an application for a new energy project. The two-party, retrospective trial-like dispute-resolution mode, which works well for an individual's dispute with another individual, does not work at all for a decision to build a coal-gasification plant. With increased caseload and complexity of issues, an individual energy case may not work its way through the regulatory process to a final decision in a time frame of any use to the litigants. Costs of construction may escalate, financing costs may change in the economy, or loss of interest by the sponsors of a new energy project may occur while the regulatory decision-making process grinds along. Simply, the process may be so burdensome that it falls of its own weight. A standard triallike hearing, with cross-examination of multiple parties and interests—a useful vehicle for sharpening issues of law and fact in definable, circumscribable matters—usually becomes obsolete when applied to the Byzantine issues of energy policy.

A classic example of a dramatic shift from adjudication to rule making is the FPC's experience with natural-gas rate regulation for producer sales in interstate commerce. Before 1954, the NGA had been interpreted by the FPC to exclude independent-producer wellhead prices from rate regulation. Rates for natural-gas sales or service by natural-gas companies (interstate pipelines) were set through adjudicatory hearings. In these hearings the pipeline company was required to demonstrate the justness and reasonableness of its rates before an administrative law judge (ALJ). Ample opportunity to cross examine or present conflicting evidence was available to customers, FPC staff, state public-service commissions, and others. After a hearing before the ALJ, he rendered an initial decision, which the FPC had the power to adopt, remand, or reverse in whole or part. After decision by the FPC, the decision, if adopted, became final within thirty days unless rehearing of the FPC was sought. If rehearing was denied, the matter was subject to appeal in the appropriate U.S. Court of Appeals. In 1954 the U.S. Supreme Court decided *Phillips Petroleum Co.* v. *Wisconsin,* which extended FPC ratemaking jurisdiction to independent producers making sales or providing service in interstate commerce—a huge number of entities previously unregulated at the federal level.[10] The FPC at first attempted to graft its pipeline-rate individual-decision process onto the establishment of rates for thousands of independent producers. As a result of the FPC's procedural response to the *Phillips* decision, the backlog of cases before the FPC on producer prices became so large that the cases filed annually, if decided on an individual basis, could not be finished until the end of the century. Seeing the futility of its approach, the FPC moved to natural-gas rate setting on a geographic regional basis, in adjudicatory hearings, where groups of producers presented their case, as did the FPC staff and intervenors. All were subject to cross-examination. Even this process became administratively cumbersome, so eventually rates for independent-producer sales were set on a nationwide basis in a nationwide rule making in 1976 and 1977. Thus, the individual adjudications after *Phillips* metamorphosed to group/regional adjudications in the 1960s and then to nationwide rates established in rule makings in the mid-1970s. The final step in the producer-pricing history came in 1978, when Congress established "maximum lawful prices" under the National Gas Policy Act, stripping the FERC (the FPC's successor) of much or its discretionary authority to set rates.

An extreme response to the problems and the limitations of the triallike hearing is use of informal rule making with its requirement of minimum notice and comment.[11] The major disadvantage with this method is that it is so open-ended that identification of the basis for a decision through references to specific evidence is often difficult, if not impossible. In response to this problem, hybrid hearings can be designed that use some adjudication, some informal, and some formal rule making.[12] For example, where some facts are particularly sensitive, limited cross-examination can be employed on certain issues, written comments can be taken on others, and oral presentations made on still others. These hybrid procedures may evolve through Congress as it passes new laws, such as the DOE Organization Act, or they may be adopted voluntarily by the agencies.[13]

Rule Makers as Policymakers

Rule making, particularly informal rule making with its scaled-down emphasis on classic due-process requirements, is not the favored mode for agency decision making.[14] Despite the existence of legitimate complaints about the trial-based adjudicatory process, the reasons for the shift away from adjudication and the consequences of the shift are somewhat unsettling. Agencies have become the primary policymakers in energy as well in economic and social issues.[15] As cases increase in complexity each branch of government vies for policymaking power, and conflicts ensue.[16]

In a real sense, the question of which branch has power to make policy is just a stopping point on a political continuum. But the quality of the decisions and policies made is directly affected by the point on the continuum where power resides. Different interest groups have various degrees of access to decision-making processes depending on where the decision-making authority rests. The degree of political accountability of the different branches necessarily colors the way decisions are made and controls which decisions are made. The greatest objection to the growth of rule making lies in the fact that this growth requires agencies (which are less democratically structured entities than Congress, for example) to exercise a greater policymaking function. Thus the question of where and how should policy be made must be asked. Answering this question is a volatile process because matters of energy policy have a significant impact on society. Arguably, policymaking should be handled through a process that facilitates an even and equitable airing of polycentric problems.[17] On the other hand, an adjudicatory approach to dispute settlement is not the ideal solution, because that mechanism is fiendishly time consuming, often inefficient, costly, and self-defeating.[18] Rule making at first glance seems both an attractive alternative to adjudication and in some cases a panacea to sluggish decision making; however there is a sense of dislocation, of omitting important data and parties in this trend toward universal rule making. Rule making is not only a means for making decision on already identifiable issues: it is a creator of original policy. Earlier we stressed that the participation in decision making is fundamentally a power itself. That power is either delegated wholesale to or usurped by administrative agencies in the rule-making process. Only in limited circumstances has the Congress recognized the risk in such delegations or usurpations and taken back the fundamental right to set policy for its creatures of delegation, the agencies, to interpret and administer.

An Introduction to Judicial Review

Once a decision by an agency becomes final, it is subject to judicial review regardless of whether it is the product of an adjudicatory or rule-making proceeding. Courts are limited by the APA as to their scope of review. A court may decide all relevant questions of law, interpret constitutional and statutory provisions, and determine the meaning of an agency action. Further, the court may compel agency action if it is unlawfully withheld or unreasonably delayed. Agencies' actions may be set aside if they are found to be:

1. arbitrary, capricious, an abuse of discretion or otherwise not in accordance with law
2. contrary to constitutional right, power, privilege, or immunity
3. in excess of statutory jurisdiction, authority, or limitations, or short of statutory right
4. without observance of procedure required by law
5. unsupported by substantial evidence in a case subject to section 556 and 557 of [the APA] or otherwise reviewed on the record of an agency hearing provided by statute
6. unwarranted by the facts to the extent that the facts are subject to trial de novo by the reviewing court.[19]

Before a court declares an agency action unlawful the court is required to review the whole record.

Courts and agencies interact in a pattern of relationship created by the APA. Federal administrative law has gained a significant force of its own because of the narrow bases of judicial review. We will demonstrate that developments in the nature of agency responsibility and procedural workings (such as the increase in rule making) further inculcate agency action with the force of law.

Courts have been chastised for interjecting themselves into agency processes.[20] Under most statutues delimiting agencies' authorities, most court review is quite circumscribed. On the other hand, Congress gives birth to the agencies, and the judiciary could be given more authority to review agency actions by virtue of modifications in the regulatory statutes.

There will be no reverse in the flow of power to agencies unless the agency-court relationship is altered by Congress. It has been historically the case that policymaking cannot be effectively accomplished through a strictly adversarial process. Thus, it appears that, until Congress acts to set policy or gives reviewing courts a broader basis on which to review agency decisions, agencies will be required to exercise a greater role in policymaking. Reform efforts to reduce that role, by reducing the use of rule making, are aimed at the wrong target.[21] Efforts by courts to impose adjudicatory formalities on rule making may exacerbate the problem. Other limitations on the exercise of agency power such as limitation of the scope of agency mandate or exercise of a legislative or executive veto can reduce the scope of agency power but will also reduce the effectiveness of the agency's attempts to fulfill its mandate. Agencies were created to deal with problems that Congress could not. The problems do not evaporate when the agency is hobbled in attempting to resolve them. Until agencies are dissolved, they must fulfill their responsibilities under the statutes they are to administer.

This opening chapter touches on the administrative law system that underpins energy decision making. Administrative law has its roots deep in our political culture, for not only do agencies settle individual disputes, they also make policies that touch us all. In energy decision making how these policies are made and the degree of administrative-agency involvement is correlated to the exercise of political power over the agency. The issue of political responsibility and accountability of the agencies and whether the agencies abide by the democratic and majoritarian ideals that pervade our Constitution arise in this search for their proper role. Administrative agencies are undeniably powerful actors in the American political system. It is undeniable that the consequences for a wrongful exercise of power by them can be staggering. With reform efforts in the field of administrative law afoot, we will explore the powers, problems, and potential of the administrative agency.

Notes

1. Although underlying assumptions (philosophical and otherwise) of economics, and, a fortiori, economic analysis of law, can be questioned we do not directly do so here. *See, e.g.,* Michelman, *Norms and Normativity in the Economic Theory of Law,* 62 Minn. L. Rev. 1015 (1978); R. Stewart & J. Krier, Environmental Law and Policy 103–07 (2d ed. 1978); Schwartz, *Economics, Wealth Distribution and Justice,* 1979 Wisc. L. Rev. 799; and C. Fried, Right and Wrong 81–107 (1978). Parenthetically, one of the founders of the modern-economic-analysis-of-law movement argues that utilitarianism is not the basis for this discipline. R. Posner, The Economics of Justice 48–115 (1981).

2. B. Ackerman & W. Hassler, Clean Coal/Dirty Air 4–7 (1981). *See also* Stewart, *The Reformation of American Administrative Law*, 88 Harv. L. Rev. 1667, 1671–76 (1975) and, Verkuil, *The Emerging Concept of Administrative Procedure*, 78 Colum. L. Rev. 258, 261–79 (1978).

3. B. Ackerman & A. Hassler, *supra* note 2, at 104. These authors call the legislation that creates this type of agency an "agency forcing statute." *Id*. at 104. The authors delineate two species of agency forcing, at 105:

Agency-forcing statues should be read in the light of the *principle of full inquiry*—requiring the fullest possible agency investigation into competing policy approaches consistent with the text of the agency-forcing statute.

To make this principle more precise, distinguish several kinds of statutory interventions within the agency-forcing category. The first and least aggressive statute simply forces the agency to focus decision-making attention on a particular question, the desirability of scrubbing for example, rather than on the countless other policy questions that might occupy its time. In contrast to this *agenda-forcing* function, more assertive statutes aim to give a particular policy solution special salience in the agency's deliberations—call this *solution-forcing*.

See also, Diver, *Policymaking Paradigms in Administrative Law,* 95 Harv. L. Rev. 393, 409–413 (1981).

4. 5 U.S.C. sec. 554 *et seq.* (1976).

5. *See,* Industrial Union Department v. American Petroleum Institute, 448 U.S. 607 (1980) (Rehnquist, J., concurring) and American Textile Manufacturers Institute Inc. v. Donovan, 101 S.Ct. 2478 (1981) (Rehnquist, J. dissenting).

6. These categories are taken from S. Breyer & R. Stewart, Administrative Law and Regulatory Policy 13–18 (1979); and, Breyer, *Analyzing Regulatory Failure: Mismatches, Less Restrictive Alternatives and Reform,* 92 Harv. L. Rev. 547 (1979).

7. 26 U.S.C. sec. 4986 *et seq.* (Supp. IV 1980).

8. See, Breyer, *supra,* note 6.

9. 5 U.S.C. sec. 553(c) (1976).

10. 347 U.S. 672 (1954).

11. The procedure for notice and comment rulemaking is:

Under section 553 of the APA, an agency develops a proposed rule, drawing on any sources of information and analysis, including business or consumer representatives, academicians, or the agency's own expertise. The agency then publishes a notice of the proposed rulemaking in the Federal Register, the matter is opened to written comment for an unspecified period, and any interested person may introduce into the record "data, views, or arguments" in support or opposition. The agency has discretion to hold oral hearings or take additional procedural steps to develop the rule further. After considering the proposal in light of the comments, the agency may withdraw the proposal, publish a revision, or promulgate a final rule accompanied by a concise statement of basis and purpose explaining its action. In this original APA model the final statement could draw also upon sources of information or argument not previously raised. Delong, *Informal Rulemaking and the Integration of Law and Policy*, 65 Va. L. Rev. 257, 258–59 (1979).

12. *See*, Williams, *"Hybrid Rulemaking" under the Administrative Procedure Act: A Legal and Empirical Analysis*, 42 U. Chi. L. Rev. 401 (1975); Delong, *supra* note 11, at 262–84 (1979); and, Stewart, *Vermont Yankee and the Evolution of Administrative Procedure*, 91 Harv. L. Rev. 1805 (1978).

13. *See*, Vermont Yankee Nuclear Power Corp. v. Natural Resources Defense Council, Inc., 435 U.S. 519 (1978).

14. *See*, Gellhorn & Robinson, *Rulemaking "Due Process": An Inconclusive Dialogue*, 48 U. Chi. L. Rev. 201 (1981) and DeLong, *supra* note 11.

15. Diver, *supra* note 3.

16. *See., e.g., Bruff, Judicial Review and the President's Statutory Powers*, 68 Va. L. Rev. 1 (1982); Bruff, *Presidential Power and Administrative Rulemaking*, 88 Yale L. J. 451 (1979); Bruff & Gellhorn, *Congressional Control of Administrative Regulation: A Study of Legislative Vetos*, 90 Harv. L. Rev. 1369 (1977); Note, *Delegation and Regulation Reform: Letting the President Change the Rules*, 89 Yale L. J. 561 (1980).

17. Fuller, *The Forms and Limits of Adjudication*, 92 Harv. L. Rev. 353, 394–95 (1978) a polycentric problem is one in which all parts of a dispute affect each other. These cannot be resolved effectively in adversarial proceedings. See also, Yellin, *High Technology and the Courts: Nuclear Power and the Need for Institutional Reform*, 94 Harv. L. Rev. 489 (1981).

18. The weakness of the adversary system for energy decision making is elaborated on in chapter 9.

19. 5 U.S.C. sec. 706 (1976).

20. Compare International Harvester Co. v. Ruckelshaus, 478 F.2d 615 (D.C. Cir. 1973) and Appalachian Power Co. v. EPA, 477 F.2d 495 (4th Cir. 1973) with Vermont Yankee Power Corp. v. Natural Resources Defense Council, Inc., 435 U.S. 519 (1978).

21. Gellhorn & Robinson, *supra* note 14, at 260–62.

2

Administrative Law and Energy

Although every branch of government has considerable influence on the promulgation, administration, and enforcement of laws, administrative agencies have moved into the forefront of those activities, especially in complex economic and social areas that require specific technical expertise. Energy law, like the agencies that spawned it, has developed on a parallel path. Until the 1973 energy crisis, most visible energy decision making generally was done on the state level through attempts to conserve resources and prevent waste and through rate decisions by public-utility commissions. Further, the federal agencies that had some energy decision-making responsibility did not coordinate their activities. Policy, therefore, was severely fragmented and often contradictory.

The Department of Energy

Prior to creation of the Department of Energy (DOE) by the 1977 Department of Energy Organization Act, the mélange of federal regulation of production, transportation, and distribution of energy resources was spread throughout a number of cabinet-level departments and agencies and administrations.[1] Jurisdiction was unequally sprinkled in an inexplicable hodge-podge among varying policymaking and regulatory entities. Any precise count of federal entities with some relevant jurisdiction over energy policy is difficult to enumerate because energy program has been defined as broadly as possible to preserve or expand the jurisdiction of the subject entity. Suffice it to say that the field of energy regulation was and even now is fragmented throughout the federal government.[2] This splintering of jurisdiction, unfortunately, did not end with the creation of a 20,000-person bureaucracy known as the DOE. The DOE, created in response to a real or apparent energy crisis, was originally designed to organize policy and regulation in a coherent centralized approach. The genesis of the DOE was the perception and policy of the Carter administration that a single cabinet-level executive department could coordinate and formulate a far-reaching national energy plan, with a primary focus on combatting American dependence on international crude-oil sources. The word *combat* and the allusion to war is used advisedly. President Carter's battle metaphor, that the energy crisis was

23

"the moral equivalent of war," was thematic in pushing through Congress several major pieces of legislation, including the legislation that established the DOE.

The DOE was not created out of whole cloth. Various existing energy agencies and energy jurisdictional fragments of departments were pulled together under the one roof of DOE with the mandate to administer and enforce what was at the time and yet remains an unresolved and changing energy policy. Both because of the variations in energy resources and technology and corresponding energy-related programs and because of the bureaucratic will to preserve existing power bases, not all pertinent agencies or parts of agencies were made a part of the DOE. Nevertheless, the creation of the DOE represented a controversial, significant effort by the Carter administration and Congress to design a cabinet-level department to oversee and regulate energy-resources, production and marketing. The centralization, at least in part, of the bureaucracy was intended to be the structural administrative foundation for a comprehensive national energy policy.

The DOE assumed virtually all the powers of the Federal Energy Administration, the Energy Research and Development Administration (ERDA), and the Federal Power Commission, thus eliminating these formerly independent agencies at least in name. Most of the jurisdictional authorities of the Federal Power Commission were transferred to the Federal Energy Regulatory Commission (FERC) which today exists as an independent and autonomous body under the mantle of the DOE. The DOE was also the recipient of powers transferred from other entities, including the departments of Interior, Housing and Urban Development, Commerce, Navy, and the ICC.

In addition to FERC, DOE has other discrete organizations within it, including the Energy Information Administration (EIA), the Office of Energy Research, the Leasing Liaison Committee, and Economic Regulatory Administration.

FERC responsibilities include regulation of gas and electricity matters under the Natural Gas Act of 1938 and the Natural Gas Policy Act of 1978 (NGPA),[3] the Federal Power Act,[4] and the Public Utility Regulatory Policies Act.[5] In addition, FERC has limited authority to affect oil-price regulations under the Emergency Petroleum Allocation Act of 1973 through appeal of DOE orders to FERC.[6] Additionally, the FERC has substantial responsibility to regulate the rates of oil pipelines under the authorities of the Interstate Commerce Act transferred to DOE from the ICC. The EIA, as its name implies, was established to collect all energy data for the department and information such as that required by the Energy Supply and Environmental Coordination Act of 1974,[7] and the Federal Energy Administration Act of 1974.[8] The Economic Regulatory

Administration under the DOE Act had residual jurisdiction to administer programs not in conflict with FERC such as crude oil and products pricing and allocation. The Leasing Liaison Committee was established as a link between DOE and Interior on the leasing of federal lands.

Structurally, then, the DOE was a hastily created, massive agency consisting of an amalgam of bits, pieces, and sometimes whole agencies. Besides creating the agglomeration, the DOE was infused by Congress with new authorities. The manner in which DOE was created immediately highlighted two significant flaws. First, the failure to include all energy-related agencies within DOE meant that, in fact, significant energy decisions could be effected by other entities particularly the department of Interior and State and the Nuclear Regulatory Commission (NRC). Second, a state of tension in the department itself among the new sibling sections representing competing technologies and philosophies quickly became painfully obvious. Pronuclear ERDA staff were suddenly competing with soft-technology staff within the same bureaucratic structure. The problems mentioned here proved to make early successful functioning of DOE a never-achieved goal that still haunts the department and the country. In part, the story of this chapter is one of interagency and intraagency conflicts. These philosophical and administrative conflicts have crippled the creation of a unified energy policy. We discuss herein two major examples of the inherent difficulties of making DOE work in pursuit of its lofty goals.

Interagency Conflict

Although there are numerous other agencies and departments that affect energy programs, several organizations totally independent of DOE have a major impact on energy policy. Three of the more substantial agencies are the Environmental Protection Agency (EPA) the NRC (the partial successor to the Atomic Energy Commission), and the Department of the Interior (DOI). The relationship between these entities and the DOE instructively points out how difficult it is to form a consensus even within a single branch of government on a broad consistent energy policy. Indeed, although many direct confrontations on energy policy spring directly from the claims of environmental advocates against the claims of proponents of energy production, the DOE has little direct impact on environmental issues. Although environmental-impact statements are required of the agency by law in major federal actions significantly affecting the environment, the EPA has the primary jurisdiction in most cases to make the ultimate decision as to whether a particular project should or should not proceed on the basis of its environmental impact.

The constant tension between these two forces alone profoundly affects the process of our national energy policy's formulation as we will discuss later.

In the area of nuclear policy the NRC, DOE, and EPA have a jurisdictional interest that is not necessarily compatible with the others. The DOE may wish to promote alternative energy sources, including nuclear power. The NRC may wish to promote nuclear power in the abstract but must do so with supreme attention to safety issues in the particular. The EPA has no statutory mandate to promote production in any form and thus may successfully impede development of a project on purely environmental grounds. Thus arises a quintessential interagency conflict of goals and regulatory policies.

The litigation culminating in *Watt* v. *Energy Action Educational Foundation,* starkly illustrates the interagency-conflict problem in energy policy.[9] As a result of the Outer Continental Shelf Lands Act Amendments of 1978 the secretary of DOE and the secretary of the Interior both have responsibility for leasing tracts of the Outer Continental Shelf (OCS) for the exploration and development of mineral resources, including oil and gas.[10] The amendments to the OCS act were intended to encourage domestic production of oil and gas to reduce dependence on foreign oil. In a manner that took full account of environmental and other concerns the OCS amendments represent an attempt to please states' environmental interests and to address social considerations, antitrust concerns, and a variety of other issues, all while promoting development of the OCS.

One goal of the amendments was to overhaul the bidding system for OCS lands. Although the federal government owns the OCS, historically the central government has not been considered to be in the best position to develop OCS resources. The OCS had therefore been explored and developed by private-sector oil and gas companies. Prior to the amendments, the bidding system for leases on OCS tracts tended to favor large capitalized private interests because generally they could outbid smaller companies through huge-lease bonus bids. The bidding system for OCS tracts thus had developed characteristics skewing power to explore and develop toward the major oil companies, particularly through heavy dependence on front-end cash-bonus-fixed royalty bidding. The system was not competitive in that it worked to inhibit entry into the lucrative OCS by smaller companies that simply could not bid the massive cash sums for front-end payments necessary to secure OCS leases. Through the OCS amendments, Congress added alternative bidding systems to the traditional system to promote competition in the OCS lease market and invested the secretary of Interior with certain discretion in selecting an appropriate bidding system. Although the DOI conducts all lease sales, the secretary of DOE, in consultation with DOI, was required to promulgate regulations governing the use of each particular new bidding system. As a result of Interior's continued use of the old cash-bonus-fixed royalty bidding system, a lawsuit was filed seeking a mandatory injunction against the secretary of DOI and requesting the court to require DOI to promulgate regulations for all alternative bidding systems authorized under the OCS amendments. The suit was commenced because of the delay in Interior's actions to implement the statutes' goals of stimulating competition in this market. The delay was attributed to a jurisdictional squabble between the DOE and DOI.[11] The U.S. District Court for the District of Columbia denied injunctive relief, and the denial was upheld on appeal. One year later the plaintiffs in the original action successfully pressed their claim for injunctive relief on the basis that the DOI had continued to delay implementing alternative bidding systems, thereby frustrating an essential purpose of the OCS amendments. The DOI and DOE conflict resulted in delay in the implementation of a directive from Congress. Only after litigation did DOI and DOE take heed and settle their internecine squabble, but the consequence of delay and uncertainty is an unstable energy program.

Intraagency Conflict

The relationship between FERC and DOE is a curious one in administrative law, creating an inevitable tension between the two entities with potential to stymie effective policymaking and consistent regulatory treatment. FERC's independence is a testament to the tenacity with which power is clutched to the breast of the bureaucracy. FERC's predecessor, the Federal Power Commission (FPC), was the prototype federal energy agency, with jurisdiction over certain hydroelectric facilities on navigable waters, wholesale electric natural-gas sales premised on the interstate nature of those facilities and transactions. FERC now has jurisdiction over these areas. The FPC exercised its power independently of any other federal agency or department, answering only to its creator, the Congress. With the transformation of the FPC to FERC, a new administrative configuration appeared, one with powers trimmed in some areas and substantially expanded in others. However, FERC was and is under the DOE umbrella, and arguably, at least, its previously fully independent decision making can be jeopardized.

Within the DOE itself, an executive agency, significant powers are delegated to the cabinet-level office of the secretary and to executive departments under its control. At the same time DOE has under its administrative canopy an independent regulatory agency. Originally, the Carter administration had proposed the abolition of the FPC as an independent regulatory agency seeking to emasculate its authorities in the form of a three-member board, whose decisions could be appealed to the secretary of DOE. The Congress reacted unfavorably to this proposal and established FERC, or "son of FPC," retaining its status as a final decision-making body. This split of authority finally arrived at by Congress meant that decision-making responsibilities (depending on the resource involved) are likewise divided. FERC, for example, fundamentally retained rate-making authority over wellhead and pipeline rates for natural gas, but the secretary of DOE exercised control over crude-oil prices and allocation. FERC has authority to develop pipeline-specific natural-gas-curtailment plans, but the secretary of DOE was to set national curtailment priorities. Even more curious is the power FERC was granted by Congress over some decisions of the secretary regarding oil and products pricing and allocations. Neither the FPC nor the FERC had any authority to establish or enforce those regulations relating to oil-pricing matters, yet FERC became the body designated to hear appeals of the secretary of DOE's decisions on those subjects. FERC's own decisions are final and are reviewable by the court; they are not reviewable by the secretary as originally envisioned under the Carter plan. Not only did FERC retain its independent status in this fashion, FERC also has a veto power over actions by the secretary that may significantly affect any function within the jurisdiction of FERC. DOE's very structure has a built-in, or institutionalized, conflict between decision makers. That conflict has the potential to fragment energy policy. Following Murphy's Law, this fragmentation will most likely occur when the need for a cohesive policy is most felt. Where an agency is broken down into units with separate domains of power but overlapping interests, conflict is inevitable. Interagency conflicts over energy development, production, and conservation are even more likely.

DOE and APA

We have discussed structural and institutional arrangements within administrative agencies that affect energy decision making and therefore energy policymaking. The very alignment of agencies within the federal constellation has a direct and dramatic impact on how the energy picture is perceived and how the country responds. In addition to the structure of these institutions there are substantive and procedural administrative rules of law that are peculiar to energy decision making.

Historically, the emergence of the APA was seen as an attempt to unify and generalize agency procedures. Every agency was given minimum standards to guide its actions, and courts were also directed on how agency actions were to be reviewed. The pattern of a unified vision of administrative procedure remains basically intact with minor modifications, some of which affect the energy decision-making process.

The DOE act in certain respects has altered the APA's applicability to DOE actions. As noted, in the last several years agency decision making has moved away from traditional adjudicatory hearings toward rule making. The increased number of cases, burgeoning case backlogs, and the need for expeditious policymaking account for the growth of the popularity of the rule-making process particularly in the energy agencies. Rule making provides a swifter vehicle for the implementation of prospective policy decisions. Rule-making procedures, particularly the informal notice and written-comment variety, have allowed the DOE and the FERC to promulgate far-reaching policy quickly. The concern among many persons affected by DOE rule making is that although it promotes the agency's convenience, it may not provide sufficient procedural due-process safeguards to them.

Subchapter V of the DOE Organization act sets out specific procedures for DOE decisions. Generally, the act makes APA applicable to DOE, including the informal rule making of section 553. Because the DOE act does not require that rules ''be made on the record after an opportunity for an agency hearing,'' the minimum requirements of notice-and-comment rule making are authorized. Under the APA, notice-and-comment rule making requires only notice of the time, place, and nature of the rule-making proceedings, of the substance of the proposed rule, or a description of the subjects and issues involved. Interested persons have an opportunity to participate through the submission of written data, views, or arguments, with the opportunity for oral presentation discretionary with an agency. However, the DOE act imposes additional requirements.[12] If the secretary of DOE determines that a substantial issue of fact or law exists or that a rule, regulation, or order is likely to have a substantial impact on the nation's economy or on large numbers of individuals or business, an opportunity for oral presentation must be provided. In the absence of the determination of substantial impact, the ''paper'' informal hearing obtains. The DOE act also imposes notice requirements that differ from the APA. When a proposed rule is published in the *Federal Register* it must be accompanied by a statement of the research, analysis, and other available information in support of the rule. When the rule is finally promulgated it must accompany a response to the major comments, criticisms, and alternatives offered during the comment period. The secretary is authorized to waive these comments if they are likely to cause harm or injury to the public health, safety, or welfare.

These additional rule-making safeguards do not apply to FERC. FERC's rule-making process for the most part follows that prescribed by the APA, although the act does provide for some variations. The FERC, in implementing the NGPA, The Natural Gas Act, and The Federal Power Act, has relied extensively on the informal rule-making process to expeditiously issue rules of general applicability. These variations encourage actions to be taken by electing the rule-making process rather than adjudication.

The DOE act highlights a troublesome issue: Can a unified administrative procedure exist to govern all federal-agency processes or should agencies be allowed by statute to fashion procedures peculiar to their mission and charge? The only significant alteration in administrative procedures in the DOE act is to promote rule making APA style with some additional procedural safeguards. The emphasis on informal rule making in the DOE act underscores Congress's preception of the need for expedition in energy decision making. Whether expedition is either appropriate or warranted, given the complexities, uncertainties, and magnitude of the issues involved, is not always clear.

Dismantling DOE

The DOE, then, was created to design and oversee the nation's response to the energy crisis. Even given the attempts to consolidate disparate agencies under one titular decision maker and to customize general administrative law to meet the needs of a particular problem, institutional conflicts exist, and rules of law work rather crudely at times. The result is a less-than-cohesive energy policy. Dismantling the DOE will lead to a further fragmentation of decision making and will contribute to an increase in conflicts. This fragmented decision making together with a greater reliance on policymaking through rule making can further weaken the legitimacy of energy decisions.

Decision making can deteriorate to an even less satisfactory level of utility and be even less helpful to the national interest. The proposals to dismantle the DOE by reshuffling the decision-making machinery to the departments of Commerce and Interior is based on several questionable assumptions. Although one cannot fault the theoretically laudatory goal of elimination of wasteful, costly, or unnecessary government controls, the real question is what constitutes a so-called unnecessary control. Separating the necessary and proper regulatory units from the duplicative or obsolete is vital to energy decision-making in the national interest.

The predicate for abolition of DOE to trim government spending and increase private investment and production is certainly superficially appealing. However, from an economic standpoint it is questionable whether DOE's dismantlement will achieve these goals. According to the Congressional Budget Office (CBO), fragmenting every decision-making process may well cause certain serious problems, including failure to make any special provision for a coordinated response to disruptions in supply of imported oil, a too-heavy reliance on market adjustment as a primary means of response, and problems regarding economic and social dislocations during the period of adjustment. Furthermore, the CBO has not asserted that dismantlement will save the U.S. government any money.

The DOE was created to streamline energy-policy decision making and to facilitate design of a comprehensive national energy policy. Dismantling the DOE reverses that movement and significantly downgrades energy as an issue of national importance.

Under the deregulatory stance underlying DOE's proposed dismantlement, private capital is assumed to be available for development of new sources of energy supply. Whether private capital is forthcoming is problematical as has been evidenced by the shelving of a number of major energy projects, including oil shale, Alaskan Gas Pipeline, tar sands, and certain soft-technology initiatives.

The potential effects that dismantling the DOE will have on research and development of alternative technologies may be dramatic. Assuming that alternative technologies are needed for a well-balanced energy program, it is not clear that development and initial entry into the marketplace will be possible without federal involvement, particularly federal financial participation. Energy produced by the so-called alternative technologies may be unable to start or stay price competitive with the standard forms of energy produced by major energy companies.

The administration's disillusionment with the U.S. Synthetic Fuels Corporation (SFC) has dampened the synthetic-fuels industry. Ironically, the SFC was the centerpiece of the prior administration's policy of shifting reliance on foreign supply sources to use of available domestic resources of all kinds. However, with Exxon's recent departure from the Colony Park oil-shale project and the decline in oil prices that industry is left with only a few developers. Whether the nation will ever develop a viable synthetic-fuels industry is now a matter of speculation.

Should the DOE and the SFC be eliminated most portions of the National Energy Act and the Energy Security Act are virtual dead letters. The administration apparently has no intention of substituting any laws that direct federal energy policy, preferring instead to rely on the forces of the market. The DOE was created precisely to centralize energy decision making. Unfortunately, centralization was only partially accomplished, thus making DOE the perfect example of fragmentation and confusion. Thus, policy never had a chance to be made cohesive because of direct conflicts of interest in the DOE or because of overlapping responsibilities that, because of bureaucratic red tape, were not timely resolved. Energy decision making was moving toward the goal of consistency and informed decision making. However the strains of the political process have placed energy decision making back into its precarious position vis à vis development of a coherent and economically and socially useful body of law.

Notes

1. 42 U.S.C. sec. 7101 *et seq.* (Supp. I, 1977, Supp. II 1978, Supp. III 1979, and Supp. IV 1980).

2. *See* 1 H. Green, Energy Law Service, Ch. 2 (1978); Aman, *Institutionalizing the Energy Crisis: Some Structural and Procedural Lessons,* 65 Cornell L. Rev. 491 (1980); Byse, *The Department of Energy Organization Act: Structure and Procedure,* 30 Ad. L. Rev. 193 (1978).

3. 15 U.S.C. secs. 717 *et seq.* (1976 & Supp. I 1977—Supp. IV 1980).

4. 16 U.S.C. secs. 791 *et seq.* (1976 & Supp. I 1977–Supp. IV 1980).

5. 15 U.S.C. secs. 751 *et seq.* (1976 & Supp. I 1977–Supp. IV 1980).

6. 15 U.S.C. secs. 753 *et seq.* (1976 & Supp. I 1977–Supp. IV 1980).

7. 15 U.S.C. secs. 791 *et seq.* (1976 & Supp. I 1977–Supp. IV 1980).

8. 15 U.S.C. secs. 761 *et seq.* (1976 & Supp. I 1977–Supp. IV 1980).

9. 50 U.S.L.W. 4031 (U.S., Dec. 1, 1981).

10. 43 U.S.C. sec. 1331 *et seq.* (1976 & Supp. I 1977–Supp. IV 1980).

11. Energy Action Education Fund v. Andrus, 631 F.2d 751, 755, 758 (D.C. Cir. 1979).

12. 42 U.S.C. sec. 7191 (Supp. I 1977–Supp. IV 1980).

3 Judicial Review of Agency Action

The basic institutional process by which energy decisions are made is a rendering of a final appealable order by the administrative agency with judicial review of agency decisions. Courts also review decisions by the legislative[1] and executive branches.[2] Courts operate as a stabilizing force, deciding disputes and acting as a check on action by other arms of government. This checking function is most prominently displayed when courts are called on to oversee agency decision making. In the federal system, even though all law must find its basis in some positive formulation—rule, regulation, statute, or constitution—these general statements of law must be interpreted, applied, and refined. Parenthetically, insofar as courts fill in gaps left by statutes and regulations they exhibit a law-making as well as a decision-making function. Given the nature of energy decisions, which, because of their complexity, involve numerous parties and a large variety of positive and normative issues, the proper role of the judiciary relative to administrative agencies is of crucial importance. We have already noted that agencies are either usurping or being forced to usurp a greater role in policymaking. How have and how should courts respond to that development?

Courts exist to provide relief to those aggrieved in our society. In this regard, courts are not reluctant to create remedies and thus fashion rights for parties involved in administrative proceedings. If an agency fails to act, a court will force action. If rights are not vindicated before an agency, courts will provide a forum. If an agency exercises unwarranted authority, a court can offer protection from the improper use of agency power. If a person is denied something to which he or she is properly entitled, a hearing procedure can be provided. Each of these actions is a judicially created remedy intended to mend the tears of inadequacy in the administrative process. Courts, therefore, generally have not been reluctant to correct agency deficiencies if, in the view of the court, the agency has not followed its charge. However, most of these corrective actions have been to protect individual-liberty or property interests rather than to further or to articulate collective policy goals.[3] There has existed a notable judicial tendency to avoid interfering—at least overtly—with public policymaking. In most cases, policy has been reserved as a province of Congress and, through Congress, the agencies. As administrative-agency politics change and the social and economic problems before them change, courts have redefined their place in the policymaking structure and have stepped, in ever-increasing instances, into the policymaking fray.

The APA and Judicial Review

When we refer to law throughout this book we invariably refer to either legislation or a decided court case. All law in the federal system must be grounded in either a constitutional provision or a statute. Since positive law is written to encompass broad classes of interest, the judiciary exists to explain and apply the general provisions contained in the Constitution and in the rules and regulations that implement the statutes. In the modern federal system, administrative agencies, the arms of Congress, are established to minister the economic and social problems that Congress has earmarked for solution through regulation. Consequently, courts more often review agency actions under a statute rather than entertain original suits challenging the constitutionality or fundamental wisdom of enacted legislation. Although a statute may authorize direct court review (as does the Emergency Petroleum Allocation Act of 1973) or preclude judicial review (as does a portion of the Regulatory Flexibility Act) the overwhelming majority of cases are first heard in the hearing rooms of an administrative agency before they are argued in court. This is the scheme envisioned in the APA, wherein the process of agency decision making combined with court review places these two institutions in a symbiotic relationship relative to policymaking. Agencies are delegated the primary responsibility for formulating policy, but they do not exclusively exercise the policymaking function. Courts, as supervisors of agency action can play a significant part in policymaking through the review process. Although courts are more likely to defer to the agency, there are times when courts are compelled to overturn an agency decision. Under what circumstances a court may do so and the extent of its authority to modify the agency decision is the subject of this chapter.

The Scope of Judicial Review

In the study of administrative law the topic of judicial review is a major focus. Issues surrounding judicial review include the authority of a court to hear a case (jurisdiction), under what circumstances a case can be brought before a court (ripeness, timing, and finality), who can bring the action (standing), and once a case is properly before the court what is the limit of the court's review (scope of review). Our primary emphasis is the scope of review. By bypassing some of the more technical areas such as standing, ripeness, timing, and finality to discuss what actually happens when a court has an agency decision properly before it we move to the heart of the marriage between courts and agencies. Depending on how expansively a court chooses to exercise its review power (within statutory limitations) an agency's action can be given a broad-stroke imprimatur or microscopic scrutiny. The more closely a court reviews an agency's actions, the more involved the judiciary becomes in decision-making and policymaking processes.

Once an administrative agency has made a final decision, presumably one within its expertise, court review becomes available. The traditional view of judicial control of administrative action was that because agencies were delegated the authority to act in its stead by Congress and because agencies were to have developed expertise in the field, a good deal of deference should be given to agency decisions. A corollary reason for the so-called rule of deference is that courts, being the least-democratic branch of government, were viewed as ill-suited to make the decisions that agencies are required to make. A court, under these basic tenets, was not to substitute its judgment for that of an agency. The extent of court review is narrowly circumscribed by the APA. The APA sets forth those instances in which agency actions can be set aside. These are cases where the agency's actions are found to be:

(a) arbitrary, capricious, an abuse of discretion or otherwise not in accordance with the law;

(b) contrary to constitutional right, power, privilege, or immunity;

(c) in excess of statutory jurisdiction, authority, or limitations, or short of statutory right;

(d) without observance or procedure required by law;

(e) unsupported by substantial evidence (in cases of formal rulemaking and adjudication); or

(f) unwarranted by the facts in cases in which the facts are subject to trial de novo.[4]

Recalling the distinction between adjudication and rule making, limited court review of adjudicatory matters makes sense. Agency adjudications usually are individualized disputes where a small number of parties are given a triallike hearing before an administrative law judge (ALJ) before being affirmed or reversed by the agency. The role of the reviewing court in circumstances where a full triallike hearing has been held is then more appropriately limited to overturning the decision when it is clearly wrong.[5] However, when the agency promulgates a rule under informal procedures, closer scrutiny may be called for by the courts. In complex technical, economic, and social areas arising in energy or environmental agency rule making there is more room for varying interpretations of the law or the facts. An agency may exhibit biases that may build up during its lifetime of regulating broad areas of the economic system. Consequently, courts have been willing to more closely scrutinize this type of far-reaching agency decision making.

At the same time that courts display and express this willingness to scrutinize agency rules they are also wary of using this power, since the issues they are called on to review are often open-ended and given to varying interpretations that the expert agency is generally in a better position to make.[6] Courts do not have the resources to gather scientific data and perform the sophisticated scientific, technological, and economic analyses that agencies were established to undertake in furtherance of congressional mandate. Thus, courts may be caught in a dilemma between the desire to oversee closely agency decision making and the desire to defer to agency expertise. This tension is not yet fully reconciled. The issue of how closely courts may scrutinize agencies and what courts may require to uphold agency decisions is unsettled. In an era of expanding agency policymaking, and the corollary increase in areas of potential error, court review itself comes under scrutiny.

The scope of review should not be so broad as to have the court acting as the beady-eyed overseer of every administrative decision, nor should it be so narrow so that the court simply rubberstamps administrative decisions. A happy medium must be reached between these two extremes.

To reach that medium, one author has suggested that two overriding considerations should be used to weigh judicial review of administrative actions. Courts should first consider the wisdom of giving a deference to the expert, the administrative agency. The agencies spend a great deal of time and public money in considering the issues. Agency staffs accumulate massive information and perform analyses of that information, which cannot be done by courts. Parties to the proceeding similarly invest in the fullness and correctness of agency decisions. It is unwise to ignore the expertise and the expense of its development. This consideration does not surrender the duty, right, or privilege of the court to reject that administrative agency's findings, but it does limit the extent to which the discretion of the expert may be scrutinized by the nonexpert judge. The second consideration leading to a narrower scope of review is simple calendar pressure. The number and complexity of cases emanating from agency decisions makes it extremely difficult to handle each case with efficiency. Without giving substantial deference to the agency experts, today's judicial decision would either become perfunctory affirmance of the administrative decision or result in such extraordinary time lags as to make the provision for review a meaningless protection.[7] This essentially means that courts should assess their ability as an institution to hear a matter and to what degree to hear it. Invariably courts limit their review. They do not, absent statutory authorization, hear agency cases anew.

The Subject of Review

Once the limited scope is determined, the reviewing body must then consider what is subject to its analysis. As a general rule, the court is to confine its review solely to that evidence available in the record. Should the reviewing body believe that pertinent information was excluded at the agency hearing, it is the court's obligation to remand that case to the agency for further development and consideration of the facts in question. Additionally, the scope of review is limited to only those issues presented to the agency. Issues presented for consideration to the court that have not been considered at the administrative level are not subject to review by the court.[8] Furthermore, review of administrative decisions is limited by the rule in *Chenery I (SEC v. Chenery Corp.)*.[9] Generally stated *Chenery I* holds that the reasoning and logic relied on by the agency is binding on the reviewing body. In other words, "the ground upon which an administrative order must be judged are those upon which the record discloses that its action was based."[10] Thus the administrative rule will be upheld or struck down on the basis of its internal logic.

Courts are not generally authorized to substitute their judgment for that of an agency. Where the record presented by an agency is insufficient, a remand to the agency for more complete facts and rationale is necessary.[11]

However, the guiding precept for review still has not been stated. The true test, the real scope of review of agency action by an adjudication or formal rule making, is grounded in the so-called substantial-evidence test. The adjudication requires the agency to develop, through the hearing process, a record on which the agency bases its decisions. The decision based on the record available to the court must be based on substantial evidence. The substantial evidence rule is as follows: "The scope of judicial review over administrative action is limited to whether or not the findings of fact underlying the administrative conclusion are based upon substantial evidence."[12] Although the rule may be easily stated it has run up against a good deal of difficulty in its application and interpretation. We do know that substantial evidence is more than a "mere scintilla." It is "such relevant evidence as a reasonable mind might accept as adequate to support a conclusion."[13] Prior to the enactment of the APA, the courts interpreted substantial evidence to mean that evidence found in the record before the courts, not the evidence in the full record before the agency. Evidence outside the record was not to be considered, resulting in a rather narrow scope of review. The sponsors of the APA were concerned with the manner in which the substantial-evidence test was being applied. Specific language was included in the APA directing the reviewing courts to evaluate the "whole record." The Supreme Court had the opportunity to evaluate the APA's directive in *Universal Camera Corp.* v. *NLRB*.[14] In that case the Court stated that the whole-record requirement meant just that: courts are to consider the entire record on review, not just those portions of the record that the agency cites in support of its decision. The reviewing court is to assess whether the facts that are a part of the agency record are supported by substantial evidence. Therefore, the substantial-evidence rule is really a rule of reasonableness. After considering everything available to the agency, the court must find the evidentiary support for the agency's decision. If it exists, then the court's scrutiny ends and the decision stands. If not, then the case (in whole or part) is either remanded to the agency with instructions or it is reversed.

When does an agency decision present itself for review without a record? This situation arises when the challenged action is not proceeded by a hearing. Two types of proceedings give rise to the recordless review: First, rule making of the notice-and-comment variety; second, informal adjudication, where the decision is made without a hearing and hence without a record. Under these circumstances the substantial-evidence test cannot be applied because there is no record capable of review. Effectively, the same criteria are used to evaluate these situations. As was stated earlier the substantial-evidence rule is based on reasonableness.

In place of the substantial-evidence test, reviewing courts may overturn informal agency actions when they are arbitrary, capricious, or unreasonable. A court may not overrule the rule-making process simply "because reasonable minds might differ on the wisdom thereof."[15] However, a court may vacate an agency rule if it appears to have been drawn arbitrarily.

This same reasonableness test is applied to those situations where there is no record because the agency decision was reached through informal adjudication. This principle was pointed out in *Citizens to Preserve Overton Park, Inc.* v. *Volpe*.[16] This case revolved around whether or not federal funds could be used to construct a highway through a park, against statutory prohibition and in light of other alternatives. A general public hearing was held to determine the community attitude concerning this project. This community meeting was not the formal hearing required by the APA. Because there was no record for review, review of agency actions when a record is absent is based on reasonableness of agency action.

The *Standard Oil* Case: A Case Study

The judiciary has figured prominently in the development of administrative law in this country. For the most part, the APA circumscribes the role of and sets standards for the courts in the review of agency actions. APA review standards must be interpreted, applied, and specially tailored by the courts and then applied to fill in the interstices of the law. When a new field of administrative law emerges, such as energy law, courts are called on to create, clarify, or refine the law and regulations of a new and untested legal system. Such policy-oriented functions of the court become more pronounced when, as in the case of most energy statutes of recent vintage, the law was written in a crisis atmosphere.

Standard Oil Co. v. *DOE* presents a useful case study of how energy decisions are made within a newly formed, complex bureaucracy and of the court's response to these decisions.[17] Although oil controls have been lifted so that the vagaries of these arcane regulations are no longer part of energy law, the *Standard Oil* case nevertheless reveals, all too clearly, how the machinery of administrative law functions relative to energy decision making. The story of *Standard Oil* shows the creation of an agency, its response to industry, and industry's response to the agency all staged before a backdrop of crisis. To carry the story further, we will see how the law eventually settled back into a stable mode. In reviewing the *Standard Oil* case, it may seem in the evolution of the DOE and energy decision making that it is difficult to conclude whether energy decision making at the agency level with judicial review works or whether the machinery of administrative law grinds along haltingly in spite of itself.

Although the *Standard Oil* case is lengthy and deals with complex and conflicting regulations, the facts can be simply stated. The Federal Energy Administration (FEA), predecessor to DOE, issued an amended regulation in 1975 on which a number of oil refineries relied. The regulation imposed a formula that refiners were required to use to set their regulated-products prices. Through this formula certain costs could be passed through to customers, and others could not be passed through by the refiners. A base price was established for the oil and refined products, and certain costs could be "banked," which meant that if the prices fell below the base price then the banked costs could be recovered later through the sale of the oil and refined products. Based on the refiners' understanding of the regulations, they adopted a so-called nonproduct-costs-first sequence of recovery of banked costs. The effect of this interpretation allowed refiners to recover nonproduct or nonoil costs before their product or oil costs. Since the oil-pricing regulations then in effect allowed refiners to raise prices to reflect a 15 May 1973 profit margin and since product costs could be banked (to be recouped at a later time), nonproduct costs could be passed through to customers up to the base price as established by the 15 May 1973 date. Nonproduct costs could not be banked. Consequently it was possible, indeed probable, that many nonproduct costs could not be passed through if the FEA's first sequence rule had to be followed. In February 1976 the FEA issued a rule that required refiners to use the product-costs-first method. The rule was prospective and retrospective for 1975. The heart of the case was whether the FEA could recover about one billion dollars of nonproduct costs that the FEA alleged were impermissibly passed through during 1975 because of the use of the wrong sequence.

On different occasions representatives of the DOE rendered different interpretations of the cost-recovery rule. Not unexpectedly the oil companies relied on the nonproduct-costs-first rule—the method most favorable to them. DOE based its position on the opposite interpretation. To break this impasse the court examined the agency's construction of the regulations at the time of their promulgation and implementation. The court adhered to a rule of interpretation requiring "contemporaneous construction." And, although as a matter of policy an agency's interpretation will normally control because it is deemed to have expertise in the area, deference is not appropriate when the agency's interpretation is plainly erroneous or inconsistent with the regulations. In the *Standard Oil* case the court found that the DOE's interpretations were ambiguous and confusing. The court therefore decided not to defer, employed an expanded scope of review, and accordingly held for the refiners. At first glance the *Standard Oil* decision is not exceptional. The rules of law applied by the court are straightforward and the outcome of the court proceeding is fair. Yet beneath the surface *Standard Oil* gives us a peculiar look at energy decision making.

Most energy cases that have arisen under the National Energy Act or its predecessors and their accompanying regulations present complex technical and economic questions to which rules of law that have developed in a different technological and economic environment must be applied. Courts must thus reconcile the two. However, in *Standard Oil,* the court was presented with an agency interpretation of a rule that misled the industry. The court refused to defer to the agency's interpretation and retroactive application. Subsequent cases also raise the issue of invalidation of agency rulings on the basis of the *Standard Oil* decision by capitalizing on the complexity inherent in the nature of energy regulations. These cases, however, were not successful as the courts reverted to their posture of deference to agency decisions.

In *UPG, Inc.* v. *Edwards,* the question was whether certain hydrocarbons occurring in natural-gas pipelines referred to as "pipeline residue" or "condensate" should be treated as "crude oil" for pricing purposes as defined in the Code of Federal Regulations.[18] In *Sauder* v. *DOE* the issue was whether a formal or de facto "unitization" agreement was necessary before an operator could benefit from the stripper-well exemption.[19] In both cases the courts deferred to the DOE's interpretation of a regulation despite industry claims that the regulations were confusing and that the industry's interpretation should be given preference.

The issues posed in these three cases serve to illustrate the pressure that is brought to bear on a legal system that is forced to untangle technically based crisis legislation. In analyzing these cases we start with a relatively simple legal principle—judicial deference. A massive bureaucracy was created virtually overnight to handle an international problem that contains political, technical, economic and social intricacies. The existing legal regime is then called on to ease this bureaucracy into place. Generally accepted rules of law, such as judicial deference to agency action, are tugged at by the realities of the inadequacy of the in-place decision-making structure.

Before the purely legal questions can be addressed the technical and procedural aspects of the case must be understood. That is simple enough compared to the next major step in the analysis. The court must know the purpose behind the legislation and then assess how the case before the court fits into the scheme. It is not unusual to find that a set of facts in a given case can satisfy the policy behind the legislation but not comply with the letter of the law of either the statute or the regulations. Such was the case in *Sauder* where the court said: "There is considerable force to Sauder's claim; indeed, the agency does not deny that had the field been properly unitized, (a technical formality), the exemption would have been available to Sauder."[20] The effect of such a pronouncement is to decide the case on a legal technicality and preserve the underlying legal rule rather than risk judicial intrusion into agency policymaking.

Thus, it is not odd to find procedural issues exalted over substantive ones as an alternative to a court putting on the policymaking mantle. In *Sauder* and *UPG* the deference rule worked in favor of DOE, even though in both cases the planitiffs had cases that satisfied the policies behind the legislation. In *Standard Oil*, despite the deference rule, the oil companies were successful, demonstrating that the agency contradicted itself. The rub is that *Standard Oil* is not the usual case. Before the plaintiffs in *Standard Oil* could prevail they had to make an unusually compelling case. Before the court could issue a ruling favorable to the refiners it had to look to the contemporaneous construction of agency rulings and delve into a province into which courts reluctantly go. This, in turn, established a rule that provided fertile ground for others harmed by DOE interpretations to plough. The parties in both *Sauder* and *UPG* attempted to benefit from the *Standard Oil* case, but the courts, reasonably, veered back to the deference standard. Although as a matter of present law the latest construction rule prevails, after *Standard Oil* the contemporaneous-construction requirement can be called on, particularly if the record is unclear. Although we see a movement away from this type of judicial scrutiny, the courts willingness to overturn agency interpretation demonstrates the underlying difficulties involved with crisis legislation and the resultant complexity and uncertainty. These cases also demonstrate how judicial review can affect policymaking. In *Standard Oil* by preferring to defer to the agency interpretation the court effected a policy that allowed the passing through of certain costs for a period of time. In *UPG* and *Sauder* the courts' deference let agency policy stand even in questionable instances.

Rule Making and Judicial Review

Today's administrative decisions are usually the products of rule making (the more policy-oriented process) rather than adjudication.[21] The major case controlling the rule making review standard for courts is *Abbot Laboratories* v. *Gardner.*[22] That case held that preenforcement review should be allowed unless there is a persuasive reason to believe that Congress intended to preclude review. The impact of that case launched a wide variety of specific legislation that provided for rule-making review. The statutory reaction to the case has produced the following.[23]

There are five types of statutes that provide for rule-making review. Those types of statutes include:

1. Legislation that confers rule-making power on the agency is silent as to judicial review.[24] These cases are then subject to the review provisions of the APA.
2. Legislation that provides for judicial review in federal district court but establishes no time frame for review.[25]
3. Legislation that provides for direct preenforcement review within a prescribed time period and explicitly preserves the jurisdiction of the

appropriate court to review the validity of regulations after the prescribed period in enforcement proceedings.[26]

4. legislation that provides for direct preenforcement review within a prescribed time period but is silent about the availability of review in enforcement proceedings or otherwise.[27]

5. Legislation that provies for direct preenforcement review within a prescribed time period and prohibits, with certain exceptions, review of the rule in an enforcement proceeding.[28]

"Hybrid" Rule Making

Aside from the matter of timing, availability, and proper review form, judicial review of rule making raises serious questions regarding administrative procedure. Assuming for the moment that courts maintain their reluctance to inject themselves too deeply into the administrative decision-making process for fear of overt policymaking then how far may courts go in remanding cases to the agency with instructions on how to proceed?

Courts are comfortable and find support in asking questions on process and in providing either guidelines or directives to agencies regarding the procedures the agencies employ or should employ. In fact, courts have become so comfortable with this mode of review that they have frequently directed agencies to reexamine certain issues because of the courts' judgment that the decision-making process was defective. Although this scheme may appear to be neutral it naturally can affect the substantive outcome of a case and, in this manner also, courts are injected into the policymaking process.

One method courts use to correct what they view as an improper agency procedure or result is to remand to the agency on the basis that procedural due process was not satisfied. Courts often spell out why a hearing was not fair and then provide guidance on how the agency can mend its procedurally defective ways. This creates an entire series of so-called hybrid cases.[29] The significant legal issue is whether this method of review by the court is legitimate.

When a court makes such a ruling and tells an agency how it should structure its decision-making process this is called "hybrid" rule making. Essentially, hybrid rule making is a court-created decision-making process. Courts review how an agency made a decision and whether the minimum requirements of the APA were met. Constitutional requirements for procedural due process are applied on the court's own volition. In this situation the court imposes on agencies requirements that are not required by the APA. This additional imposition of decision-making requirements has not gone unchecked. Courts that overstep their standard of review can and have been chastised. Courts cannot make wholesale reforms in administrative law nor may they totally restructure agency decision making. Rather, they can oversee the functioning of established processes and correct malfeasances or misfeasances in the process.

Vermont Yankee

In *Vermont Yankee Nuclear Power Corp.* v. *Natural Resources Defense Council, Inc.* the Supreme Court reversed the Court of Appeals for the District of Columbia Circuit because the D.C. Circuit overstepped its bounds in reviewing two decisions of the NRC.[30] The effect of the D.C. Circuit's decisions was to invalidate the NRC's grant of licenses to two power plants. The APA sets out the minimum procedural requirements that an agency must follow in conducting its rule-making proceedings. These requirements were satisfied by the NRC. Although agencies have the discretion to expand procedural rights, reviewing courts are generally not free to impose additional requirements. The Supreme Court did not put an absolute ban on the reviewing court's power to impose further procedural rights, but it said that such circumstances, "if they exist," were extremely rare.

In *Vermont Yankee,* the NRC, pursuant to the Atomic Energy Act, has the authority to issue construction and operation licenses for power plants. Within the context of these licensing procedures the NRC undertakes the environmental review required by the National Environmental Policy Act (NEPA). Excluded from consideration at the licensing hearing was the issue of the environmental effects of the operation required to reprocess fuel and waste disposal resulting from the reprocessing operations.

The NRC then instituted rule-making proceedings to consider the environmental reprocessing and waste-disposal issues among others. In the notice of proposed rule making the NRC stated that the proposed rules were based on a staff study of the uranium fuel cycle and indicated that hearings on the rule making would not be open to cross-examination, but that the staff study would be made available prior to the hearings so that it could be reviewed and commented on or criticized. Participants were allowed to present their positions in writing and orally if time permitted. At the conclusion of the hearing a transcript would be made available and the record would be open for thirty days to allow the filing of supplemental written statements. After the hearing one of two proposed rules was adopted.

The grant of the license to the Vermont Yankee plant was challenged on the basis that the NRC had to deal with the reprocessing and disposal issues in individual licensing proceedings. The D.C. Circuit, reviewing the NRC's decision, invalidated the grant of the licenses because of the NRC's failure to document certain potential environmental impacts of the reprocessing and waste disposal in that case.

The Supreme Court reviewed the D.C. Circuit's decision on certiorari, and stated that the Court of Appeals overturned the rule based on its view that the agency procedures were inadequate. Although the lower court did not order specific procedures it did suggest additional procedural devices such as cross-examination, informal conferences, and the use of outside experts and remanded the case to the NRC on the basis that it found that parties did not have an opportunity to participate in a "meaningful way." Although a court can remand to an agency because of an inadequate record, the Supreme Court said that, in the absence of a substantial justification, which was not enumerated, the reviewing court could not dictate agency procedures. The Supreme Court underscored the institutional significance surrounding judicial review by noting that the determination of whether commitment to nuclear energy was a wise policy or not was a congressional, not a judicial matter, and that Congress had delegated the responsibility for this decision to the NRC. The Supreme Court clearly noted the very sensitive policy position in which reviewing courts find themselves. Under the catch phrase of "procedural fairness" the reviewing court can have a serious and substantial impact on decisions of an agency by forcing the agency to rehear issues in a new light or with a particular emphasis.

We have noted a shift in administrative law previously. Agencies are becoming more imbued with a policymaking role, and courts have responded to that shift by requiring more-detailed hearing procedures in the rule-making/policymaking process.[31] How has *Vermont Yankee* influenced that shift? In one sense, because the decision reinforces the already narrow scope of judicial review by restricting the basis on which the reviewing court can overturn agency decision, *Vermont Yankee* retards this shift. A reviewing court also is limited in what demands can be made of an agency faced with a decision of complex technical, as well as value, choices. Can or should the court require the agency to take a hard look at the issues? Should the courts take a hard look themselves? Or, since agencies are to be afforded great discretion, should courts review agency decisions with a kid-glove approach? Further, is the hard-look standard justified because of the changes in administrative structure and process? Should this type of court-agency interaction permit the creation of hybrid rule making or must this await voluntary agency adoption or legislative mandate?

Energy and Judicial Review

The persistent question arising in all administrative law is what is the appropriate standard of review? What should the standard be in energy cases? The tapestry of complex, technical issues that affect energy decisions cause this question to arise more frequently in the energy/environmental area than in virtually any other area of administrative law. The actions of the energy agency are unusually complex, uncertain, and legislative in nature. Courts are not generally structured or technically educated to handle these types of cases.[32] This fact mitigates in favor of a greater deference by the court to the decisions of the agencies. At the same time, because agencies are dealing with exceptionally complex matters, there is more room for error even by the technically astute. Perhaps the courts should take a harder look at their decisions and at their decision-making processes. The result of the *Vermont Yankee* decision is to limit the area in which the courts can force the agencies to adopt procedures outside the APA's requirements. The trend toward rule making complicates matters insofar as agencies are engaged in more policy formation.[33]

One court described two extremes of judicial review of rule-making actions that involve a large element of policy choice when those actions are not shown to be demonstrably correct.[34] At one extreme is the following:

> The Administrator may apply his expertise to draw conclusions from suspected, not completely substantiated, relationships between facts, from trends among facts, from theoretical projections from imperfect data, from probative preliminary data not yet certifiable as ''fact'' and the like.[35]

Given this differential attitude the court will affirm regulations, if rational, even given necessarily speculative agency predictions in the social sciences. At the other extreme the court will conduct a more exacting inquiry into agency methodology, ''where the facts pertinent to [a] standard's feasibility are available and easily discoverable by conventional technical means.''[36] Courts often feel they are faced with a case between the two extremes. In *NRDC* v. *EPA* the court was asked to review EPA decisions regarding the likely sequence of further technological development of a pollution-control device known as a ''trap oxidizer.'' The court felt both that deference was necessary and that they should review the EPA's methodology. The court held:

> We think that the EPA will have demonstrated the reasonableness of its basis for prediction if it answers any theoretical objections to the trap-oxidizer method, identifies the major steps necessary in refinement of the device, and offers plausible reasons for believing that each of those steps can be completed in the time available.[37]

Another serious problem in the case concerned the lead time for the development of the pollution-control device. The time period was uncertain, creating an ambivalent situation for the court. The court could second-guess the agency or ask it to provide reasonable estimates. The court chose the latter.

The Regulatory Reform Act, presently sponsored by three fourths of the Senate, amends the judicial-review section of the APA by adding the following to the provisions describing the circumstances under which an agency's actions may be set aside by a reviewing court:

> [When the agency action is] (F) without substantial support in the rule-making file, viewed as a whole, for the asserted or necessary factual basis, as distinguished from the policy or legal basis, of a rule adopted in a proceeding subject to section 553 of this title.[38]

The rationale for this addition is best given by its sponsor, Senator Dale Bumpers:

> A fundamental premise of our system of government is that the courts interpret and apply the law; they are the ultimate authority on all legal questions. It simply makes sense for courts to decide independently whether an agency has exceeded its authority, without deference to the agency's interpretation regarding the extent of its authority. It is folly to expect an agency to be objective about the limits on its authority, and many court decisions encourage Federal Bureaucrats to abuse their power. A recent opinion of the U.S. Supreme Court presents a good example. In Environmental Protection Agency against National Crushed Stone Association, decided only 5 months ago, the Court had this to say:
>
> "When faced with a problem of statutory construction, this court shows great deference to the interpretation given the statute by the officers or agency charged with its administration."
>
> In my view, this is not the way Congress intended the system to work. The Court, not the Agency itself, should decide whether the Agency has overstepped its authority, and the language of section 5 of this bill makes this clear.[39]

This new section recognizes the distinction between fact and policy and leaves the agency its discretionary authority in making policy choices. However, it requires the reviewing court to take a hard look at the factual bases for the agency rule. Thus, where the finding of fact is necessary to the rule the court must analyze the factual predicate for the rule. Where the agency's policy choice would fail to satisfy the "arbitrary, capricious and abuse of discretion" standard, absent such a factual finding, where the "finding of fact" is an asserted basis of the rule, the factual findings must meet the substantial-support standard of the regulatory-reform legislation.

Judicial Attitudes toward Policymaking

Energy decisions and their peculiar nature deserve special note. Energy decisions generally are not two-sided disputes over a simple matter of property damage or about the extent of an individual's entitlement or about the resolution of a past dispute. Rather, energy decisions are multilayer, many-party, future-looking bundles of positive and normative issues. The very nature of the decisions that energy agencies must make and on which the courts must pass judgment affects how courts envision their scope of review. The decisions of the energy agency not only present scientific and technical issues but they are imbued with delicate social, political, and economic issues. Not surprisingly, the intensity and priority of these issues will vary according to which individual or interest group raises the issues and with the forum that must make a decision. Because energy decisions frequently affect such fundamental social institutions such as the economy and the extent of government intervention in society, agencies are given a broad policymaking agenda by Congress. In part, this expansion of the exercise of policymaking power is reflected in the use of rule making. Consequently, courts, when confronted with an opportunity to review an agency action, are confronted with a perplexing problem. The traditional mode of judicial review calls for great deference or what has been called the "soft glance."[40] Courts, constrained by the APA, are willing to let the experts (ostensibly the agency) control the decision. However, precisely because agencies exercise such significant power and because rule-making proceedings are so open-ended and polycentric, courts more often feel the compulsion to scrutinize closely the energy agency's actions—the so-called hard-look approach.[41]

The type of judicial review that a court chooses can determine the outcome of the matter. Further, there are no precise rules to guide courts in fashioning their scope of review. In *Ethyl Corporation* v. *EPA,* for example, the court reviewed the EPA's determination requiring a reduction in the lead content in gasoline additives.[42] The court was willing, if not eager, to defer to the agency's decision:

> Where a statute is precautionary in nature, the evidence difficult to come by, uncertain, or conflicting because it is on the frontiers of scientific knowledge, the regulations designed to protect the public health, and the decision that of an expert administrator, we will not demand rigorous step-by-step proof of cause and effect.[43]

That is a compelling argument for deference. Yet the question arises, would the court have used the same minimal scrutiny if the EPA were increasing the lead content in gasoline while knowing that it was increasing a health risk? The simple posing of the question raises a subtle yet profound political issue: What criteria do courts use in deciding the degree of review to apply in a given case? Courts can confine themselves to reviewing the record and satisfying themselves that enough evidence exists to validate an outcome, or they can limit their oversight to observing whether the procedural requirements of the relevant statutes were properly followed. More aggressive courts can ask whether affected or aggrieved persons were adequately represented, whether the burden of proof was allocated properly, and whether it was satisfied. There are numerous variables that a court must take into account, and many of the variables present an opening for a court to consciously or unconsciously rework the agency's actions. The degree of explicitness that a court uses in reviewing the work of an agency directly affects the quality of law, the legitimacy of the process of judicial review, and the nature of the policy that is ultimately designed.

The conclusion emerging from analysis of court opinions is that different judges have developed very different personal philosophies about how to work within a system that requires a court to review an expert agency's decision in a case with scientific, technical, economic, or social complexities. The late Judge Harold Leventhal, a member of the Court of Appeals of the D.C. Circuit[44] examined this question in a penetrating look at decision making in the context of environmental law.,[45] Leventhal wrote the *Greater Boston* opinion first enunciating the hard-look standard.[46] Leventhal was clear to note in a later explication of the decision that court review is supervisory only. The court is not to make its own findings or select its own policies. The supervisory function

> begins with enforcing the requirement of reasonable procedure, fair notice and opportunity to the parties to present their case, and it includes examining the evidence and fact findings to see both that the evidentiary fact findings are supported by the record and that they provide a rational basis for inferences of ultimate fact.[47]

Then the court must study the record attentively, including the evidence on technical and specialist matters to ensure that the agency has genuinely engaged in reasoned decision making with regard to all the material facts and issues. The hard-look concept does not put the court in the role of central supervising decision maker, rather the court oversees the process and forces the agency to take a hard look at the issues in the case.

Because the issues involved in energy decisions are scientifically and technically complex, as they are in environmental law, courts easily recognize that they are not technicians and cannot decide technological disputes or draw on their own knowledge for a ruling on whether an agency's determination is proper.[48] There is something of a hidden assumption in the quotation, and Leventhal explored this point. Although it is true that courts (especially appellate) are neither designed nor equipped to do the basic fact finding necessary to test or evaluate a scientific hypothesis, it is also true that agencies are not necessarily in vastly superior positions. Most often the more scientifically complex the case is, the more subject to the vagaries of proof it is. Although courts cannot conduct the initial scientific or technical inquiries they do have special expertise in methods of proof and about the processes by which matters are proven. Thus, no matter how narrowly one may wish to define the scope of judicial review, a court should examine the entire record to identify the issues and choices made by the agency, to determine whether there has been a disregard of legislative intent, to assure itself that the parties were offered a reasonable opportunity to be heard, and to determine whether there has been a reasonable assessment of the interrelated policy and legal questions.[49]

The chief judge of the D.C. Circuit, David Bazelon, is an equally distinguished jurist who has another philosophy on the scope of judicial review. In an article that sets out his view of the proper method for review of agency decisions, he noticed the interdependence of science and values. Scientific or technical decisions involve painful value choices and pose difficult policy problems; they are further complicated by the intervention of government regulation.[50] Although scientists may be in the best position to conduct the basic research and assess the costs and benefits of an individual innovation, they are not necessarily the best evaluators of how the innovation should be applied to society. In part the evaluation process and the policy analysis are done by administrative agencies, and not infrequently courts are asked to step into that process. Like Leventhal, Bazelon eschews any design that suggests that the court substitute its judgment for that of the experts. And, Bazelon goes further by arguing that the courts should not substitute their own value preferences for those of the agency, to which the legislature has delegated decision-making power and responsibility.[51] He then goes on to outline the proper role for courts and judges:

> What courts and judges can do, however—and do well when conscious of their role and limitations—is scrutinize and monitor the decision-making process to make sure that it is thorough, complete, and rational; that all relevant information has been considered; and that insofar as possible, those who will be affected by a decision have had an opportunity to participate in it.[52]

The consensus is that one way to manage complex, value-laden decisions that are difficult to understand and that contain a number of uncertainties is to construct a process that makes fair decisions. It is not as necessary that the ultimately correct or right decision be made from an empirical, technical, or scientific perspective as much as it is that issues are fairly presented and interested parties are given the opportunity to participate.

Notes

1. *See* Consumers Energy Council of America v. FERC, 673 F.2d 425 (D.C. Cir. 1982) (Court holds unconstitutional one-house-veto provision of Natural Gas Policy Act of 1978.)

2. *See* Independent Gasoline Marketers Council v. Duncan, 492 F.Supp. 614 (D.D.C. 1980) (review of President Carter's imposition of a 10 percent conservation fee).

3. Stewart & Sunstein, *Public Programs and Private Rights,* 95 Harv. L. Rev. 1195 (1982).

4. 5 U.S.C. sec. 706 (1976).

5. Courts have held that the arbitrary-and-capricious standard and the substantial-evidence standard may converge in an informal rule making. ECEE, Inc. v. FERC, 611 F.2d 554, 565 (5th Cir. 1980); National Small Shipments Traffic Conference, Inc. v. CAB, 618 F.2d 819, 826–27, (D.C. Cir. 1980).

6. The court does not inquire into the wisdom of the regulation that the agency promulgates. "[It] inquires into the soundness of the reasoning by which the Commission reaches its conclusions only to ascertain that the latter are rationally supported." United States v. Allegheny-Ludlum Steel Corp., 406 U.S. 742, 749 (1972).

7. B. Schwartz, Administrative Law 578–80 (1976).

8. FPC v. Colorado Interstate Gas Co., 348 U.S. 492, 498 (1955); Consolidated Gas Supply Corp. v. FERC, 611 F.2d 951, 958–59 (4th Cir. 1979).

9. SEC v. Chenery Corp., 318 U.S. 80 (1943).

10. *Id*. at 87.

11. Sun Oil Co. v. FPC, 445 F.2d 764 (D.C. Cir. 1971); American Electric Power v. FERC, 675 F.2d 1226 (D.C. Cir. 1982). (Order denying rehearing April 23, 1982).

12. B. Schwartz, *supra* note 7, at 592.

13. Consolidated Edison Co. v. NLRB, 305 U.S. 197, 229 (1938).

14. Universal Camera Corp. v. NLRB, 340 U.S. 474 (1951).

15. FCC v. Schreiber, 381 U.S. 279, 292 (1965).

16. 401 U.S. 402 (1971).

17. Standard Oil Co. v. DOE, 596 F.2d 1029 (Temp. Emer. Ct. App. 1978).

18. 647 F.2d 147 (Temp. Emer. Ct. App. 1981).

19. 648 F.2d 1341 (Temp. Emer. Ct. App. 1981).

20. *Id*. at 1346 (parenthesis added).

21. Davis, *Judicial Review of Rulemaking: New Patterns and New Problems* 1981 Duke L.J. 279.

22. 387 U.S. 136 (1967).

23. This discussion is based on Davis *supra* note 21.

24. *See, e.g.,* 5 U.S.C. sec. 1302 (Supp. II 1978) (conferring power on the office of Personnel Management to prescribe and enforce various types of regulations for the administration of the provisions of Title 5, but making no mention of any special judicial-review procedures); 12 U.S.C. sec. 1902 (1976) (conferring rule-making power on the Board of Governors of the Federal Reserve System under the National Credit Union Central Liquidity Facility Act); 42 U.S.C. sec. 1302 (1976) (conferring rule-making authority on the secretaries of Labor, Health and Human Services, and the Treasury to "make and publish such rules and regulations as may be necessary for the efficient administration of the functions with which each is charged under this Chapter").

25. Department of Energy Organization Act, 42 U.S.C. sec. 7192(g) (Supp. II 1978) (conferring power on the district courts of the United States to resolve cases or controversies arising "under rules, regulations, or orders" issued by the Federal Energy Regulatory Commission).

26. Magnuson-Moss Warranty–Federal Trade Commission Improvement Act, 15 U.S.C. sec. 57a(e) (1976); Toxic Substances Control Act, 15 U.S.C. sec. 2618 (1976).

27. The preenforcement review may be in the court of appeals or in

the district court. Orders Review Act, 28 U.S.C. secs. 2341–53 (1976), as amended by the Hobbs Act, 28 U.S.C. sec. 2342 (Supp. II 1978) (court of appeals) and the Marine Mammal Protection Act, 16 U.S.C. sec. 1374(d)(6) (1976), (district court).

28. Federal Mine Safety and Health Amendments Act, 30 U.S.C. sec. 811(d) (Supp. II 1978).

29. Williams, *"Hybrid Rulemaking" under the Administrative Procedure Act: A Legal and Empirical Analysis,* 42 U. Chi. L. Rev. 401 (1975).

30. 435 U.S. 519 (1978).

31. *See* Stewart, *Vermont Yankee and the Evolution of Administrative Procedure,* 91 Harv. L. Rev. 1805 (1978); Byse, *Vermont Yankee and the Evolution of Administrative Procedure: A Somewhat Different View,* 91 Harv. L. Rev. 1823 (1978); and, Breyer, *Vermont Yankee and the Courts' Role in the Nuclear Energy Controversy,* 91 Harv. L. Rev. 1833 (1978).

32. Yellin, *High Technology and the Courts: Nuclear Power and the Need for Institutional Reform,* 94 Harv. L. Rev. 489 (1981); Rogers, *Benefits, Costs and Risks: Oversight of Health and Environmental Decisionmaking,* 4 Harv. Envtl. L. Rev. 191 (1980).

33. DeLong, *Informal Rulemaking and the Integration of Law and Policy,* 65 Va. L. Rev. 257, 294 (1979). *See also* B. Ackerman & W. Hassler, Clean Coal/Dirty Air, Ch. 7 (1981); Diver, *Policymaking Paradigms in Administrative Law,* 95 Harv. L. Rev. 393 (1981).

34. NRDC v. EPA, 655 F.2d 318, 329 (D.C. Cir. 1981).

35. *Id.* at 329 (quoting Ethyl Corp. v. EPA, 541 F.2d 1, 28 (D.C. Cir.) *cert. denied,* 426 U.S. 941 (1976)).

36. *Id.* (quoting National Lime Ass'n v. EPA, 627 F.2d 416, 454 (D.C. Cir. 1980)).

37. *Id.* at 331–332, 333.

38. S. 1080, 97th Cong., 1st Sess. 127 Cong. Rec. at S4228 (daily ed. Apr. 30, 1981).

39. *Id.* at S4239.

40. Rodgers, *Benefits, Costs and Risks: Oversight of Health and Environmental Decisionmaking,* 4 Harv. Envtl. L. Rev. 191, 216–18 (1980). This has also been referred to as the "kid-glove" approach. *See* Shell Oil Co. v. FPC, 520 F.2d 1061 (5th Cir. 1975).

41. Greater Boston Television Corp. v. FCC, 444 F.2d 841 (D.C. Cir. 1970) *cert. denied,* 403 U.S. 923 (1971).

42. 541 F.2d 1 (D.C. Cir. 1976).

43. *Id.* at 28.

44. The District of Columbia Circuit of the U.S. Court of Appeals sits in a unique position in federal administrative law. Many agency decisions are appealed to this court, which historically has had a pro-consumer reputation. In many respects it sets the policies of the field of federal administrative law.

45. Leventhal, *Environmental Decisionmaking and the Role of the Courts,* 122 U. Pa. L. Rev. 509 (1974).

46. Greater Boston Television Corp. v. FCC, 444 F.2d 841 (D.C. Cir. 1970) *cert. denied,* 403 U.S. 923 (1971).

47. Leventhal, *supra* note 45, at 511.

48. *Id.* at 532.

49. *Id.* at 541.

50. Bazelon, *Coping with Technology through the Legal Process,* 62 Corn. L. Rev. 817, 819 (1977).

51. *Id.* at 822.

52. *Id.* at 823.

4 Regulatory Failure, Deregulation, and Regulatory Reform

Government involvement in the affairs of industry is cyclical. The presumption in favor of the free market gives way to government regulation in the face of a perception of market failure. When regulation does not achieve its goals or when the goals apparently become obsolete, society is faced with regulatory failure, the breakdown in the process. The inability of a regulator to set standards or rules that will imitate as closely as possible a truly competitive market is one notable example of the fundamental failure of regulation. An unsuccessful attempt to provide useful outside controls that could in theory, but did not in reality, correct an ailing market has been witnessed repeatedly in the regulatory world. Regulatory failure also may take the form of excessive regulation. In an attempt to provide a competitive market the regulator may overreact and impose a plethora of regulations that chokes the market, causes stagnation or confusion to the point that the cure of regulation may be worse than the sickness of a noncompetitive market.

Viewed in this light, regulatory failure of corrective actions employed by the agencies aggravate the inefficiencies in the market. Regulations may be too costly to impose, and thus price signals are distorted. Costs to the consumer may rise inappropriately, or the profits of industry may precipitously decline, forcing industry to reduce supplies or services when they are needed by the society.

Two responses to regulatory failure are available: deregulation and regulatory reform. This chapter discusses certain instances of regulatory failure and analyzes the two approaches to remedying this deficiency.

Regulatory Failure

Instances of regulatory failure occur when the law itself or regulations and procedures are inefficient, ineffective, or out of date.[1] A built-in check exists to correct those failures—judicial review. However, in view of the multitude of cases handled by the numerous agencies, lack of resources to appeal numerous cases, the complexity of the cases, and the limited scope of review accorded a court by the Administrative Procedure Act (APA), legitimate questions exist about the actual utility of judicial review in repairing an ailing regulatory structure. Should the basic structure of administrative law be changed to more quickly reflect current realities of the success or defeat of regulation?[2]

The following discussion is designed to put forward a number of situations that tend to create regulatory failure or perceptions of regulatory ineptness or misfeasance. Further, we set out some remedies proposed and attempted that may improve the functioning of agencies.

The Captured Agency

Specific agencies were created to handle specific, often technical, problems. Who is better qualified to assess the safety of a nuclear-power plant than a nuclear engineer on the staff of the Nuclear Regulatory Commission (NRC)? Who better to serve as general counsel of the Federal Energy Regulatory Commission (FERC) than a lawyer who has practiced before the agency, may have served on the staff years before, and has clients that are involved in FERC matters? Who knows more about the oil and gas industry than a producer of oil and gas who may seek appointment as a federal policymaker in the departments of Energy (DOE) or of the Interior (DOI)?

Unfortunately, the appointment of an individual who has actively engaged in the oil or gas business or the delegation to a person who has been an employee of the NRC for decades of major decisions on nuclear-plant safety is not necessarily noncontroversial or appropriate. In the case of the oil and gas producer who may be under consideration for appointment to the DOE or DOI, cries of "bias" will undoubtedly arise in the Senate confirmation hearings. In the case of the NRC engineer, complaints of antibusiness, antiindustry bias as a result of bureaucratic inbreeding are bound to arise if the engineer's recommendations on safety issues go contrary to the utility's interests. In the case of the lawyer wishing to become general counsel of the agency before which he or she has practiced, substantial questions of conflicts of interest or self dealing may and should arise.

These problems may be labelled "inbreeding" and "incest." This instance of regulatory failure has become synonymous with the terms *agency capture* and the *revolving-door problem* through which lawyers or technical personnel move back and forth from private practice to government. The appearance of impropriety in agency or department appointments, particularly at senior levels, can subvert the public's confidence in the legitimacy of agency decisions. The insinuation of incest between the regulators and the regulated likewise may undermine the agency's internal functioning if such allegations are not dealt with in a straightforward, candid way. Direct conflicts of interest, such as participation while in government service in a matter in which the lawyer participated, must be avoided, of course. More difficult are situations where the lawyer must act as a dispassionate general counsel, who makes recommendations on general matters such as a rule-making proposal that may profoundly affect a former client's interests. The important principle that must be observed is scrupulous avoidance of situations where the credibility and impartiality of the individual and agency are besmirched. The DOE act and the Ethics in Government Act seek to accomplish these and other goals. However, to avoid conflict, bias, and prejudice in the decision-making process, many qualified, properly motivated individuals who may have been trained by working in or on behalf of a regulated industry may shy away from the controversy and refuse to enter government service. Additionally, during the term of service of those who do not fear to tread into energy policymaking, harassment from special interests of one type or another, particularly with congressional or media support, may drive otherwise committed public servants from office or make their stay so miserable as to be nonproductive to agency, country, or self.

The case of the nuclear engineer is an example of potential inbreeding. The engineer faces a dilemma: May an individual make adverse decisions to the industry that is being regulated or make decisions adverse to the agency that employs her or him and still expect to obtain or retain employment or be promoted by either agency or industry or both? The tension created by inbreeding, where the employee is afraid to say no to either agency or industry, may produce an environment not of informed advocacy but rather of "wishy-washy" compromise and perhaps cooptation.

The case of the DOE or DOI appointee is a variation on this theme. All this is not to say that the bureaucratic milieu created by administrative agencies is of itself good or evil. Rather it is to say that institutionalization may have self-sustaining forces, existing independently of the agency's mandate, and these self-sustaining forces may hamper the agency. The negative impact can arise in a number of ways: fear of making a wrong decision; inordinate concern about market ability of an agency employee in his profession after government service; focusing on perceptions of action rather than action; and narrowing choices to conform to agency or industry expectations. The worst-possible outcome for an agency relying on industry-trained appointees is a public view that the agency's charge and the mission of the regulated firm are one and the same. If issues are regarded in the same light and discussed in the same language and analyzed with the same methodologies, the press, the Congress (or its arm the GAO), or the public will most certainly object, and the legitimacy of the decision and of the decision-making process will be questioned.

Thus, the concerns about the agency and the industry's relationship are grounded in legitimate issues: predisposition to listen and give more credence to the arguments of former senior employees of the agency; the fear of agency employees that they may not be able to get a job in the industry if they make decisions unfavorable to it; and the public mistrust of an agency that is perceived as being in the power of the regulated industry because of appointments and long-standing relationships between the two. However, it is simplistic and short-sighted to argue that those who have worked for the industry cannot make a dispassionate, truly in-the-public-interest decision. Further, the safeguards that have been employed to deal with the problems of conflicts and prejudice may result in overkill and an aura of skepticism and mistrust, severely hampering decision making in the agency. At the same time, if the industry-agency tie does in fact exist, anyone who challenges industry or agency (for example, a public-interest group) is seen as an outsider, unfriendly and not to be afforded the same privileges as the regulated industry.

Decisions and Uncertainty

Agencies must make decisions in the face of great underlying uncertainty. Even a specialized agency with high levels of expertise, like FERC, cannot easily find answers to hard questions. The questions may involve the costs to consumers of certificating a $30-billion pipeline from Alaska or the effect on national security of failing to approve the pipeline construction. The agency has been told by Congress that it is the body to make an expert decision. Thus, a decision must be made. However, the terrifying uncertainties of complexity, changing circumstances, and technological insufficiency plague the decision from its inception and the agency in perpetuity if it does not make the right choice or fails to make any choice.

The agency must make decisions on incredibly complex economic and technological matters when crucial evidence is missing or when information is simply unknown and probably unknowable. The manner in which agencies regulate in the face of uncertainty is discussed more fully in chapter 9. However, if, in deciding such issues, the agency gambles incorrectly, it risks misallocating huge resources, raising costs astronomically and unduly, or imposing harm on society or groups within society that would otherwise not occur in a free-market context. In the example of the Alaskan natural-gas pipeline the harm to the environment that may be caused by improper routing or inadequate construction is only one factor that must be weighed against the benefit to the consumer of having a secure domestic energy supply of significant proportions.

Weakness of Judicial Review

Judicial appellate review is removed, at least one step, from fact finding, and the scope of review requires that a great deal of deference be given to agency decisions. As a consequence, the case law that develops does not effect a rigorous, consistent examination of the effectiveness and efficiency of agency decisions. It is the rare appellate-court opinion that does not devote extensive efforts to a discussion of procedural matters and technical niceties rather than frontally probing substantive issues originally before the agency. The appellate process is yet another step in ineffective agency regulation. The judicial-review process usually cannot scrutinize agency doings sufficiently to make a meaningful statement about the propriety and wisdom of its actions.

Inefficient Regulation

Other instances of regulatory failure can be ascribed to simple inefficiency. The term *inefficiency* is used here in its economic sense: Does the particular administrative regime result in net economic benefits to society, or is the cost of the administrative program so high as to offset any gained benefits?[3] All costs of federal decision making generally must be borne by taxpayers rather than imposed on consumers of a product or service or on the owners of the firm that supplies that product or service. A valid question exists as to whether it is in the public interest to have society at large pick up the costs that could be precisely distributed in a competitive market? Regulatory costs could be imposed on the individual or firm appearing before the agency rather than imposed on tax-paying society. In the broader sense, cost accrues when agencies delay decision. Proposals exist to charge a fee for services such as the issuance of advisory opinions, adjustments from regulations, filings for applications, and other matters requiring agency attention. Federal agencies have the authority to charge fees for such services pursuant to the Independent Office Appropriations Act of 1952.[4] For example, about twelve years elapse before a nuclear-power plant becomes operational, in large part because of the time necessary to obtain all agency authorization. Granted, the issues involved in nuclear licensing may be complex and delicate. However, is twelve years of regulatory navel-gazing, which, in terms of real dollars can double or triple the cost of the plant over that time, worth it? Such delay is often so burdensome as to smother the desire to proceed. Is it justifiable politically to allow opponents to the construction of new energy projects to kill a project through strangulation in the tentacles of the administrative agencies' deliberations? The issue then becomes whether administrative law should delay and obstruct or whether the law should be used directly and explicitly to deal with difficult issues.

Another example of inefficiency is the agency-to-agency ping-pong game played at the federal and state levels as well as between these levels. For example, before an oil-shale plant comes on line, numerous federal, state, and local permits are needed from such agencies as the DOE, DOI (and various organs within those agencies), and the EPA. State mining and environmental approvals are required, and local zoning and environmental and building codes must be followed. It is not efficient to add to the cost of such a project those costs that result because of the conflicting demands that can occur within and between these levels of agency action and review. Nor is the duplication of administrative costs efficient.

Lack of Political Accountability

Agencies also fail because they may take actions considered antidemocratic because of the lessened political accountability of the agencies. Delegated their authority by Congress, agencies are thus removed a step from the electorate. The electorate does not give agencies a direct mandate; although this isolation is remedied in part by making agency actions open to the public scrutiny, serious questions remain as to the effectiveness of public access and participation. A homeowner upset with increased fuel bills cannot challenge that bill effectively before the energy agency with jurisdiction. The average individual is not conversant with the vagaries of rate design and return, declining-block rates, and marginal-cost pricing. Even if they are familiar with the terminology, individuals generally are incapable of evaluating a public utility's performance or accounting methods. A cadre of experts to dissect, analyze, and criticize is usually necessary to make any intelligent evaluation of the propriety of a utility's filings. Further, a concerned individual is seldom accorded the same real opportunity to be heard that the regulated company is given. Industry, as a result of familiarity with agency idiosyncracies, the revolving door, and the environment of camaraderie, cooperation, and compromise with agency personnal, have a voice more likely to be heard clearly than that of a concerned individual or small group of consumers.

Additionally, the costs of challenging a company's filings with an agency may be so high that individuals do not play at all in the regulatory game between the insiders—that is, the agency and industry. Is the answer to be found in group representation? If so, are groups forceful advocates in agency surroundings? Further, must concerned individuals compromise some of their beliefs to further those of the group?

Deregulation

Deregulation is the undoing, removal, or reduction of influence imposed by the government on a particular industry. It is an attempt to unravel the regulatory tapestry government has woven; a tapestry that arguably has such great imperfections as to be a failure. Industries affected by deregulation include airlines, trucking, railroads, banking, communications, crude oil, natural gas, and electric-power generation.

This book has discussed two forms of regulation—economic and social. In terms of deregulation, our comments are directed primarily toward economic regulation, because most deregulation efforts are price oriented. Deregulation of economic restrictions poses most difficult problems; the government upsets the status quo by permitting the market to set prices and allocate resources. The transition from the government-created market to the so-called free market has the potential to throw the economic system into a state of disequilibrium. In the case of social regulation restrictions can be lifted, but the economic marketplace is likely to remain intact.

Economic deregulation requires transition from a regulated, controlled, and predictable world (to the industry) to free-market unknowables and unpredictables: "Obviously, if an industry which government has shielded from competition for several decades were suddenly given complete pricing freedom, simultaneous with the removal of regulatory barriers to entry, a potential for sudden dramatic price increases would exist during the transition period to effective competitive entry."[5] A classic example of the division of opinion on basic effects of deregulation of an industry is the current debate over decontrol of producer prices for natural gas. In the natural-gas industry the Natural Gas Policy Act (NGPA) was designed to deregulate the producer prices at a leisurely pace stretching the process over a decade. Recently, however, political concerns have brought the possibility of immediate deregulation and the repeal of the NGPA to front-line consideration. Proponents of immediate deregulation argue that it will produce an estimated net annual welfare gain of $3.5 to 6 billion, eliminate administrative costs of enforcing the complicated pricing scheme, and better allocate natural gas. Opponents counter that the transfer of wealth from consumers to producers and holders of interests in so-called old gas would earn unjustified economic rents.[6] Industry argues that rapid deregulation will stimulate development, produce truer price signals to consumers, and promote the discovery and production of reserves. Opponents of more rapid decontrol express concern about the effects of more rapid deregulation on consumers. All agree that deregulation now or later means higher prices. Opponents of a speedier decontrol schedule believe that price increases will be dramatic and, given current gas-rate designs, will have a more serious negative impact on residential users than on either industrial or commercial users. Opponents also argue that deregulation will not promote competition in the gas industry as it is presently structured.

The proponents of deregulation of the gas industry's producer prices could approach the problems of more rapid modification of the market with the following maxims in mind: If the process of deregulation is structured properly the transition to a freer market setting can be eased. First, the more slowly the market structure is changed the easier the transition to decontrolled status will be. Second, where cross-subsidization of various industry elements is extensive, the elimination of regulations across-the-board makes the transition easier. Third, if the number of parties adversely affected by the transition is small then the negative consequences and costs imposed on them can be eased with some form of compensation. Finally, transition to decontrol will be smoother if the effect of deregulation is to make the target industry more competitive rather than more concentrated.[7]

Recently, deregulation of the electric-power-generating industry has received extensive consideration in regulatory circles. Proponents of electric-generating-industry deregulation, such as FERC Commissioner David Hughes, realize that such a deregulation program would have to be treated as experimental, be confined to a small segment of the industry, for example, bulk transmission or generation, and be keyed to promoting competitive markets.

Transition problems manifest themselves in a number of areas, the most serious being price-equilibrium and market-entry difficulties.[8] The most vocal and obvious fear of consumers of petroleum and petroleum-related products about decontrol of crude oil is that prices will increase dramatically. In industries in which consumers do not have much demand elasticity, where consumers must bear heavy price increases or forgo the product or service because there are few or no substitutes, deep concern about the effects of deregulation may be warranted. A concomitant problem is that if established firms have increased pricing flexibility then entry barriers to new competitors will be erected. Two solutions to this problem present themselves, sequencing—that is allowing a phased decontrol of prices such as that envisioned in the NGPA—and market segmentation—defining different geographical, product, or service areas for the removal of restrictions.

Professors Gaskins and Voytko in an article about the deregulation transition argue that the crude-oil-decontrol program and the NGPA with its pricing provisions aimed at encouraging investment in certain types of production actually created inefficient allocations of investments among types of production. The problem, they argue, may be avoided by not artificially isolating and creating price differentials between products within an industry. The inefficiencies in allocation of investment could be either reduced or eliminated by limiting the size or duration of the differentials or by utilizing a market-segmentation approach.[9]

A final problem is the "loser" in a deregulation program. For example,

> [c]rude oil decontrol and the deregulation of natural gas involves the most massive transfers of any regulatory change we have seen. Over the course of several decades, hundreds of billions of dollars, formerly held by oil users as a result of crude oil and natural gas price controls, will be returned to producers allowed to charge the market price.[10]

The authors also note that there are other shifts as well. Our domestic petrochemical industry, which benefited from low crude-oil prices, will see that advantage disappear. Also, small refiners whose profitability depended on federal subsidies will lose that support. On the positive side, coal and nuclear power will find better and more competitive markets.

In this case either so-called side payments or direct subsidies to provide for some type of compensation can and in some instances should be made to ease the way if there is a legitimate reason to protect a particular class of loser. In the case of small consumers of gas or heating oil, some subsidization to enable them to pay fuel bills may be necessary. In the case of small refiners or crude-oil resellers, who were the beneficiaries of the entitlements and crude-oil-price-control program, it appears that little legitimate economic purpose exists for continued underwriting of their activities by other companies, consumers, or society. An example of an indirect side payment is the Crude Oil Windfall Profits Tax of 1980. The law was enacted to siphon away gains from crude-oil-price rises in the form of an excise tax, which the federal government redistributes to the public at large.

Diversification

Utilities in the past decade have sought to diversify their activities beyond the classic utility-related operations. Diversification has become a middle path between decontrol and total regulatory reform. The utility may seek to expand into either utility-associated or nonassociated fields. An electric utility investing in coal fields and mines is diversified in a way that is associated with the utility industry, whereas investment in real estate, trucking, shipbuilding, or manufacturing is probably not. Utilities view diversification as a way of shoring up their financial position in an economy that has been less conducive to healthy utility investment than it once was. Diversification is seen as one way to attract capital investment in overall operations.

The concept of diversification varies in its application, depending on the industry in question. The telecommunications industry is highly diversified and is becoming more so because of technological advances in the field. The telecommunications business is changing rapidly in the deregulated environment—and pending settlement or other final resolution of the AT&T case is likely to become a more competitive industry.

The natural-gas industry is usually considered fairly diversified, because much exploratory and drilling activity is virtually unregulated, and, typically, portions of the industry are segmented from one another. The electric-utility industry classically has been considered to be the least diversified of the lot.

Philosophically at least diversification should present few problems to the regulator at the federal or state level. Utilities are regulated in the public interest and are given the opportunity to earn a fair rate of return on their regulated products and services as long as they are prudently managed. However, herein lies the principal practical problem. Given an ideology that encourages free enterprise and capital investment by utilities in the private unregulated sector, should regulators have the opportunity to review those management decisions to protect the public the utility serves—the ratepayers? Although the activities the utility pursues may be unregulated, the funds to undertake investments in the unregulated sector are usually provided by utility-related earnings from the ratepayer. Thus, in industries such as the electric-utility industry that are exploring diversification as a means to escape regulatory controls in the hopes of attracting capital, substantial questions remain as to the oversight necessary by the regulatory agency with jurisdiction over the utility operations.

Regulatory Tools

Decontrol is one species of regulatory reform. Generally, we have used the term to denote a rearrangement or lessening of government intervention into an industry or its segments rather than a final, complete deletion of a regulatory scheme. To make some sense of regulatory reforms a brief description of regulatory tools intended to correct market imperfections is included here.[11] The primary goal of these regulatory devices is economic efficiency.[12] You will note that reform can come about in various ways. Substantive methodological and procedural reforms all play parts in correcting flaws in the market and increasing economic efficiency.

Perhaps the most widely used method of economic regulation today is cost-of-service ratemaking. Cost-of-service rate making is an analysis system whereby the regulator determines the operating costs of a business and then adds in a fair amount of profit. The process serves as a price-setting mechanism for a particular good or service.

Cost-of-service regulation attempts to create or recreate a well-functioning competitive market, particularly in an industry that has the potential of developing monopolistic characteristics. However, cost-of-service rate making is not without problems. The obvious problem is that there is no settled, fail-safe way of determining a just and reasonable rate of return. Hundreds of federal, state-agency, and judicial decisions have wrestled with the concept since its introduction. Every state has its version of a public-service commission that, like federal agencies and the judiciary, has developed varying notions of what constitutes a just and reasonable rate. Each industry, and the agency that regulates it, has idiosyncracies that affect the rate-making process; and as the economy changes and as technology changes even more, adjustments and equilibrations must be made.

For example, in setting electric rates for power produced from nuclear generators, not only cost of generation but costs for the future decommissioning of a plant or the cleanup costs must now be factored into the just and reasonable rate. Different agencies address the problem of who pays the just and reasonable rate and when it is paid. Also, classic cost-of-service rate making may not provide adequate incentive for the efficient production of product or provision of service. The guaranteed reasonable rate of return for a prudently managed company may destroy the incentive for innovation, allowing a company and its management to sink into the comfort of a low-risk, low-reward business. In addition, price setting by its nature is based on historical events, particularly the company's past experience of costs and revenues, and does not take into account future problems such as inflation unless adjusted by regulatory fiat.

[T]he difficulty of making economic predictions about changes in demand and costs . . . . make it impossible for the regulator to replicate

the price and output results of a hypothetically competitive world. Under
a competitive regime, prices adjust fairly rapidly, . . . prices are based
on present cost, changes in demand resulting from changes in price will
be taken into account as they occur, and firms experiment with different
rate structures.[13]

With cost-of-service rate making, however, prices remain stable for
a fixed period of time, and these set prices may not yield the expected
revenue because of demand changes or market conditions, and firms find
it difficult to experiment with different prices.

A second type of regulatory tool to correct market inefficiency is
historically based price regulation. Classically, this system is used by the
government to set price controls affecting a wide array of firms. Although
the system superficially functions well in the early stages of its application, over time problems arise. This type of regulatory control functions
in the early stages because it is based on past events that have a controlling
effect on the immediate future functioning of the regulated industry. In
addition, the system may function well because the terms of the regulation
are applied evenly across the board—thus it tends to become self-en-
forcing.

However, over the long-term this system has not proven effective.
First, regulators are faced with the problem of how to price new products
or services. These new items have no historical base for the imposition
of a price. Therefore, the producers must either wait until all the old
items are sold or have the regulator set a price and hope that it will return
a profit. Another problem inherent in this system is the inability to establish a proper price of two identical items that may have been produced
at different times or under different circumstances. Two identical items
produced at different times, for example, may have significant cost differences simply because of inflation. Therefore the problem becomes one
of which product is sold first and to whom. Also, because of the change
in production or inflation and the price restrictions placed on these items,
the company and the regulator may be faced with deteriorating profitability.

Finally, producers subject to these price regulations begin to look for
areas that are not regulated to sell their products. As a result, the regulatory
system tries to expand regulation or close loopholes.

A third regulatory tool developed in the administrative system is the
use of a public-interest standard. The public-interest standard is used most
effectively when the demand for a product is much greater than the
supply. Like the concept of the just and reasonable rate, this is a subjective
method of selecting either which firm is best qualified to provide or
receive a product or service or who has the greatest need. A public-
interest standard, by definition, must be general to respond to many

interests. The element of generality inherent in such a broad standard means that if the agency does not interpret the standard wisely, certain classes or groups will be favored and others will be disadvantaged. If it is too general the standard can collapse into meaninglessness.

The public-interest standard may raise political-accountability problems. If the standard is established in the law by Congress then it must be implemented by the agency. Implementation of an ill-defined standard leads to conflicts in interpretation, which may be reviewed by the courts or by the electorate itself. However, if the agency sets the standard, it is done by an arm of government one step removed from the electorate. Further, despite the fact that a regulator may compile a list of criteria that appear balanced prior to making the subjective decision as to what is in the public interest, there are no guidelines as to the weight to be given particular criteria. Because of the lack of structure, the decision can turn solely on arbitrary selection. The result may be that public-interest standards are set, consciously or unconsciously, with a bureaucratic bias—one that favors compromise and following the path of least resistance. Public interest then becomes only what is in the eye of the regulator. Public interest in truth may evolve into the interest of the incumbent. The regulator may favor the interest with a proven track record rather than the untried.

Allocation based on an historical predicate is another mechanism employed by regulating agencies to iron out marketplace wrinkles. Historically based allocation is similar to historically based price setting and has many of the same problems. The major problem with both historically based allocation and price setting is that it ignores change, growth, and decline in firms, technology and the economy.

Perhaps the most fundamental problem with allocation is that at best it is merely a temporary solution. It is difficult to gauge the proper duration of such allocation, and the longer allocations occur the more dependent firms become on the system. At some point reliance may turn into entitlement, and a new market configuration may appear.

Individualized screening is another device applied by agencies in seeking a better mode of regulation. A vast array of imprecise standards requires regulators to screen out, on a case-by-case basis, those individuals or products that do not meet sometimes vague and often complex regulatory standards. Individualized screening is a costly device, and the development of nonarbitrary screening criteria can be arduous. Thus, regulators are put in the position of including or excluding more of the class to be screened than is economically efficient. Additionally, because the regulator-screener must rely on scientific tests and methodologies, which may or may not be accurate or applicable, the regulator may once again be dependent on subjective judgment.

Regulatory Reform

Regulatory failure is a popular theme of politicians and students of government. The reasons for the occurrence of regulatory failure are varied and intertwined. However, it is possible to identify a number of discrete causes for the breakdown of the process of regulation. Improper planning, speculative regulations, bias-toward the past and reliance on historical solutions in the face of a constantly changing present and future, misinterpretation and misapplication of data, and simply making the incorrect subjective decision are all factors that either jointly or severally may turn a regulatory program into a failure. If the wrong regulatory tool is used to fix a particular market-machine, either the tool or the machine will break. In its purest sense, regulatory reform seeks the right tool or forces the would-be mechanic to leave the machine alone.

Regulatory reform may proceed along two major paths: (1) Fundamental shifts in regulatory goals and foundations—movement away from regulating or changing the effects of the market function to a change in the market itself to seek a more competitive exchange between buyers and sellers—and (2) reform of regulatory process—refinement and tooling of the devices employed by agencies in regulating.

Antitrust regulation is a form of government action that seeks to achieve the conditions of a competitive marketplace. Although antitrust regulation has been touted as the patent medicine to cure virtually all American economic ills, as an alternative mode of government decision making its effectiveness is questionable. Antitrust litigation and remedies are extremely costly and very time consuming. After a dozen years of antitrust litigation brought by the Department of Justice against International Business Machines (IBM) the lawsuit was dropped by a newly appointed antitrust official in a new administration. After a decade of investigation of the eight major oil companies, billions of dollars in legal fees, consultant fees, government expenditures, and general drain on both the companies and the government, the case has gone nowhere and proven little. The magnitude of the litigation belies the results in many monumental antitrust cases. Antitrust may be effective when dealing with moderately large corporations or with excessive competition. But it is doubtful whether or not antitrust policing is an effective remedy for such occurrences as spillovers, inadequate or misleading information, or when the size and resources of a firm, such as IBM or AT&T or the eight major oil companies, exceed those of the government or private party that seeks to invoke antitrust remedies.

Another structural way of reforming regulation is the imposition or removal of taxes on a particular industry. Traditionally used to raise revenue, taxes have the equally prominent goal of encouraging or discouraging a particular type of conduct. Taxes have been used extensively in the energy field as regulating devices, although taxes in and of themselves do not prohibit outright the use or production of any given product. On the contrary, if a particular industry or individual is willing to pay the additional tax for the privilege to produce a particular product he may do so. Thus, in the case of a government wishing to discourage reliance on a particular fuel, taxation of use is a natural regulatory policy. For a government interested in encouraging development of a particular energy-supply source, tax benefits are a sure step to encourage development.

A final draconian solution to market defects is government ownership and operation of a resource or industry. No adversary relation between regulator and firm exists—both become as one. This approach is, at least in U.S. society, probably politically and economically unacceptable. The concept of nationalization is not one with which many Americans are enamoured, and it is a devastating indictment of the ability of government to regulate and the regulated to be governed. Further, the prevailing orthodoxy of American capitalism is that private-sector management is far more efficient and effective than government-sponsored, -supported or dominated firms, because the profit incentive present in private enterprise is eliminated. The profit incentive, it is believed, increases production, sharpens management, brings down costs, encourages technological innovation, and fosters competition. Thus, the nationalization option as a regulatory reform is not under active consideration in the upper echelons of policymaking.

The antitrust and taxation modes of governance are broad-based structural methods employed in the hope of attaining a free, desirable market. The other method of achieving regulatory reforms is systemic, seeking the alteration of the process of agency decision making or the nature and scope of judicial review.

As discussed in chapters 1 and 2, agency decision making occurs in two basic modes, adjudication and rule making. Rule making has become dominant as a process, a trend criticized on the grounds that it gives the agency too much policymaking power with a lack of due-process safeguards. Thus, regulatory reform directed at agency process has sought alternatives to rule making as it presently exists in most federal agencies.

Another proposal surfacing in studies of the agency process is a move away from adversarial decision making to the bargaining process. The use of negotiation in regulatory processes, particularly in informal rule making, also would be encouraged.[14]

By institutionalizing the negotiation methodology over an adversary mode of dispute resolution, it is hypothesized that the interest-representation model of administrative process will replace the traditional process.[15] The thrust behind the interest-representation model is that instead of agency administrators and their staffs developing rules, views of those interested individuals or groups directly affected would more directly control the rules. The interest-representation model does not use economic efficiency as its guiding norm. Rather, political and social interests, including public confidence in the decision-making process, are paramount.

The benefits of regulation by negotiation include the promise of superior substantive outcomes. Complex problems may be brought to a more satisfactory resolution by the input and compromise of those directly affected by the rule. Instead of decided winners and losers, the hallmark of the litigation process, negotiations might yield compromise solutions that accomodate all interested parties. Thus, the solution should reach a higher level of acceptability. Further, the process, if structured correctly, is more democratic than either rule making or adjudication.[16]

Regulatory reforms also include institutional reforms, such as legislative and executive vetos of agency action to promote political accountability[17] or procedural reforms such as restructuring the APA.[18]

Because the impact of regulatory programs varies wildly depending on the nature of the regulated company, Congress enacted the Regulatory Flexibility Act in January 1981.[19] The act recognizes that agency decision making will have varying impacts depending on the nature and size of a firm within an industry.

The prior discussion of regulatory reform is based on three ideas: identify goals, identify failures, and use a regulatory-reform strategy to meet those goals.[20] The goal implicit in this discussion of regulatory tools is founded on the tenet that competition in the market is preferable to government regulation. However, if government regulation is needed, then the least-restrictive method of regulation should be used. This grand strategem concentrates on economic regulation. Thus it is guided by a principle of economic efficiency or wealth maximization. The failure of regulators to recognize differences in scale can adversely affect competition in the market, by preventing entry and discouraging innovation, for example. Thus, the act tailors regulatory requirements to the scale of a business. The act requires that whenever an agency begins the rule-making process, it must prepare and make available for public comment an "initial regulatory flexibility analysis" describing the impact of the proposed rule on small entities. The factors to be included in the flexibility analysis include such information as a statement of the objectives of the proposed rule, the number of entities to be affected, and an identification of all relevant federal rules that may duplicate or overlap the proposed rule. When an agency promulgates a final rule then a "final flexibility analysis'' must be filed. The act also explicitly limits the scope of judicial review by barring review in some instances to reduce the possibility that the law might be used as a delaying tactic.

A major proposed legislative reform effort is S. 1080, the Regulatory Reform Act of 1981, which has been sponsored by three-fourths of the Senate.[21] The bill was generated in response to criticisms that regulatory agencies have added to the costs of production and to prices to consumers without significantly improving the health and safety of production and consumption. Also it was felt that costs of compliance seriously undermine agency effectiveness. This proposal, then, follows the lead of Executive Order 12,291 issued 17 February 1981 and imposes a cost-benefit-analysis requirement for agency actions. Another dramatic change in process in S. 1080 concerns judicial review. In addition to setting aside agency actions under the circumstances prescribed in the APA, the reviewing court is authorized to set aside agency actions that are without substantial support in the rule-making file when reviewed as a whole. This review pertains to the asserted or necessary factual basis of an agency action as distinguished from the policy or legal basis. The effect of this standard is that courts will have a greatly expanded scope of review of rule-making proceedings. Also, courts would be given authority to ''independently'' decide all relevant questions of law, interpret constitutional and statutory provisions, and determine the meaning or applicability of the terms of an agency action. This means that no burden of proof shifts to the court and that the courts do not necessarily defer to agencies on legal issues. The effect of S. 1080 is to further entwine courts in agency decision making.

Notes

1. *See generally,* J. Tomain, Energy Law in a Nutshell 80–85 (1981).

2. *See,* G. Calabresi, A Common Law for the Age of Statutes (1981).

3. *See,* ABA Commission on Law and the Economy, Federal Regulation: Roads to Reform (Final Report, 1978).

4. In scattered sections of 12, 31, 36, 42, 49 and 50 U.S.C. (1976).

5. Gaskins & Voytko, *Managing the Transition to Deregulation,* 44 Law and Contemp. Probs. 9, 11 (1981).

6. Hollis, *Natural Gas: Options, Issues, Risks,* 1980 Petroleum

Independent 51. Pierce, *Natural Gas Regulation, Deregulation, and Contracts,* 68 Va. L. Rev. 63, 73 (1982).

7. Magat, *Introduction: Managing the Transition to Deregulation,* 44 Law and Contemp. Probs. 1 at 4 (1981).

8. The discussion of transition problems is taken from Gaskins & Voytko, *supra* note 3, at 11–30.

9. Other problems discussed by Gaskins & Voytko include unequal competitive opportunities, uncertainty, "lumpiness" (deregulating segments of an industry gradually rather than entire industry), slow industry response, and complete deregulation of an industry. A full discussion of winners and losers appears in L. Thurow, the Zero-Sum Society (1980).

10. Gaskins & Voytko, *supra* note 6, at 17.

11. The basis of this discussion is, Breyer, *Analyzing Regulatory Failure: Mismatches, Less Restrictive Alternatives, and Reform,* 92 Harv. L. Rev. 547 (1979).

12. The phrase *economic efficiency* is far from being unambiguous. It can mean wealth maximization. The Pareto-superiority criterion means that an allocation of resources is efficient which makes at least one person better off and no one is worse off. The Kaldor-Hicks criterion of efficiency is a variation of Pareto superiority, and it states that an allocation is efficient when gains are large enough to offset loses and that losers could be compensated by winners.

13. Breyer, *supra* note 11, at 565.

14. Note, *Rethinking Regulation: Negotiation as an Alternative to Traditional Rulemaking,* 94 Harv. L. Rev. 1871 (1981).

15. Stewart, *The Reformation of Administrative Law,* 88 Harv. L. Rev. 1669 (1975).

16. *Rethinking Regulation, supra* note 14, at 1876–78.

17. *A Fresh Look at Federal Regulatory Strategies,* 32 Ad. L. Rev. at 186–90 (Comments of William F. Kennedy).

18. *Id.* at 287–381.

19. 5 U.S.C. sec. 601. The president has also implemented a methodological change for executive branch agencies with Executive Order 12,291, which requires executive-branch agencies to adopt cost-benefit analysis. This is discussed in chapter 7.

20. *A Fresh Look at Federal Regulatory Strategies,* 32 Ad. L. Rev. 165, 166–72 (1980) (comments of Stephen Breyer).

21. The bill and senatorial comments appear in 127 Cong. Rec. S4228–S4242, (daily ed. April 30, 1981).

5 Decision Making in a Federal System

Energy decision making is about the allocation and use of power as much as it is about pricing and allocation of natural resources. There are many legal influences that affect how policy is formed. The federal institutional framework within which decisions are made and the methodologies employed by those institutions directly affect the outcome of decisions and therefore affect the resulting policy. Another factor that contributes to the shaping of a national energy policy is the political and constitutional fact that numerous sovereigns have input in our federal system. Although the federal government has asserted a heavy hand in energy policymaking with the passage of the National Energy Act and the Energy Security Act, these acts only partially displace the role of the states regarding energy decisions.[1] With President Reagan's call for a ''new federalism'' and with his plan to dismantle the Department of Energy the proper allocation of power between the states and the federal government over energy policy must be examined.

Federalism

Any energy-policy design that purports to be comprehensive must confront the inherent tension that exists between the states and the federal government in determining how best to produce, transport, and use energy resources. Federalism is less a doctrine or rule of law than it is a geophysical and geopolitical reality. For the uninitiated, federalism describes the allocation of power between the states and the central government. A theoretical given is that the people of this country are the repositories of all power. They then ceded some power to the states, which are the basic governmental units of sovereignty. The states in turn delegated enumerated powers to the federal government while explicitly retaining all undelegated power.[2] However, since Chief Justice John Marshall's decision in *Gibbons* v. *Ogden* the phenomenal growth of the federal government's power has been legitimized.[3] Much of the rise of the dominance of the central government has been because of the perceived need to reduce competition between the states so that national commerce and national markets could operate smoothly, thus making the United States a viable commercial participant in world markets.

Federalism centers around a debate between centralized and decentralized or noncentralized decision making. To assess whether the allocation of power between federal and state governments is proper, basic questions must be posed and answered. Will centralization or decentralization result in:

a more efficient allocation and distribution of resources?

a better and more effective representation of interest groups?

a more effective and efficient resolution of spillover effects and externalities?

a better statement and preservation of moral ideals and political values?[4]

Unquestionably, these are difficult questions, founded in values that to some extent may be incompatible. As a society, we may reach a consensus, for example, that a central agency can make decisions more efficiently regarding nuclear power in an economic sense. That is, the federal Nuclear Regulatory Commission (NRC) can make nuclear-power decisions more cheaply than several states can. At the same time, as a society we can agree that nuclear power presents so many delicate moral and philosophical issues that a decentralized decision-making structure more effectively gauges the will of the people. It is precisely this sort of conflict between an economic calculus and political and social variables inherent in the legal rules that institutionalizes the concept of federalism. In this chapter we will explore three issues that exemplify the difficulties surrounding energy decision making in a federal system. We conclude that these institutionalized frictions impede the formulation of a comprehensive national energy policy.

State Taxation of National Resources

Recently the U.S. Supreme Court handed down three opinions on state taxation of natural resources.[5] As constitutional law each case is remarkably consistent; as energy policy they are not. They are consistent because these cases deal with the same rules of law and the rule is fairly uniformly applied, but as energy policy the cases go in opposite directions. Indeed they cannot help but be inconsistent, because there are too many conflicting variables operating simultaneously within any given energy policy. At one analytic level an argument can be made (and has been made) that the so-called energy crisis requires a concerted national effort to promote domestic production, to move away from dependence on foreign sources, and to price resources efficiently and reasonably. Thus, the role of the states in formulating and carrying out a national energy policy should be subservient to national interests. These three severance-tax cases do not further that national-energy-policy picture. They could not be true to that portrayal of an energy policy and be faithful to constitutional law at the same time.

Commerce-clause analysis is fairly straightforward. To avoid the commercial balkanization of the states, the U.S. Constitution gives precedence to national commercial interests. If a state's commercial policy or practice can be shown to interfere with interstate commerce the parochial state interest must fall. States, in this regard, cannot discriminate in favor of their citizens over citizens of other states.[6]

In a 1977 case the Supreme Court established a functional four-part test for assessing the constitutionality of state-taxation cases. The Court considers ''not the formal language of the tax statute but rather its practical effect and [sustains] a tax against Commerce Clause challenge when the tax is applied to an activity with a substantial nexus with the taxing state, is fairly apportioned, does not discriminate against interstate commerce, and is fairly related to the services provided by the state.''[7] In the three cases that will be discussed, Louisiana's first-use tax violated this test, but Montana's severance tax and the severance tax imposed by the Jicarilla Apache Tribe did not. In the Louisiana case the state imposed a tax of 7 cents per thousand cubic feet of natural gas on the so-called first use of any gas imported into Louisiana that was not previously taxed by any other state or the federal government. This tax was equal to the state severance tax on Louisiana gas producers. The primary effect of the tax was on gas produced in federal Outer Continental Shelf (OCS) areas, processed within Louisiana boundaries, and moved into interstate commerce. The purpose of the tax was to reimburse the people of Louisiana for damages to the state's coastal areas and waters, to compensate the state for costs incurred in protecting these resources, and to equalize competition between gas produced in Louisiana, which was subject to the 7-cent state severance tax, and gas produced elsewhere, which was not subject to the severance tax. The effect of the tax, because of credits and exemptions, was that Louisiana consumers were not burdened by the tax but out-of-state purchasers were. The Court held that the first-use tax unquestionably discriminated against interstate commerce as a result of the tax credits and exemptions. As a matter of constitutional law the case is properly decided. The effect of the tax was to give local interests a competitive advantage, and thus it was violative of the antidiscrimination and procompetition aspects of the commerce clause.

Montana's severance tax, imposed on each ton of coal mined within the state fared better. There are various rates of taxation depending on the value, energy content, and method of extraction of the coal, and the rate may equal, at a maximum, 30 percent of the contract price of the coal. Appellant coal companies in the case argued that Montana's severance tax discriminated against interstate commerce because 90 percent of the coal mined in Montana is shipped out of state and with the coal so goes the tax burden. The Court noted that unlike *Maryland* v. *Louisiana,* all coal producers in Montana were taxed similarly. Again the Montana case follows constitutional law, as does the Louisiana case. Yet clearly the impact on a national energy policy of each case is disparate. The invalidation of the Louisiana tax fosters a national energy market by eliminating discrimination between local and out-of-state producers—yet Montana's tax structure burdens the national energy market by shifting the tax bite out of state. Adherence to the ideal of federalism, then, puts national energy policymaking in a curious and anomalous position. The Supreme Court allows state taxation to affect interstate commerce as long as the locals are equally burdened. Presumably, Louisiana could also burden out-of-state gas producers as long as local gas producers had to pay the same taxes, thereby encouraging the imposition of a tax whose result is to burden the development of a national energy policy geared toward promoting domestic production.

Thus, what we see is a substantive-law rule, dealing with the limits of a state's ability to tax, that is applied consistently as a matter of law but that has conflicting consequences as a matter of policy and may even defeat the purposes of the policy. In part this is because policy options conflict themselves. Another reason, the one we focus on here, is that substantive-law rules and the institutional structure within which those rules are applied have a nature and force of their own, which may not, and in this case do not, comport with a national energy policy. Part of the reasoning behind the commerce clause is the promotion of national markets. A conflicting reason is more overtly political—to preserve and promote, at least partially, the sovereignty of the states.[8]

The political nature of these severance-tax cases is more apparent in *Merrion* v. *Jicarilla Apache Tribe*. The tribe imposed a severance tax on any oil and natural gas severed or removed from tribal lands situated in New Mexico. Long-term leasees challenged that tax as being contrary to the commerce clause. The Supreme Court held that taxing power was an inherent attribute of tribal sovereignty and that the tax satisfied the *Complete Auto Transit* test. In deciding the case the Court's primary and natural concern centered around the discussion of the unique status of indian tribes in this country and of the need to protect their attributes of sovereignty. The Court viewed the power to tax as an "essential instrument of self-government and territorial management."[9] Clearly, the desire for the preservation of sovereign integrity outweighed the desire for an economically efficient national energy policy. The reason for the disparity is the doctrine and reality of federalism.

The Supremacy Clause

Another rule of law that embodies the federalist spirit is the supremacy clause.[10] The essential effect of this clause is to have the federal government preempt the exercise of power by the states. Based on the notion that the states have given up certain powers to the federal government, the states may not interfere with the exercise of that power by the federal government. Analysis of supremacy-clause cases begins with identifying which power the federal government is exercising. There must be some constitutional basis for the federal government's assertion of power. If that prerequisite is not extant, the activity is ultra vires or beyond the power of the federal government. The expansive scope of the commerce clause is usually sufficient to provide a power source. Next, the issue becomes whether state and federal regulations can coexist or whether federal regulation has supplanted and excluded state regulation.

Like any generally worded provision the supremacy clause is open to interpretation and misinterpretation. The basic area for disagreement is where the so-called power line between the federal and state governments should be drawn. There are two variations on this theme: first, whether the federal government may regulate an area that has been traditionally left to the states, and second, whether states may regulate where federal regulation already exists but the extent of such regulation has not been determined.

The federal courts have been consistent in sustaining federal energy legislation against constitutional attacks. Once the federal government demonstrates a national need for regulation it is a short step to legitimize federal intervention. To justfiy this imposition all Congress must demonstrate is that the means of regulation selected are reasonably related to the goal of regulating interstate commerce. In *Hodel* v. *Virginia Mining and Reclamation Assoc., Inc.*[11] and *Hodel* v. *Indiana,*[12] the Supreme Court sustained the validity of the 1977 Surface Mining Control and Reclamation Act against various constitutional challenges, including arguments by the states that the Tenth Amendment protected their right to regulate coal mining on private land from federal encroachment: "Although such congressional enactments obviously curtail or prohibit the states' prerogatives to make legislative choices respecting subjects the states may consider important, the Supremacy Clause permits no other result."[13] Other recent energy legislation that has been challenged includes the Powerplant and Industrial Fuel Use Act[14]; Natural Gas Policy Act of 1978 (NGPA)[15]; and the Public Utilities Regulatory Policies Act of 1978 (PURPA).[16] It was alleged in each case that federal intrusion into areas of traditional state regulation is impermissible. In *Atlanta Gas Light Co.* v. *DOE*,[17] the Court of Appeals upheld the Fuel Use Act, intended to conserve oil and natural gas, by prohibiting the use of these resources in certain installations, at the same time encouraging the use of coal. In *Atlanta Gas* the plaintiffs argued that a prohibition on the use of natural gas for lighting purposes was beyond federal control because of the inherently local nature of their business. Even conceding the local nature of this industry, the fact that it affects interstate commerce (here the national concern with the shortage of natural gas) means that it is no longer immune from regulation by the central government: "More importantly, the relatively small gas savings resulting from the Fuel Use Act must be considered as an integral part of a much broader federal regulatory program aimed at shifting our nation's energy consumption toward fuels that are more plentiful and accessible than natural gas."[18]

The NGPA was likewise sustained by the Tenth Circuit.[19] Since 1954 federal regulation of natural-gas sales was limited to those made in interstate commerce. Intrastate sales were left to be regulated by the states, if at all. As a result of these dual regulatory systems different markets with marked price disparities arose, and those disparities eventually created market dislocations. One purpose of the NGPA was to unify the intrastate and interstate markets through direct and indirect regulation of sales and other transactions in both markets. This attempt at unification was attacked by Texas, Oklahoma, and Louisiana as interfering with each state's jurisdiction. Following *Hodel* the Court of Appeals rejected these arguments and sustained the act.

PURPA originally faired less well in Mississippi when the U.S. District Court for the Southern District declared it unconstitutional. The decision of the lower court has been reversed in a split decision by the Supreme Court sustaining the constitutionality of PURPA.[20] Thus the first federal intrusion into the rate-making processes of electric- and natural-gas-regulatory-commissions utilities has been authorized. It is hardly surprising that federal energy legislation is having such an easy go of it in the courts—after all, central markets always have been preferable theoretically to fragmented ones.

The focus on federalism changes significantly when a state attempts to undertake regulation in an area that the federal government is already regulating. Under the banner of cooperative federalism both governments may regulate as long as the states do not interfere or conflict with an area that is the subject of legitimate federal regulation. If state law does conflict then the federal regulation preempts that of the states.

There is no more obvious area for conflict between state and federal regulation than that of nuclear energy. Historically, the development and regulation of nuclear power was controlled by the military. After World War II and the Korean War scientists sought to pass on the benefits of nuclear power used in military activities through commercial utilization. To facilitate the development of this field the Atomic Energy Act was passed and the federal Atomic Energy Commission was created. "Our Friend the Atom" was the hope for a safe and technologically expansive future—and the federal government was to be at the helm for this voyage. The voyage, recently, has not been as smooth as it was envisioned three decades ago. As fears increase regarding reactor "incidents," transportation, and waste management, many citizens have expressed deep concern about the role of the federal government in bringing nuclear power into their lives. To remedy perceived inadequacies state legislatures have attempted to pass a variety of laws regarding many aspects of nuclear regulation only to have the bulk of this legislation declared invalid under the preemption doctrine. A recent and controversial exception is *Pacific Legal Foundation* v. *State Energy Resources Conservation & Development Commission*.[21] The case is controversial because most decided cases and prevailing scholarship indicate how pervasive (if not inclusive) federal regulation is in this field.[22] The Court of Appeals held that the California statutes that imposed a moratorium on the construction of new nuclear plants until a state agency found a satisfactory method of waste disposal were not preempted.

Like the discussion of the severance-tax cases, cases that deal with issues of federalism (Tenth Amendment, supremacy clause, and preemption) are not difficult to reconcile as a matter of law. In the nuclear-power field centralized decision making as fostered by preemption is the norm as a matter of law. As policy though, the movement toward decentralization is gaining momentum in instances where federal agencies simply fail to provide adequate safeguards for nuclear-energy use and control.

The principle of federalism is broad enough to allow federal and state involvement in the same aspects of the policymaking process. The National Energy Act, whose various parts are now being sustained by judicial decree, promotes centralized decision making. However, President Reagan's "new federalism" initiatives conflict with that premise, and the proposal to dismantle DOE seeks to decentralize energy-policy decision making.

Fast Tracking

A final example of the dichotomy between centralization and decentralization of energy decision making is the history of a failed legislative proposal known as "fast tracking." The perceived energy crisis of the 1970s was precipitated by two complementary events. Domestic production of crude oil and natural gas decreased. To supplement the limited supplies resulting from lagging domestic production, the United States became dependent on foreign sources of crude oil. Thus, our present energy programs and policies have as their chief characteristic the goal of reversing these twin developments. National energy programs are intended to increase the domestic supply of resources and to reduce dependence on foreign sources, particularly in a potentially unstable world.

Fast tracking is one regulatory response to these problems. *Fast tracking* denotes a streamlining and speeding up of administrative and other institutional permit processes to promote energy development. It is a response that is predominantly structural rather than substantive, directed to knocking down the obstacles created by the bureaucratic mind set. The bureaucratic mentality, characterized by a welter of overlapping, duplicative, and sometimes inconsistent administrative rules and regulations, reaches deep into our legal, political, and economic cultures. The rise of entitlements, the expansion of the number and types of rules and regulations, the increase in the variety of regulatory tools, and the concomitant increase in intergovernmental and intragovermental and interagency and intraagency conflicts exist throughout the alphabet soup of agencies at the federal and state level.

These conflicts cause delay in taking action. These delays mean increased costs, a slow-down in the production of energy, and a slow-down in the implementation and testing of new technologies. This is the down side. Delay, however, can also bring benefits. Delay ensures more time to test new ideas and complex technologies, more public participation and hence more democratic decision-making processes, as well as more reflective procedures before a commitment is made. Thus, fast tracking that intends to coordinate governmental activities, reduce duplication, expedite processes, and remove or reduce agency conflicts to mobilize energy in a time of crisis is not so compelling as to minimize the serious problems that inhere in speeding up the regulatory process.

We might view fast tracking as a government's impatient response to the energy crisis, realizing itself through greater centralization. As a society we may feel the energy pinch as it is reflected in higher costs in our utility bills and at the gas pump. These are some immediate effects. However, we are also becoming aware of longer-term effects such as rapid and permanent depletion of our natural resources. There are other less noticeable, yet nonetheless real long-term effects of the energy crisis, and as a society we are forced to deal with distributional and transgenerational issues as well. How does fast tracking fit into this scheme?

We explore this issue by review of the Priority Energy Project Act

(PEPA) on the federal level and the Colorado Joint Review Process (CJRP) on the state level.

Federal Fast Tracking—Its Benefits and Pitfalls

At the federal level, the concept of fast tracking has been bandied about for several years. In June 1979 the 96th Congress introduced S. 1806 which was entitled the Energy Mobilization Board Act. This bill was seen as a complementary part of President Carter's Energy Security Act proposals as outlined in his presidential energy message on 15 and 16 July 1979. In that message the president announced his proposals for the development of synthetic fuels and for the development of alternative technologies. Both of these strategies require a serious commitment from all levels of government. In the case of synthetic-fuels development the large-scale and often interstate nature of the physical plants and equipment mean that numerous governmental permits are required at every level of government. In addition, the development of alternative technologies, some of which are also large-scale operations, may require government-backed financial support. To expedite these developments the Energy Mobilization Board (EMB) proposed by S. 1806 was a device to cut through ''red tape'' and avoid ''bureaucratic delays.'' This proposal never passed yet it is illustrative of the role that the central government may play in formulating a national energy policy. What society must ask itself is at what cost does centralization come?

The bill, as amended, was reintroduced as S. 1308 and was rejected by the Senate-House Conference Committee in June 1980. However, on 10 March 1981 Senator Jackson introduced S. 688, entitled the Priority Energy Project Act (PEPA), which is another yet similar proposal for fast-tracking legislation.

Although none of the proposals became law, their makeup reflects much about current political and social attitudes toward the role of government in energy decision-making processes. The bills indicate the general dismay over bureaucratic delay and duplication, impatience with administrative processes, and the perceived need for expedition. The problems presented by such proposals go far beyond either the real technical difficulties of implementation or the natural bureaucratic resistance to loss of power over an established domain. The more problematic and troubling issues posed by fast-tracking legislation go to the fundamental division of power and responsibility between major agencies such as the Department of Energy and the Environmental Protection Agency as well as between federal and state and local governments.

The purposes of S. 668 are straightforward enough: to increase the national security by reducing dependence on foreign oil; to coordinate and simplify the approval process for nonnuclear energy facilities; and to facilitate the integration of federal, state, and local procedures. PEPA also created an EMB to oversee the expediting process.

The process under S. 668 starts when the EMB designated a proposal as an ''energy project,'' broadly defined in the act as a ''priority energy project.'' To make such a finding the EMB was to determine that a particular project or class of projects is in ''the national interest,'' which was further defined to be a project that directly or indirectly reduces U.S. dependence on foreign oil. The interested project sponsor was simply to apply to the EMB for the designation if the applicant believed that the normal approval requirements would substantially delay a final decision and that critical regulatory problems were likely to be encountered. The adequacy of the application was not subjected to judicial review.

Because of the totally voluntary nature of PEPA, fast tracking could only be instituted through a request by an individual who wished a priority designation. Once the request had been presented, the EMB was to publish a notice in the *Federal Register* and to allow for public comment on the proposal. EMB was to evaluate the proposal in light of the public comments and either approve or disapprove the priority-designation request.

This designation, although an agency decision, was not subject to the environmental-impact-statement requirement of the National Environmental Policy Act. Thus, the EMB's decision to designate an application as a priority energy project was exempted from two significant types of oversight—judicial review and NEPA analysis. Whether expedition is worth a reduction in these types of review of either large projects or untested technologies is a question yet unanswered.

Finally, after a priority designation is made, the EMB was to announce a schedule of all deadlines affecting that particular project. The schedule, known as the Project Decision Schedule (PDS) is the heart of the PEPA. The PDS sets filing dates and permit requirements with a view toward the elimination of unnecessary duplication of applications for permits from various local, state, and federal agencies and toward the uniform collection of data.

Once the EMB published a PDS, if a project qualified as major federal action under NEPA then it became subject to NEPA's requirement of an environmental-impact statement. The EMB was authorized to require the preparation of one final statement to satisfy all federal, state, and local environmental report requirements.

The EMB was to require legislative-type rather than trial-type hearings by the affected agencies, thus taking the decision-making process away from the adversarial process and toward consensus finding.

The obvious source of potential conflict was between the EMB's PDS and the permit schedules of other federal, state, or local agencies. PEPA granted the EMB the authority to make the necessary decisions regarding the progress of a particular project to take any required action and to bring an enforcement action in U.S. district court when an agency either failed to make a timely decision according to the PDS or was reasonably likely to fail to do so. Further, the EMB could have intervened in any federal-, state-, or local-agency proceeding that involved a subject-energy project.

The bulk of EMB's power was directed explicitly toward restructuring the energy decision-making process to run more smoothly and quickly. Little substantive power was to be at EMB's disposal, although EMB was given authority to waive the application of any federal, state, or local laws enacted after the commencement of construction of a ''critical energy facility'' on an EMB finding that the waiver was necessary to ensure timely and cost-effective completion and that the waiver will not endanger public health or safety. EMB could also recommend to the president the suspension, modification, or amendment of certain federal laws that present a substantial impediment to a project.

These latter powers to have been granted to the EMB would have allowed a superagency to supersede other agencies, presenting vast areas of controversy. It is hard to justify duplicative, expensive, time-consuming review of a single project by many overlapping agencies. It is, however, much less compelling to argue that agencies cannot exercise their jurisdictional powers in the absence of threats by an ''all-knowing'' oversight bureau.

Federal fast-tracking legislation presents serious and significant legal and policy problems. First, and most prominent, is the degree of direct federal involvement in state and local decision making processes looming in such a proposal. Specifically, PEPA empowers the federal government to exert its influence and control over state and local governments as needed to ensure that such governments comply with the PDS. The federal government could therefore affect how state or local agencies make decisions concerning such typically local matters as licensing and site selection.

Second, if the preemption contemplated by PEPA were to be given effect, the financial, environmental, or social well-being of a given community could be adversely affected. Because the federal government is less familiar with the needs and socioeconomic makeup of a particular area, federal reign over energy decision making is apt to overvalue, undervalue, or ignore the community's interests. In its haste to see a particular facility constructed, the federal government could easily sacrifice or impair long-standing local social and economic interests.[23]

A third consequence of fast tracking in the energy-development area is the effect it could have on the mix of technologies available to resolve the energy problem. A statutory scheme modeled on PEPA could well narrow such a mix over the short and middle terms. Under PEPA, priority energy projects would invariably be large scale, and multi-billion-dollar enterprises would be commonplace. Those more likely to enter such a market are large energy companies, including the major oil companies. Their primary interests, however, may not lie in developing wholly innovative alternative or transitional technologies or sources but rather in developing oil and gas substitutes and in such pursuits as acquiring substantial coal and oil-shale holdings. Thus, lower cost, softer-path technologies or resource substitutes may be trampled over in the care and feeding of the large-scale energy projects contemplated in federal fast-tracking proposals. States and their local subdivisions could more easily accomodate small-scale and alternative technologies such as solar development and gasohol. Ultimately, PEPA concerns the kind of energy future and society suggested for the twenty-first century. To the extent that an adopted fast-track program provides an economic, regulatory, and legal advantage to priority-designated projects, it can be expected that projects so designated could form the dominant energy technologies for the future. A fast-track technological bias will be created. Since the authority to grant fast-track status would rest with the federal government, control over the mix would necessarily reflect federal policies and might result in a drive to "nationalize" energy.[24]

Fourth, a PEPA-like statutue would establish an artificial dichtomy between priority and nonpriority projects. Those with the favored designation and an expedited schedule would be, relatively speaking, less costly to complete because of a shortened regulatory lag.

Fifth, fast tracking reduces the degree and efficacy of public participation otherwise available in several respects. First, an entity such as the EMB would increase the federal presence as already described. Local interests and concerns may not be heard as clearly, if they are heard at all. Second, the number of hearings would be curtailed. Third, if the EMB was forced to make the decisions in lieu of the local or state government because of the latter's failure to meet a deadline then representation of local interests may be severely limited. Finally, if laws are modified or waived, previously established rights of public participation have been eliminated.

The final policy problem is the impact of fast tracking on the environment. Those energy projects that receive priority status would be able to obtain a time preference over nonpriority projects. The time preference would have allowed the project to begin construction at an early point and, as a result, the new facility would begin to disseminate pollutants earlier as well. The pollutants emitted by the earlier-designated projects gain an advantage in the calculation of the acceptable limit of pollutants in an area.[25]

PEPA has been examined for its constitutionality. In its preamble PEPA asserted that its purpose is to regulate interstate and foreign commerce, to promote the national defense, and to increase national security; thus, it can be said that PEPA's roots are in the commerce clause. An argument can also be made that PEPA can find support in the war-powers clause among others.[26] All a reviewing court must find is that there is a rational basis for a congressional finding that the regulated activity affects interstate commerce. Under this rational-basis standard large-scale energy-production facilities would be immune from the reach of Congress in only rare instances. In a 1979 memorandum the Department of Justice argued that the commerce clause is a sufficient grant of federal power to allow an EMB to exercise the broad authority contemplated for it under an act like PEPA.[27] The Supreme Court has also suggested that the commerce clause would provide a sufficient basis for the federal regulation of priority energy projects: "Even activity that is purely intrastate in character may be regulated by Congress, where the activity, combined with like conduct by others similarly situated, affects commerce among the states or with foreign nations."[28] More recently, the severance-tax cases support this view.

Thus, although the exercise of federal power must be based on a constitutional provision, as suggested, the commerce clause has been construed to be a grant of very broad authority to Congress to legislate. The clause must have some limits. An exercise of power claimed under authority of the commerce clause may run afoul of other constitutional provision, such as the Tenth Amendment. The Tenth Amendment reserves to the states all powers the Constitution does not delegate to the federal government. In *National League of Cities* v. *Usery,* the Supreme Court made clear that there are limits to the authority of the federal government to regulate state agencies pursuant to its commerce-clause powers in an opinion that raises some question as to whether a federal agency such as EMB could constitutionality supersede state and local decision making.[29] PEPA provided that if a state or local agency (as well as a federal agency) fails to meet a PDS deadline, then the EMB can make the necessary decision. After *National League of Cities* it is questionable whether such displacement of state or local decision making by the EMB could pass constitutional muster.

Although ample precedent exists for the federal setting of standards that displace those of state or local governments, *National League of Cities* deals with a different sort of situation. *National League* addresses the issue of how far the federal government can go in taking over state functions. PEPA would have directed the EMB to step into state or local decision-making processes in the event of a missed deadline and perform the needed function. *National League* would arguably prohibit this. However, *National League of Cities* is a 5–4 opinion that has been analyzed and at present no clear consensus has emerged establishing its precedential value in the area of energy regulation. Moreover, rewording of PEPA-like proposals might avoid the *National League* problem altogether.

More recently, in *Hodel* v. *Virginia Surface Mining and Reclamation Association, Inc.,* the Court addressed the Tenth Amendment.

> As the District itself acknowledged, the steep-slope provisions of the Surface Mining Act govern only the activities of coal mine operators who are private individuals and businesses. Moreover, the States are not compelled to enforce the steep-slope standards, to expend any State funds, or to participate in the federal regulatory program in any manner whatsoever. If a State does not wish to submit a proposed permanent program that complies with the Act and implementing regulations, the full regulatory burden will be borne by the Federal Government. Thus, there can be no suggestion that the Act commandeers the legislative processes of the States by directly compelling them to enact and enforce a federal regulatory program. The most that can be said is that the Surface Mining Act establishes a program of cooperative federalism that allows the States, within limits established by federal minimum standards, to enact and administer their own regulatory programs, structured to meet their own particular needs. (Citations omitted.)[30]

The open question is whether the states see a proposal such as the EMB as ''cooperative'' or as a negation of their vital jurisdictional prerogatives.

A Model for State Fast Tracking

One instance of an existing fast-track program that has had some opportunity to be tested operationally and legally is the Colorado Joint Review Process (CJRP). The CJRP creates an intragovernmental review board designed to coordinate review and decision-making processes between local, state, and federal governments within each level of government. It is to provide interest groups with opportunities to become involved in all phases of project planning; provide an informal forum in which government, industry, the public and special-interest groups have an opportunity to discuss issues and concerns on a regular basis; provide industry with an alternative to conventional methods of obtaining required governmental decisions; and promote conflict resolution through cooperation and compromise.[31]

The CJRP manual was written pursuant to a grant from the Department of Energy to promote coordination between federal, state, and local governments. As the manual states, the intent is to create not a new decision-making authority but rather a process where flexibility is key. To this end the CJRP is a completely voluntary process—neither a proponent of an energy project not any governmental agency is legally obligated to participate in the CJRP, nor are they bound by any agreements entered into as part of the process. Additionally, at any point any of the parties may withdraw from the program without legal consequences. Given the voluntary nature of this program, communication, cooperation, and compromise are of paramount importance, and this spirit informs a new mode of decision making. (In part III we discuss the values inherent in complex decision making and suggest alternatives to the legalistic adversarial model of dispute resolution and government regulation.)

The CJRP addresses three major problems. First, it attempts to examine the interrelationship of the various environmental and land-use laws to reduce conflict and duplication. Second, an attempt is made to improve public participation by allowing formal access at points where the public is not put into an automatic adversary posture and before project plans are firmly established. Third, project proponents are encouraged to approach the government and the public early in the planning stages to increase communication and to reduce delays. In addressing these and other concerns the CJRP process operates in three stages.

Once a proponent has made a request for joint review, then the executive director of the relevant state agency must determine whether the proposed project qualifies for joint review. In many situations the director rendering it is the director of Natural Resources. The Colorado Department of Natural Resources (DNR) has a joint-review staff to coordinate these efforts. However, this is not a hard-and-fast rule; if another agency would be more appropriate to handle the decision, they may do so.

Stage I, essentially a screening process, begins after the director receives a written request for joint review and a completed project-information questionnaire from the proponent party. This questionnaire is the basis for the director's final decision as to whether joint review should be offered. The questionnaire will aide the director to determine such factors as project scope, required permits, responsible government agencies, jurisdictions affected, and current project phase.

Once this questionnaire is submitted, it is reviewed to determine if the proposed project should be considered major, and therefore qualify for CJRP. Colorado has established three criteria for a major project: First, the project must include, but need not be limited to, metals and uranium mining and milling, oil-shale and/or coal mining and processing (major may also apply to coal gasification, coal liquefaction, petroleum-upgrading facilities, and refineries).[32] Second, the project must require government action of some type. This government action may include the granting of "permits, approval, review, resolution, certificate, license, consultation, clearance, or other regulatory activity required by any agency at any level of government."[33] Third, it must be determined that the proposed project is "major," has significant impacts on public health and safety, or may become more significant in the interest, awareness, or controversy it generates, thereby increasing its importance.[34]

After the initial papers are filed by the proponent, the government machinery begins to function. The director then informs the governor's office that a proposed project is being considered for joint review. Additional meetings with key agencies at the federal, state, and local levels are arranged. These meetings are to identify those agencies that may be involved in that particular CJRP. These meetings are also conducted in an attempt to assess early support for the project and to solicit intergovernmental participation.

During the second stage of the fast track a detailed schedule of guidelines is compiled. This PDS, like that contemplated in the federal system, provides for coordinated regulatory processes and public participation. Also, the PDS is designed to coordinate administrative processes into one logical, interrelated sequence of events through organization of a joint-review-project team. This team is comprised of lead or coordinating agencies from the federal, local, and state levels of government. The project proponent is considered an ex officio member of the team but is not a formal member.

Once the lead coordinating agencies have been contacted and identified, the director of the DNR is to prepare a joint agreement outlining general concepts and procedures to be followed by the CJRP team. The role and responsibilities of each team member are enumerated, and a team leader is identified. Team leaders can be either state or local officials, and there are arguments supporting each leadership choice. The considerations relative to a division of powers between state and local team leadership parallel those discussed earlier between federal and state roles in energy production. Proponents of state leadership can point to the fact that impacts from certain projects may involve two or more counties or states. In such cases, the state, as a higher authority, will have more leverage to negotiate compromises and minimize jurisdictional disputes. Finally, the state may be responsible for broader or more substantial decisions than its local-government counterparts.

The advantages of local leadership are that most projects will be conducted within the regulatory jurisdiction of a county and thus will require a major land-use decision from the board of county commissioners. Further, most projects will result in substantial social, economic, political, and quality-of-life impacts that will affect local communities and citizens explicitly. Lastly, the accessibility of the local leadership to the community will encourage an active and healthy grass-roots involvement in the governmental and public-review process.

The joint agreement will describe the statutory and regulatory jurisdiction, duties, and responsibilities of each permitting and nonpermitting agency at each level of government as well as the general project schedule of the proponent before the affected agencies.

Following the initial steps of stage II there are a number of meetings planned between project-proponent and government leaders with additional public-information meetings. One of the purposes of the CJRP is to provide the public with early opportunities for project review. Even prior to this point in stage II there have been several public-participation and information efforts, including public notices, two public CJRP meetings, and a major news release. The public-information meetings are the first major formal activities in the public-participation program designed to provide the public with an opportunity to learn about the project from the proponent and government officials early in the process.

The final stage is the implementation of the PDS. The PDS prepared in stage II need not be followed methodically to ensure an efficient fast track. The CJRP by its very definition is merely a procedural tool to improve coordination and cooperation between all levels of government, thereby expediting decision making and improving the quality of governmental and public reviews.

Implementation of a PDS depends on active leadership from the CJRP team. During implementation, the team is responsible for:

1. Ensuring that the agencies are communicating with each other and the proponent
2. promoting coordination activities
3. preparing agreements to coordinate various activities
4. providing agencies with administrative assistance in organizing and conducting coordination activities
5. promoting, organizing, and conducting public-participation activities
6. updating the PDS in accordance with changes requested by the agencies and/or proponent

As the coordinating body, the CJRP team is not vested with any legal authority or power to influence the activities of individual agencies or the proponent. All CJRP activities affecting or involving the proponent or individual agencies must be conducted by voluntary agreement of the appropriate parties. The team must rely on its powers of persuasion, coordination, and logic to accomplish identified goals.

The policy and legal problems presented by state fast tracking are similar to those at the federal level. Some projects and types of projects are favored; consequently different interest groups with different political power bases are given access to this process. The voluntary nature of the CJRP eliminates many legal obstacles but poses its own problem. Is it efficacious? Without an enforcement mechanism any agency or the project sponsor can terminate the process. If a government bias for industry develops, then even with increased and earlier public participation the quality and effectiveness of public participation may be diluted.

The CJRP at least has made an attempt to provide for public participation, whereas the federal fast-tracking proposal made no such specific provision for it.

The Colorado experiment in fast tracking is likely to be analyzed for its effectiveness and is certain to provide a working model for future proposals to speed up and make more cohesive and consistent federal energy decision making.

Thinking about Centralization

Is fast tracking a way of streamlining the machinations of a congested bureaucracy? In one respect yes. Fast tracking can reduce the amount of delay inherent in a bureaucracy. The real question, however, is whether we are willing to pay the price in a due-process sense for a more economically efficient system. Fast tracking can solve some of the problems we face today, but at the same time it may well create the problems of tomorrow. Energy issues and the laws implementing energy policy are of paramount importance, but an effective, well-reasoned decision-making system, particularly to administer energy law and policy, is essential also. Fast tracking is merely a short-term answer to a long-term problem.

Fast tracking is a government scratching an impatient itch. However, the efficacy of this type of structural fix is questionable. Fast-tracking laws may move at cross purposes. They espouse as their central purpose a streamlining of a multitude of processes; thus it seeks simplicity with elegance of method as a goal. Neither simplicity nor elegance can be achieved if the fast-tracking proposals force agencies, issues, and interests into working together when they cannot. By attempting to combine three levels of government as well as the interagency functions within those levels, frictions will necessarily arise. In and of itself friction is neither wholly undesirable nor unhealthy. However, if, in the process, political powers are chafed raw with infighting and futile activity, the process will break down. At the same time fast tracking often adds complexity to energy decision making. The creation of a new bureaucracy is almost a necessity as exemplified by the federal PEPA proposal and the new administrative structure necessary for Colorado's CJRP experiment.

Other contradictions exist. Fast tracking is earmarked for either so-called priority or major projects. These will invariably be large-scale complex projects that are intended to increase resource production. This means the speeding up of processes to install new, complex technological mixes that may not be the most socially desirable or the best suited for long-term energy and economic stability. All these decisions are made at the hands of administrative agencies at least one step removed from the electorate and thus less politically accountable.

Instead of creating new bureaucracies and structures, identification and elimination of those laws, rules, and regulations that cause unnecessary duplication, pose impassible conflicts, or create delay because of unwarranted overlap would be a simpler, more direct path. That choice of action is preferable to the creation of a new bureaucracy that, at the federal level, has the power to change, modify, or suspend laws. The concept of seeing and dispensing with contradictory or cumbersome laws is more attractive in a system already plagued with too many decision-making entities than building yet another addition to a complex system. The process of clarifying or eliminating certain obsolete or ill-conceived laws forces the political process to work. Legislatures must then be accountable for taking corrective action instead of passing the problem on to a newly established agency.[35]

Notes

1. Both these acts contain several major pieces of legislation. The popular names of the National Energy Act are: Energy Tax Act of 1978; National Energy Conservation Policy Act; Natural Gas Policy Act of 1978; Powerplant and Industrial Fuel Use Act of 1978; and the Public Utility Regulatory Policies Act of 1978. The popular names of the Energy Security Act are: Defense Production Act Amendments of 1980; United States Synthetic Fuels Corporation Act of 1980; Biomass Energy and Alcohol Fuels Act of 1980; Solar Energy and Energy Conservation Act of 1980; Solar Energy Energy Conservation Bank Act; Geothermal Energy Act of 1980; and, the Acid Precipitation Act of 1980

2. U.S. Const. Amend. X.

3. 22 U.S. (9 Wheat.) 1 (1824).

4. Stewart, *Pyramids of Sacrifice? Problems of Federalism in Mandating State Implementation of National Environmental Policy,* 86 Yale L.J. 1196, 1210–22 (1977).

5. Maryland v. Louisiana, 101 S.Ct. 2114 (1981); Commonwealth

Edison Co. v. Montana, 101 S.Ct. 2946 (1980); and, Merriron v. Jicarilla
Apache Tribe, 102 S.Ct. 894 (1982).

6. U.S. Const. Art. I, sec. 8, cl. 3. L. Tribe, American Constitutional Law 239–44, 344–47, 376–89 (1978).

7. Complete Auto Transit, Inc. v. Brady, 430 U.S. 274, 279 (1977).

8. States cannot be overwhelmed by self-interest. When New Hampshire restricted the exportation of hydroelectric energy produced in that state the Supreme Court held that maneuver to be violative of the commerce clause. New England Power Co. v. New Hampshire, 50 U.S.L.W. 4223 (U.S. Feb. 24, 1982).

9. 102 S.Ct. 894, 901 (1982).

10. U.S. Const. Art. VI.

11. 101 S.Ct. 2352 (1981).

12. 101 S.Ct. 2376 (1981).

13. 101 S.Ct. 2352, 2367 (1981).

14. 42 U.S.C. sec. 8301 *et seq.* (Supp. IV 1980).

15. 15 U.S.C. sec. 3301 *et seq.* (Supp. IV 1980).

16. In scattered sections of 15, 16, 30, 42 and 43 U.S.C.

17. 666 F.2d 1359 (11th Cir. 1982).

18. *Id.* at 1367.

19. Oklahoma v. FERC, 494 F.2d 636 (W.D. Ok. 1980).

20. Mississippi v. FERC, 50 U.S.L.W. 4566 (U.S. June 1, 1982).

21. 659 F.2d 903 (9th Cir. 1981) *cert. granted* 50 U.S.L.W. 3994 (U.S. June 22, 1982).

22. *See* Northern States Power Co. v. Minnesota, 447 F.2d 1143 (8th Cir. 1971), *aff'd mem.* 405 U.S. 1035 (1972); *Symposium Federalism and Energy,* 18 Ariz. L. Rev. 283 (1976); Note, *Nuclear Power Regulation—Defining the Scope of State Authority,* 18 Ariz. L. Rev. 987 (1976); Tussey, *State Regulation of Nuclear Power Plants,* 82 A.L.R.3d 75 (1978).

23. *See generally* Watson, *Measuring and Mitigating Socio-Economic Environmental Impacts of Constructing Energy Projects: An Emerging Regulatory Issue,* 10 Nat. Resources L. 393 (1978).

24. Fischer, *Allocating Decisionmaking in the Field of Energy Resource Development: Some Questions and Suggestions,* 22 Ariz. L. Rev. 785 (1981).

25. *Id.*

26. *Id.*

27. Dept. of Justice Memorandum, *Constitutionality of the Energy Mobilization Board Proposal,* 125 Cong. Rec. S13884–87 (daily ed. Oct. 2, 1979).

28. Fry v. United States, 421 U.S. 542, 547 (1975).

29. 426 U.S. 833 (1976).

30. 101 S.Ct. 2352, 2366 (1981).

31. Colorado Dept. of Natural Resources, Colorado's Joint Review Process, 7 (1980) (JRP Manual).

32. *Id*. at 13.

33. *Id*.

34. *Id*. at 14.

35. See L. Thomas, *On Meddling*, in The Medusa and The Snail, 90–93 (Bantam ed. 1980).

Part II
Decision-Making
Methodologies

6   Rate Making

Part II discusses three predominant methodologies used by energy decision makers—rate making, cost-benefit analysis, and enforcement. To fully appreciate the nature and implications of energy decisions one must have some familiarity not only with the substantive rules and espoused policies that are energy related but also with the institutional structure within which decisions are made and with the methods employed by those institutions. Once a foundation has been laid that describes the structures and methodologies we can then proceed to discuss the values inherent (explicitly and implicitly) in energy decision making.

Regulators have a panoply of mechanisms to implement an energy policy. Licenses, permits, concessions, standards that force a change in technology, criminal sanctions, reporting requirements, and taxes are all used by administrative agencies. In the energy field one of the most pervasive tools is rate making. Rate making is the device by which the government sets the price at which a firm can sell its regulated good or service. In a free and competitive market this price-setting function also affects the supply of goods and services. Herein lies the trade-off. Government regulation is premised on the concept of market failure, and rate-making attempts to correct the economic dislocations caused by those failures. Public utilities, for example, because they generally are the only firm in a service area, are seen to be natural monopolies, serve a captured market, and therefore could set prices above those that would obtain in a competitive environment. The rate-making process insures the utility that it will have a service area or market as long as it operates prudently in exchange for price and service regulation by government. The premise underlying reliance on rate making is the government's attempt to imitate the free market's price-setting function.

Rate making was one of the first major government interventions in economic or business regulation. Most rate making occurs at the state level before state utility commissions. However, the Federal Energy Regulatory Commission (FERC) has rate-making powers in natural-gas, crude-oil-pipeline, and electricity energy areas. Because the vast majority of rate-making decisions occur at the state level, this chapter is somewhat of a departure from our overall theme of federal energy decision making.

However, the significance of state regulation of public-utility rates is so important that we include a discussion of their activities and their effects on overall national energy policy.

Rate-Making Functions

There are four traditional rate-making functions.[1] In Bonbright's terminology these functions are:

1. Producer motivation or capital attraction
2. efficiency incentive
3. demand control or consumer rationing
4. income distributive

The conceptual picture that emerges in the rate-making experience is that of a government agency attempting to create a competitive market. Politically, our society believes in the virtues of free and competitive markets and that, given such markets, prices will be set that are reasonable to consumers and will produce fair profits for producers. At the same time goods and services will be allocated and distributed fairly and equitably. This is the theory and ideal of open, free markets. Public utilities, because of their large scale and tendency toward the exercise of monopoly power, do not operate competitively. Therefore the government steps in to create such a market through the rate-making process.

Production Motivation or Capital Attraction

Public utilities are overwhelmingly privately owned. Nearly 80 percent of the electricity produced in this country and 90–95 percent of natural gas is sold by private-investor-owned utilities. The remainder is produced or sold by government-owned or government-controlled utilities or co-operatives. Thus, some incentive for the utility industry is necessary for it to continue to attract capital to stay functional. One goal of rate making is to provide that incentive. One way of encouraging energy producers and sellers to stay in the public-utility business is to allow producers or sellers to market their product or service at rates that will provide a reasonable profit to them. Rates cannot be set so low as to preclude a reasonable return on the utility owners' investment.[2] Such price setting runs afoul of the U.S. constitutional prohibition against the taking of private property for public use without just compensation in derogation of the Fifth Amendment. Rates precluding a reasonable profit effectively take capital away from owners and transfer it to the utilities' customers, who thus pay rates below cost for the utilities' product or service. No entity can survive under such circumstances. Thus, the production-motivation function of rate making is designed to make this business opportunity attractive. Implicit in the constitutional proscription is that a properly managed public utility will make money, thereby reducing the business risk. It must be noted, however, that with reduced risk also comes a reduction in the rate of return that would be appropriate for a high-risk business.

The corollary goal in this regard is capital attraction. Rates must be set at a sufficient level to attract not only managers and operators but also investors. Individual and institutional investors must have some reason for putting their investment dollars in a regulated public utility as opposed to an unregulated enterprise. The central reason for investment in regulated utilities provided by the rate-making process is the reduction in business risks. Virtually any diversified investment portfolio will contain some utility stocks or bonds. The return on common stock or on debentures generally will be less than those of a comparable business in exchange for a greater safety of investment.

Following the Three Mile Island (TMI) disaster the electric-utility industry suffered a serious blow, being viewed as a substantially less-secure investment. Briefly, the costs of cleaning up TMI, the costs of replacement power, and the lost capital investment in plant and equipment from TMI were staggering. The group of utilities that own TMI did not have the financial capability to absorb all those costs. The costs cannot be passed through automatically to the ratepayers nor can they be satisfied solely by the shareholders. The federal government as well as the states of Pennsylvania and New Jersey are being called on to render financial assistance to TMI's owners. State or federal policy can make investment in a nuclear-power plant profitable or not, depending on the treatment of the calculations that make up the revenue requirement of a utility. By simply excluding flow through of costs incurred in a plant mishap such as TMI, government action can virtually preclude the possibility of private investment in nuclear facilities. Thus investments in utilities have undergone a significant transformation following the questions raised by the TMI incident. The costs involved in large-scale nuclear power plants or other massive-scale generation facilities strain the assets of a public utility, and this strain increases the investment risk. Those large costs also impose a strain on the rate-making process. Rate makers, those government agencies responsible for setting the public-utility rates, are being called on increasingly to raise rates and to increase the rate of return so that the utility industry will find a suitable amount of investment capital. The system can go only so far in responding to these investment needs as TMI demonstrates. The rate of return can be raised to attract investors only insofar as the rates can be reasonably passed through to customers. Once customers can no longer afford to pay for the product the rate structure collapses. Thus the regulatory process if not carefully calibrated can kill the goose that lays the golden egg of profit for the utility—the beleaguered ratepayer.

Efficiency Incentive

The premise behind rate making is the fashioning of an artificial free market. Part of that market ideal is that rates will be set in such a manner as to keep costs low. Low costs in turn mean lower prices and relatively higher profits. The incentive for low costs is to provide the best service or product at a price at or below that of the costs of a comparable product thereby increasing profits. The problem in the field of public utilities, particularly the electric utility, is that generally there are no comparable products in a given service area. With the usual situation, one utility pervades a particular geographic market. Rate makers make what appear to be educated guesses as to the efficient price. The price most closely reflecting costs and allowing a reasonable profit while avoiding waste is the efficient price. It is a price that treats both consumers and producers fairly. It is also a price that allows for the maximum distribution and allocation of products throughout the market.

Demand Control

A maxim of classical economics is that price inversely affects demand. Generally speaking, the higher the price is the lower the demand is. This relationship is also known as price elasticity. The ratio between price and demand is not necessarily 1 to 1. Rather some goods or services are more elastic or inelastic than others. The products of utilities, for example, are relatively inelastic, that is, consumers of natural gas, gasoline, and electricity do not respond lockstep with fluctuations in prices. However, studies by the Department of Energy (DOE) and other organizations indicate that some conservation has occurred in response to higher energy prices. As a technology-based society, grown dependent on the products of public utilities to operate our homes and businesses, we are forced by circumstances beyond our control to absorb and respond to energy-price escalations. Demand eventually will fall off as prices continue to increase; people limit their driving, demand more-fuel-efficient vehicles, curtail use of some electric luxury items, and become aware of the necessity to use energy more sparingly or be willing to pay the price of continued high consumption. The rate-making process must be sensitive to this price-demand relationship.

At the height of the energy crisis, energy policymakers were faced with the twin problems of loosening the grip of OPEC and increasing national energy independence by promoting domestic crude-oil production. Given the limited resources available domestically, prices also had to be geared to affect consumer demand. Eventually this was done by lifting some oil-price regulations and permitting certain categories of oil to be priced at the world-market level. This meant higher prices, which resulted in two effects: (1) domestic production of newer crude oil was stimulated, and (2) consumer demand declined, thus encouraging conservation as part of an overall energy policy.

Each of the three rate-making functions identified earlier share the common assumption that economic efficiency is the primary goal. Implicit in that assumption is the premise that the more wealth that is created, the better off society will be. A growing gross national product (GNP) theoretically translates into a better life. Rate making based on these premises speaks in the language of economic efficiency. Economics, however, is only a part of a social construct. It is a way of viewing the world, it is not the world itself. Limiting analysis only to positive economics closes our eyes to other overtly political and social issues. Although rate making is based on faith in the free market, it must not ignore some of the problems that inhere in an imperfect world. Rate making can, and does, recognize normative issues in a system that is guided by the precept of economic efficiency as well.

Income Distribution

The simple act of purchasing any product or service has the effect of transferring wealth from one individual to another. If done on a large scale, many individuals may transfer wealth to a few individuals, and economic dislocations can occur. In the public-utility industry, this phenomenon occurs on a large scale when customer-ratepayers transfer money to the owner-shareholders in exchange for utility services. Rate making affects this transfer in two basic ways. First, the rates that are set determine how much wealth moves from the customer to the utility. Second, since public utilities serve various groups of customers, the rates also affect how wealth moves among those groups. The concept of wealth distribution between classes of customers will be more fully discussed when we talk about rate structure and rate design. Here a brief description will be given.

Public utilities serve various types of customers, including industrial, commercial, and residential consumers. Within each group further divisions can be made. In the residential classification some consumers are renters, others are owners, and among owners some own vacation homes. What distinguishes these classifications for utility-rate-making purposes more than anything else is cost of service. On a per-unit-of-energy basis, it costs relatively more to serve the small user, such as a homeowner, than it does to serve the large user, such as an industrial plant. Also, price elasticity varies among different classes of users. The homeowner with the all-electric home would find it more severely burdensome on an individual basis to convert to gas heating than would an industrial user converting from oil or gas to coal. Such transition costs are more easily assumed by the industrial plant and can be passed on to purchasers of the industrial user's product. Thus, industrials are generally more price elastic than the individual homeowners, who cannot pass on costs of fuel conversion.

Costs can be shifted from one group within a classification to another. This is known as subsidization or cross-subsidization. An example of cross-subsidization occurs with railroad rates. Once the preeminent mover of passengers, railroads now earn the bulk of their income hauling freight. Yet the railroads are still faced with large capital investments in plant (rails) and equipment (cars) devoted to passenger service. Through the rate-making process railroads are allowed to shift some costs of the less profitable and unprofitable passenger service to the profitable freight service.[3]

Energy costs bite into more of the spending dollar of the homeowner than they do for the industrial user. Given this set of variables what happens when energy costs double? Are they passed through equally to all classes of customers? Is this fair? Is is fair to double the energy costs of elderly people on fixed incomes, or should individual homeowners be subsidized by industrial and commercial users? If the rate maker believes the situation to be inequitable, then rate making can be used to adjust costs and shift the burden among classes of customers. This shifting of the cost burden effects a redistribution of income and furthers a normative or equitable policy more than an inflexible efficiency-based rate-making goal does. However, there are risks in pursuing such a goal. If industrial users bear too much of the burden of increased costs from one source, they may seek alternatives and leave the utility's system. When that occurs, the remaining customers on the system must pick up the increased allocable share of the utility's fixed costs. Thus, well-intentioned efforts to distribute burdens of increasing energy costs must be carefully programmed to ensure that the process does not backfire.

Rate-Making Formula

Although this formula can use various variables the standard mathematical formulation for ratemaking is $R = O + (B)r$.[4] Once the variables are defined it is child's play to find the revenue requirement R by adding operating expenses O to the rate base B multiplied by the rate of return r. The trick is in finding acceptable or satisfactory definitions for the remaining variables. The end product of this formulation is to devise a sum, the revenue requirement R, that compensates the regulated firm on its regulated goods or services at a rate that gives the public utility the opportunity to stay in business and make a profit. What constitutes O is relatively noncontroversial compared with the other variables. Operating costs must be recaptured if the firm is to stay operational. The costs involved with the production of the regulated product are plugged into the revenue requirement. Occasionally there are gray areas. Costs incurred in operating and maintaining the firm must be recouped if the business is to continue to operate. Yet should all costs be attributed to the rate payers or should some be absorbed by the shareholders (owners)? Generally, only those costs of operation associated with the prudent management of the firm, with good faith presumed, are considered appropriate for pass-through to the ratepayer. The costs for poorly managed or mismanaged firms should be charged to the shareholders. The obvious difficulty is in judging when a firm has been improperly managed. It is not easy to attribute business losses or increased business risks to imprudent management in a scarcity economy. The presumption of good faith makes sense but not necessarily for economic reasons. Who is in a better position to decide the proper scale of executive salaries, the utility's board of directors or the courts? This good-faith presumption lets the firm run itself absent a showing of abuse of discretion by managers—the imposition of this presumption does not necessarily comport with economic efficiency, because the presumption of good faith by its nature allows a certain amount of inefficiency just short of abuse of discretion.

Occasionally, public-service commissions or legislatures step in to settle questions concerning operating expenses. The New York Public Service Commission, for example, promulgated an order that prohibited electric utilities from using bill inserts to argue its position on controversial issues such as its pronuclear policy. This was struck down by the U.S. Supreme Court as violative of the First Amendment.[5] Yet the issue of who should bear these expenses is not settled. The Public Utility Regulatory Policy Act (PURPA) favors collecting these expenses from shareholders rather than the ratepayers. Again, this preference is not based on efficiency criteria but rather on a political value choice being made that owners rather than ratepayers should bear the costs.

The more controversial variables in the rate-making formula are represented by B and r. What goes into the rate base (B) and what constitutes a reasonable rate of return (r) are issues consuming the bulk of the decision-making process of utility commissions. Of the two, r, is relatively easy to calculate insofar as it reflects the current cost of money in the marketplace. Calculating r involves ascertaining the debt/equity ratio of the company, that is, how much common stock, preferred stock, and bonds the firm has earmarked for its regulated business. Then, a so-called fair rate of return based on what comparable stocks and bonds are yielding in the market is reviewed. These figures are eventually combined, in a rather subjective process, to produce r. This is the figure that first catches the eye of an investor. If an investor is earning substantially less yield per investment dollar (even given a relatively safe investment) such an investment will be unattractive. Thus the rate of return must be competitive, even for the relatively sheltered utility investment.

The determination of what constitutes rate base, however, presents more difficult issues and choices. Because many utility plants are in need of expansion or need to be rebuilt, large capital expenditures may be required. Thus the way B is handled will become even more controversial over time. Long Island Lighting Co. (Lilco), for example, has a B of $1.9 billion. The company has under construction a nuclear plant that is scheduled to become operational about mid-1983. The plant was predicted to cost several hundred million dollars. Now predictions are that it will cost over $2.5 billion. What happens when this $2.5 billion is put into B together with operating costs associated with the plant? The effect is to more than double the rate base. Thus an increased R (revenue requirement) for the company results with a concomitant immense rate increase to Lilco's consumers. Compounding the difficulty is the fact that no one can predict now whether or not the energy-cost savings projected to result from the plant will ever materialize.

An example of the current controversy surrounding the B calculation is how to handle what is known as construction work in progress (CWIP). Basically, B is comprised of the capital investment or assets "used and useful" to the firm in producing its products or service. Thus, the depreciated value of plant and equipment used relative to the regulated product currently in use fits neatly into the rate base. When the firm produces both regulated and unregulated products this calculation may become less mathematically precise but still may be ascertained. The harder issue is what to do with capital that is invested and being used in plants under construction. Should a utility start earning a return on investment in CWIP immediately, or should it be compensated through another regulating device known as allowance for funds used during construction (AFUDC)? The latter regulatory policy delays the return a utility may earn on funds applied to construction. Public utilities are the most capital-intensive sector of the economy. Statistics regarding the enormity of the economic effects of investment required in the electric-utility industry alone are staggering. Total plant investment and equipment is now running about $35 billion per year. The nation's electrical-utility-plant systems sap one-fifth of total nationwide construction expenditures, one-third of all long-term private financing, and one-half of all new common stock issued.[6] Many public-utility plants are reaching the end of their useful life. Further, with double-digit inflation, decline in demand, high construction costs, regulatory delays, and high interest rates for borrowed money, the amount of capital devoted to plant construction is enormous. This is acutely felt in the nuclear-power industry, where regulatory lag can last over a decade. Should the firm be allowed a return on investment for money that is used for plant expenditures that are not on line and may never be on line?

The CWIP issue is but one point on the continuum of the energy decision-making process. In a real sense it is exemplary of rate-making methodology. The basic tenet of utility rate making is that utilities are important providers of products and services necessary to maintain and improve our life-style and our economy—hence utility financial health is essential. Regulators use CWIP and accelerated depreciation as techniques that contribute to the financial soundness of a utility. The prefatory remarks in a General Accounting Office (GAO) report on the CWIP issue reiterate the thinking surrounding the decision-making methodology designed to support the health of the industry: ''The financial indicators of the electric utility industry have deteriorated due to high inflation, high interest rates, accelerating construction costs, decline in demand, and a less than adequate rate of return. This has led to uncertainty about the industry's ability to attract investment capital.''[7] The GAO report recommends the inclusion of some CWIP in the rate base. A basic question in the conclusion reached is whether the outcome of the report is predetermined by the portrayal of the problem. The methodology employed—the manner in which the issue is framed by the GAO—is indicative of the manner in which energy decisions are made. Rate making and a fortiori the CWIP issue revolve around the financial plight of the utility industry. There is built into the analysis a bias to encourage industry growth. The issue of whether growth is in the best interests of the country is not really explored or questioned. Thus, obviously the fundamental question is sidestepped. Is it in the interests of the country to rebuild old plants or to create potential new large electric dinosaurs? Is it efficient to expand existing plants or should a utility convert to nuclear power on a large scale? Is there a need for more power supply within a country whose population is stabilizing? Can power be transmitted from one part of the country to another efficiently without new plant construction to serve new or sporadic requirements for power? Is there a positive connection between energy growth and economic growth? Are there alternative energy-efficient and energy-saving measures available to offset any new demand rather than add more electricity generation? Can the electric-power-generation industry be deregulated and still serve the country's needs? All these questions are the underlying perplexing issues of the rate-making process yet they may be ignored or only superficially answered. More often than not they are simply not asked in rate-making proceedings. The failure to ask these grander questions commits the decision maker to a path of continuing to support the growth of the existing utility industry. Society would be better served if the rate maker were to ask whether new financial incentives were needed or desirable from a broad perspective rather than inquiring only whether the utility is capable of attracting new capital. Electric utilities' capital needs have caused most state commissions and FERC to allow some CWIP in the rate base. The GAO has also recommended to the FERC to establish a rule-making proceeding to allow CWIP in the rate base on a case-by-case basis. The point we are emphasizing here is that CWIP is only the iceberg's tip in the broad ocean of issues that regulators should now confront.

Another current issue of marked financial magnitude regarding rate-base calculation is how to treat nuclear-plant-decommissioning expenses. Simply explained, once a nuclear plant has lived its useful life and has reached an unacceptable level of radioactivity, its operations must wind down and the plant must be deactivated. Decommissioning can be accomplished by either dismantling the plant or burying the entire site in concrete. Obviously either course is complex and expensive. Prior to the TMI incident, plant-decommissioning problems were not considered imminent, and costs for decommissioning were estimated at about $50 million per plant. The financial implications from TMI demonstrated the invalidity of those assumptions. First, the need to clean up or decommission a plant may arise anytime. Second, cleanup costs can run into billions rather than millions of dollars. The NRC has been studying the decommissioning issue in a rule-making proceeding started in 1978. The rule making is somewhat appropriate because the NRC is the body most expert in the technical aspects of nuclear matters. However, the NRC has no rate-making authority and has no jurisdiction over how utilities should carry these costs. Should those future-looking payments be included in the rate base now and paid for by present users, or should a utility be forced to wait to include decommissioning costs until the need is more immediate? Such difficult issues are the stuff of the rate-base conundrum. Not only do these issues deal in economic realities they have far ranging sociopolitical consequences as well.

Rate Design

The rate-making formula will produce a firm's rate level overall. However, it is important to recall that public utilities have various classes of customers. Each class has different demand components and different costs associated with it. Generally a user's energy bill consists of three elements: (1) customer costs (the utility's cost of serving a customer); (2) energy costs (cost of fuel used by a customer); and (3) the customer's demand costs (costs based on the rate of consumption). Therefore utilities bill different classes of customers differently. The overall rate package for different classes is the *rate design*. It is the "determination of specific rates and the relationships between the rates."[8] Issues of rate level are predominantly economic and economic in a positive sense. The objective is a rate-level assessment to meet the firm's revenue requirement. Rate design is economic but imbued with normative values. Various rate designs accomplish different economic as well as social objectives. Rate designs can further environmental and social policies and can affect what resources are used to generate electricity and how wealth is eventually distributed among classes of customers.[9]

Declining-Block Rate

The declining-block rate shown in figure 6–1 is the historic pricing design developed to reward large users of energy with lower per-unit charges. Note that the higher prices are charged in the initial blocks. This means that the more energy a consumer uses the less per kilowatt a unit of energy costs. In an era of cheap energy, this rate design allowed a utility to capture its costs in the early segments of the rate schedule. Declining-block rates are promotional rates, because they encourage energy use. If energy costs are a small part of a consumer's budget the rate is attractive. Such a design also promotes the development of luxury products associated with a particular fuel, such as outdoor gas grills and lighting and all-electric homes. The obvious effect of this design is to increase demand, promote the growth of the utility industry and associated products, and contribute to sustaining a heavily energy-dependent economy. It may also

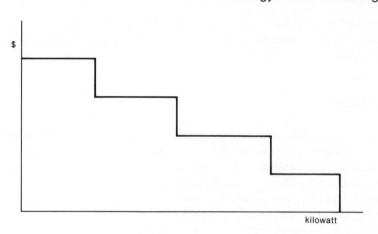

Figure 6–1. The Declining-Block Rate.

produce waste. Since the energy crunch this rate design has come under attack because of the potential encouragement of waste and because users, even large users, feel the pinch or gouge that energy costs extract from their budgets.

From a distributional standpoint the small users effectively subsidize the larger users. Since the utility recoups its costs in the early blocks, the users that consume more pay a lower average cost.

Inverted-Block Rate

As its name implies, the inverted-block design is the opposite of the declining-block method, and it resembles a staircase rising from left to right. The design was suggested as a way of combatting promotional rates. It is a conservation measure because the more energy that is consumed the more it costs per unit, thus discouraging use. Consequently, the distributional effects of this rate between classes of customers is opposite of that fostered by the declining-block rate. Residential users may tailor their use to consume minimal amounts of a resource. The larger industrial users, even though they consume a proportionately larger amount of energy, still thus effect a subsidization of residential users. The effect of this process is to pick up a portion of the smaller residential users' utility costs. A public-service commission that sees its mission as redistributing the energy-cost burden between classes of customers thus has a ready vehicle with this type of rate design. Naturally, a wholescale redistribution effort most likely will not go too far in its shifting of costs from one class to another. There will come a point where the larger user will find it more efficient for it to switch to another source of energy. If an electric utility is required to use an inverted-rate schedule, thus imposing a burden on the large users, at some point it will be cheaper for the industrial plant to convert to oil, natural gas, or coal or to use its waste heat through the form of cogeneration.[10] Rate design, then, is not a sterile formula with only positive economic consequences; inherent in the process are normative issues that the regulator cannot and should not ignore, including those related to social, political, and environmental matters.

Lifeline Rates

The term *lifeline* applied to utility rates can be taken literally. It means giving individual utility customers a lifeline to the outside world by providing basic, minimal electric service at low cost. Because energy prices have risen sharply within the last decade and because of high inflation, utility consumers find it increasingly difficult to pay the higher energy bills. Almost inevitably, utility bills consume a larger and larger portion of their income, especially consumers on fixed incomes, like many elderly citizens. Lifeline rates are intended to provide to such people a minimum amount of guaranteed service at an affordable price. To the extent that the lifeline rate is not cost based, it means that other classes of utility customers are directly subsidizing this group of consumers.

Rate making and rate design has been grounded in the idea that rates are cost based and that consumers each pay their way. With lifeline rates a conscious decision is made in this limited instance to abandon those precepts and further a social-welfare goal.

Time-of-Day Rates

Time-of-day rates or seasonal rates are, theoretically, cost based. These rates are an outgrowth of the economic concept of marginal-cost pricing. The marginal cost of an item is the cost of producing one more unit or the cost savings in producing one unit less. Applied to energy resources it means that whatever it costs the utility to produce another kilowatt of electricity, for example, that will be the price that the user pays. In the electric-utility industry, because electricity cannot be stored for very long, it is important to generate only enough energy as will be needed. Needs for energy, however, both throughout the day and seasonally, are uneven. In the summer, for example, a greater demand is made on most utilities because of increased use of power associated with air conditioning, and, during the day, more electricity is used at one time than another. The time span when demand is greatest is a peak period, which may be calculated on a daily, monthly, seasonal, or yearly basis. A greater strain is put on the utility to produce peak power, and the costs of producing peak power use. Time-of-day rate design attempts to charge users for the cost of using electricity when they use it. Theoretically, consumers using electricity at off-peak periods should pay less for the cheaper base-load use than those using peak power. Monitoring time-of-day use presents an economically difficult problem. New forms of metering are needed. At this point the costs of installing the necessary metering may well outweigh the cost savings envisioned by time-of-day proponents. With the technological advances in the microprocessor industry, metering costs should decline to the point where monitoring time-of-day or seasonal rates becomes cost effective.

Incentive Rate of Return (IROR)

Prior to the energy crisis, in an era when fuel was considered cheap, fuel and service could be provided with relative economic ease. In fact, fuel prices were so low that often utilities would compete in providing amenities and offering better quality of service. Today neither situation obtains. Rates have skyrocketed, and many believe the quality of service is declining.[11] Regulators, whose standard is to set rates in the public interest, have one eye on the financial health charts of ailing energy industries and the other on the pocketbooks of the ratepayers. The hard question is how both masters can be served. One proposal is the so-called IROR. In New York, an IROR plan was proposed by the Public Service Commission for a nuclear-power plant, the Nine Mile 2 plant in Oswego, New York. The plant, an 1,100-megawatt generator, was estimated to cost $356 million. After delays and the economic disaster of the 1970s, costs are now estimated at over $4 billion. The IROR is a system of rewards and penalties assuming a $4.6-billion-target completion cost. If there are cost overruns, then the shareholders must absorb those losses because they will not be allowed in the rate of return. Conversely, if there are underruns, then the shareholders will receive some benefits.

IROR's can also be used to further other objectives as well. In California, by statute, utilities investing in renewable resources such as solar, geothermal, wind, and hydropower or in environmentally beneficial generating systems, are allowed an award of an additional 0.5 to 1 percent on the rate of return by the public-service commission.[12] If the plant fails to promote the development of statutorily designated beneficial-energy programs, the plant can be penalized.

The IROR scheme then is also a way to promote certain types of energy projects through a system of rewards and penalties based on the rate formula. This is also a way to encourage efficient utility management.

Public Utility Regulatory Policies Act

The Public Utility Regulatory Policies Act (PURPA) represents the first attempt to involve the federal government directly in the rate-making process at the retail level.[13] Prior to enactment of PURPA, the federal government exercised limited rate-making authority, confining itself primarily to the setting of wholesale electricity and natural-gas rates for those energy resources sold or transported in interstate commerce. The remainder of all rate-making power resided in the states. With the PURPA initiative, the government greatly broadened its intervention into state rate-making processes.

The basic thrust of PURPA is to set those standards and implement those concepts the Congress believes would benefit the rate-making process. Among the purposes of PURPA are the conservation of electric energy and natural gas, equitable rates to electricity and natural-gas consumers, and an increase in the efficiency in the use of resources by electric utilities. These PURPA objectives are to be achieved through rate making at the federal and state levels.

Electric Utilities and Rate Making

PURPA requires each state regulatory authority (the state's public-service commission or public-utility commission) as well as nonregulated public utilities to consider certain rate standards. After such consideration, the regulatory entity must make a determination as to whether or not the standard is appropriate to implement. PURPA does not require the implementation of the standards, and it specifically states that the regulatory body may find that a standard is not appropriate. PURPA does require, if the entity declines to implement a standard, that it state its reasons for declination in writing for public inspection. The six federal standards to be considered include:

1. Cost-of-service rates. Rates must reflect to the maximum extent practicable the costs of providing electric service to each class of customers. This includes identification of differences in costs attributable to time-of-day and seasonal use as well as differences in customer demand and energy components.

2. declining-block rate. The federal standard prohibits this rate design

for the energy component unless the utility demonstrates that its energy costs decrease as consumption increases.

3. time-of-day rates. Rates shall reflect the costs of providing electric service at different times of the day unless the rates are not cost effective, that is, the long-run cost savings exceed the metering and associated monitoring costs.

4. seasonal rates. Rates shall reflect costs on a seasonal basis.

5. interruptible rates. Electric utilities shall offer industrial and commercial customers a rate that reflects the cost of providing interruptible service to a given class of customer.

6. load-management techniques. Electric utilities shall, to the extent this is cost effective, tell consumers how they can increase their energy efficiency.

PURPA also establishes certain mandatory proscriptions. Master metering (the practice of putting all energy use by various users in a single building through a single meter) in new buildings is severely limited as are certain automatic-fuel-adjustment clauses. Electric utilities must provide information regarding rate schedules, and termination of service procedures are established by PURPA. Promotional and political advertising expenses may be recovered only from the shareholders. Lifeline rates are permitted by PURPA.

Natural-Gas Utilities

PURPA is less encompassing in its approach to natural-gas rate making; the act proposes only two federal standards. The standards shall be adopted after notice and a public hearing if the regulatory authority or nonregulated utility determines that adoption is appropriate and consistent with state law. These standards are: (1) no utility may terminate gas service except pursuant to PURPA and (2) promotional and political advertising costs can be recovered only from the shareholders and are not to be included in the rate base or included as operating expenses.

PURPA has been held constitutional by the Supreme Court, despite its clear interference in and demands on state utility commissions. The Court found that Congress's desire to allow limited federal regulation of retail sales of electricity and natural gas and of the relationships between cogenerating and electric utilities was essential to protect the national economy and interstate commerce. Further, the Court held that if Congress may require a state administrative body to consider proposed federal regulation as a condition to the state's continued involvement in a preemptive field, the use of certain procedures could likewise be demanded.

Although PURPA's goals have at least in part been implemented, recent reductions in budget and basic lack of commitment to PURPA have resulted in nonenforcement or even lack of encouragement of many of its goals by DOE. FERC, however, has been quite active in its implementation of those provisions of the law applicable to it. Particularly FERC has implemented and administered provisions of PURPA dealing with cogeneration and small power-production facilities.

The Rate-Making Process in Perspective

Because the rate-making process is so difficult to modify and federal standards are difficult to apply, commissions may gravitate toward quantification and positive issues rather than full expositions of normative and value issues. In rate making, issues of rate design and rate structure directly affect noneconomic concerns such as redistribution of wealth, subsidization of classes of consumers, subsidization within classes, environmental protection, and conservation. Even then, many assumptions are left unexamined or promoted by default. Once a utility commission narrows a rate-making case to its traditional scope, the questions of the need for power, adequacy of existing plants, decreasing demand, and alternative sources of energy may be examined in only a superficial manner.

The methodology embodied in a simple arithmetic calculation then can obscure deeper issues. The predominant way this occurs is by using a methodology wedded by its language and nature to economic analysis. The institutions that are called on to utilize this methodology comfortably acquiesce in this formula because it at least appears understandable and it simplifies what is at heart a polycentric decision. The formula can hide huge, complex social issues.

Finally, given that most rate making is done at the state level and that several federal agencies also exercise this function, rate-making standards are not uniformly applied. Different public-service commissions utilize different accounting standards, different depreciation methods, treat CWIP differently, and compute the rate of return differently as well. Application of a simple formula becomes subjective and complex in practice. The manner in which the formula is manipulated has various economic effects, and the way regulatory bodies choose to handle it may be guided by political expediences. Thus although rate making purports to be an economic calculus and is written in the language of economics, that is only part of the story.

Notes

1. J. Bonbright, Principles of Public Utility Rates (1961). *See also,* A.J.G. Priest, Principles of Public Utility Regulation (1969).

2. *See, e.g.,* Smyth v. Ames, 169 U.S. 466 (1898); Missouri *ex rel.* Southwestern Bell Tel. Co. v. Public Serv. Comm'n of Missouri, 262 U.S. 276 (1923); and Federal Power Comm'n v. Hope Natural Gas Co., 320 U.S. 591 (1944).

3. *See* Railroad Rehabilitation and Revitalization Act, 49 U.S.C. sec. 10101 *et seq.* (Supp. III 1979); Houston Lighting & Power Co. v. United States, 606 F.2d 1131 (D.C. Cir. 1979), *cert. denied* 444 U.S. 1073 (1980); and San Antonio v. United States, 631 F.2d 831 (D.C. Cir. 1980).

4. R. Pierce, G. Allison, & P. Martin, Economic Regulation: Energy, Transportation and Utilities 130 (1976).

5. Consolidated Edison Co. v. Public Service Commission of New York, 447 U.S. 530 (1980).

6. National Electric Reliability Study, vol. 1 (Final Report, February 1980).

7. General Accounting Office, Federal Energy Regulatory Commission Need to Act on the Construction Work-In-Progess Issue (EMD-81-123, Sept. 23, 1981).

8. C. Phillips, The Economics of Regulation 130 (1965).

9. For a thorough and illuminating article on rate design, see Aman & Howard, *Natural Gas and Electric Utility Rate Reform: Taxation through Ratemaking?,* 28 Hastings L.J. 1085 (1977).

10. The Public Utility Regulatory Policies Act of 1978 contains section 210, which actively encourages cogeneration through rate making and other policies.

11. A. Carrow & P. MacAvoy, The Decline of Service in the Regulated Industries (1981).

12. California Public Utilities Code sec. 454(a) (West 1968).

13. In scattered sections of 15, 16, 30, 42, and 43 U.S.C.

7 Cost-Benefit Analysis

Cost-benefit analysis seeks to ascertain whether the social and economic benefits of a particular project outweigh the costs. Cost-benefit analysis therefore is a decision-making methodology often relied on by the public sector. Such analysis generally seeks to answer whether among competing projects, which, if any, should be undertaken. In the arena of government decisions, the test of profitability cannot serve as a useful device for measuring whether to act. Therefore, cost-benefit analysis can be a useful, albeit inherently limited, process.[1]

A distinguishing factor in public-sector cost-benefit analysis is the requirement that a public-interest standard be applied to the equation: Will the decision to invest X dollars and Y amount of resources (time, labor, and so on) not only be economically beneficial but will it also serve the public interest? Also, since energy resources are regarded as scarce resources, cost-benefit analysis must ask a corollary question: Between competing policies or sets of policies, what is the best allocation of resources? At the very least, cost-benefit analysis is a useful tool for extracting information about public policies to be used by public-sector (government) decision makers. However, even at its most revered status, cost-benefit analysis cannot be called on by decision makers as the sole decision-making method. Too much reliance on cost-benefit analysis is at best wrongheaded and at worst pernicious.

Stages of Analysis

Cost-benefit analysis can be divided into four stages: identification, classification, quantification, and presentation. First, the various effects of a proposed project are identified. Costs, benefits, and risks must be identified. Although risks can be translated into costs, such a maneuver taken uncritically is unwise. For example, in assessing the wisdom of locating a nuclear-waste-disposal facility at geographic point A or B, for example, a calculation that translates risks to costs may yield a result that indicates that point A is less costly than point B. However, by making that translation the decision is made on the basis of the relative costs and benefits of locating the disposal site at point A or B; the analysis does not directly address the question of whether the risk itself is acceptable.

Although economically it may cost less to locate the plant at point A, more people may live in the immediately surrounding area. In the event of a catastrophic accident choosing point A therefore is clearly riskier. Or it may be less costly to locate at point B but more people will be subject to continuing low-level radiation exposure. More to the point, the translation from risks to costs absorbs the underlying assumption that the risks at either point are acceptable.

Next, the effects are quantified, and the easiest to understand and most commonly used denominator is the dollar. Obviously we recognize that all things cannot be measured in monetary terms. The value of a life from an accounting standpoint, that is, how much a person earns in a projected lifetime, may be ascertained, but surely no one can confidently hope to know the value of a life. Also, the system does not take into account the fact that money means different things to different individuals. Certainly the value of a hundred dollars to a millionaire is quite different from the value of an equal sum to an unemployed welfare father. Even between two people similarly situated financially, the value of money differs between the frugal daughter and the prodigal son. Thus, quantification is also a tricky stage.

The final major stage is the presentation of information, that is, the outlining of assumptions on which the presentation is being made and the implications of those assumptions. Present at this stage are both problems of interpretation and selection of data, which will differ depending upon who is doing the interpretation.

Although economics forms the basis for cost-benefit analysis, it is more accurate to say that welfare economics is at the center of the analysis. This brand of economics asks the question of how society, rather than a private individual or private firm, can allocate scarce resources to maximize social wellbeing. Whether public-sector decision makers have sufficient information to know which decision will make society better and which will make society worse is a problematic issue. The core question decision makers must answer accountably is whether society has been improved or harmed by the decision. Between two policies, A and B, for example, it may readily be determined that A is superior to B. Yet, it may not be so easy to determine if A is a useful choice or whether no choice is wisest. One barometer of whether the decision is correct is that of economic efficiency. Does choice A result in a net increase in the value of goods and services produced? This value is measured by that crude yardstick of economic demand, people's willingness to pay. This measure has severe conceptual problems in attempting to equate subjective value. It also assumes a given distribution of income. Thus, two fundamental assumptions of cost-benefit analysis are that people know what is best for them and they always choose it and that the given distribution of income is acceptable.[2]

The concept of benefit can be elusive. The decision to encourage coal production in a western state, for example, may increase revenues, promote industrial development, and reduce our dependence on foreign oil. For the sake of argument we can assume that no untoward environmental harm will occur. Thus, a pro-coal-development decision benefits everyone without hurting anyone. This is known as a Pareto superior decision and is of net benefit. Reality, however, is hardly so neat. Environmental harms, such as air and water pollution, are inevitable. If the benefits are so great as to outweigh the losses there is still a net benefit. A criterion used in cost-benefit analysis, the Kaldor-Hicks criterion, states that society has benefited if those persons that are made worse off could be compensated by those benefited and the decision still yield a net positive result. Again the question goes unanswered whether this environmental harm is acceptable even though there is a net benefit. It was assumed by the cost-benefit methodology that a net benefit means that the coal-production decision was correct.

This brief introduction to the conceptual difficulties and to certain problematic assumptions bring into question the validity of cost-benefit analysis as the sole decision-making tool. We argue that a finding that a net benefit occurs should not be substituted as the answer to energy problems. The analysis cannot make decisions, indeed only the decision makers can do that. What the analysis can do is to provide data and information and raise questions about particular projects. If group X is worse off, group Y benefits, and a net benefit is achieved, should the project then include some compensation for group X? Should the decision be foregone? If certain variables cannot be quantified can a decision be made? If so, on what methodology will the decision rest? Decisions about the aesthetics of the project, or the value of a life, or the appropriate level of risk, can then be made outside the scope of cost-benefit analysis by a different methodology, for example, some appointed director's subjective decision, or so-called expert opinion, or a vote, and so on. Furthermore, the types of issues raised by cost-benefit analysis tend to be more normative and value oriented and are less capable of decision making by a system that depends on quantification. Such value issues require different decision-making methods, some of which we explore in part III.

A Critique of Cost-Benefit Analysis

This methodology has not been without its critics. The criticisms center not so much around what the analysis can do, that is, gather data and information and highlight sensitive normative and positive issues, as much as on its application and misplaced emphasis by decision makers. And although advocates of cost-benefit analysis do not view it as a divinely inspired methodology, they have relied on it to assess masses of complex and conflicting data. The critics of the method likewise do not impugn the contributions it is capable of making to an overall decision-making methodology. Rather, reticence exists about the temptation of decision makers to rely exclusively on the cost-benefit equation, focusing only on economic efficiency. The method should not be used to obscure the delicate moral, value, and social issues that arise in decisions regarding the allocation of scarce resources. The critique of cost-benefit analysis is based on a political and philosophical question: Is this method, emphasizing hard, idealized objective data, desirable in a pluralistic democracy? Do we want, can we afford, a society—or for our purposes a legal regime—that favors so-called scientific facts arrived at by quantified calculations?

In this context, we must watch to see where decision-making power shifts. Will it move away from democratic assemblies, such as federal and state legislatures, toward scientific and technological communities or toward specialized bureaucratic institutions? Does cost-benefit analysis raise the hoary prospects of reliance on the decision-making ability of a sterile technology?

Criticism of cost-benefit analysis starts with the difficulties of identifying benefits in the equation. A fundamental requirement of cost-benefit analysis is the accurate identification and measurement of benefits and costs. However, each category of benefits, direct, indirect, and intangible are difficult to measure.[3] For example, how should a decision be made as to whether to require a coal-gasification plant to install elaborate pollution-control equipment? Direct benefits might include the contribution to the GNP of the value of the domestic production of a natural-gas substitute and the providing of jobs to workers associated with the plant. If the decision is made to enforce the environmental requirement strictly some plants may never be built because the cost of installation of the equipment is so high. We might also assume that, because coal gas may be a useful commodity, research, time, and money will be spent looking for cleaner ways to process coal gas. How is the money required to develop effective antipollution devices industrywide to be carried in the cost-benefit equation? Is that cost a cost of the decision because the money would not have been spent otherwise? Or, is it truly a benefit to society in that a new industry is created, that is, coal-gasification antipollution research and development. If the antipollution research and development is successful, there will be not only a cleaner environment and additional gas supplies but also the socially desirable goal of more competition in the industry. As a result the price of the goal gas should go down to consumers.

This hypothetical sets out the dilemma of the identification problem. What constitutes a benefit? How far out should the equation go to find the benefits?

The identification of costs poses a similar set of problems, the hardest issue being where to draw the line in the search. Using the coal-gasification-plant example, an obvious direct cost is the cost of labor and materials to construct the plant. However, the array of enumerable costs just begins at that point. Coal-gasification plants may rely on coal supplied from strip- or deep-mining operations. In the case of coal supplied from strip-mine sources, the heavy environmental effects of that process must be factored in. If coal is supplied to the plant from a deep mine, statistics indicate that a certain number of coal miners will be killed or injured in coal-mine accidents. Should the proportionate share of deaths and injuries be allocated to the plant as a cost factor? Next, almost all coal-gas plants rely heavily on massive quantities of water in the gasification and transport process. In the west at least, heavy draw down of scarce water supplies must be considered a cost. A less direct potential cost is found in the fact that a number of plants may never come on line if environmental standards are strictly applied. This constitutes a possible lost opportunity cost that must be considered if the plant is not built. Should this indirect and intangible cost be included? Or should the costs attendant with industry concentration, that is, those that arise because only the largest firms will be able to install such devices, be included? Another difficulty arises when a decision not to require the environmental controls is made. What are the costs attributable to pollution immediately around the site, the adverse impact on the health of the workers, the consequences of pollution further removed from the plant, and the costs of lost life expectancy or illness?

These latter costs raise yet another set of identification problems— the identification of risks. Although a prediction can be made that some people will suffer health effects from absorption of the pollutants from the proposed plant, we do not know how many people will be affected, for what period of time, nor do we know the extent of the adverse health effects other than by formulating a very general opinion as to the risks involved. Assume however that these risks, with reasonable mathematical precision, can be predicted. How should they be properly translated into a part of the mathematical equation? For example, in construction of a liquified-natural-gas (LNG) regasification plant, certification by FERC is required if the gas flows in a commingled interstate stream from the plant. Let us assume that the tankers bringing the LNG to the regasification plant sail through narrow banks in a heavily populated area. Scientific calculations indicate that there exists a one-in-a-million chance that a ship may collide with another ship or object, explode, and send a fireball over the population center, killing some portion of the people and destroying property in a horrendous explosion and conflagration. Simply factoring in the chance of the disaster into the cost-benefit calculation falls far short of the fundamental moral choice involved in plant certification. Even more complex is the identification of the less-knowable possible costs such as genetic damage that may result from exposure to a heretofore unexperienced chemical and biological phenomenon such as the LNG dispute. Is there a risk that these decisions may involve creation of processes and products that outstrip society's ability to assimilate them? If so, what are the risks involved with imposing such scientifically sophisticated technologies on society? And who should decide? And what decision-making methodology should be used? Does cost-benefit analysis carry with it a predisposition to a certain outcome or to certain types of outcomes? Clearly it is more positive, scientific, and technologically oriented. Should not that bias be taken into account by the decision maker in his more comprehensive analysis?

The next stage of the cost-benefit analysis, quantification, presents the obvious problem that all things cannot be quantified. The deeper problem is that by trying to quantify such things as the value of a single life we run the risk of impairing the qualitative values of the subject.[4] Who, for example, would care to be responsible for parceling out medicine in short supply to those affected by a nuclear disaster based only on quantifiable data about a person? Another quantification problem is that for some things price simply cannot be set because markets do not exist in which to set prices. How reliable is it to price the costs and benefits of a research-center study for the genetic results of exposure to nuclear radiation in massive doses?

It may also be clear that the presentation and interpretation of the data are equally, if not more, subjective. There is simply no way to dispense with human influence in the equation. Who selects and interprets data and information is a vital factor capable of opening up the equation to a host of subjective criteria that may corrupt the neat, empirical nature of the cost-benefit formula.

Criticism of the cost-benefit analysis should be put in perspective. A critique of cost-benefit analysis does not suggest that the method itself is totally deficient. Rather it is obvious that the method is not a closed system insulated from the vagaries of subjectivity. This critique merely admonishes decision makers to take heed of the normative issues that arise in the process. Indeed, cost-benefit analysis can be useful to highlight the normative issues. Moreover, if the analysis is used well it will make the normative issues, such as whether this is a good project, explicit for decision makers, which will, or should, in turn, force decision makers to state explicitly the reasons for their choices.[5]

The Case of the Liquid-Metal Fast-Breeder Reactor

The liquid-metal-fast-breeder-reactor program (LMFBR) provides a case in point. The cost-benefit analysis for this program appears in a study for the Joint Economic Committee of Congress. The LMFBR is a nuclear-power device that creates more fuel than it consumes. It creates plutonium, a highly toxic and extremely long-lasting manmade element, taken from reprocessed fuel rods from conventional nuclear plants or processed prior to use in the LMFBR. Currently, only light-water reactors (LWRs) are commercially used in the United States. Because the supply of uranium is finite the LMFBR presents a nice alternative for the use of an exhaustible resource. The LMFBR is attractive basically because it could keep the cost of electric operation down as fuel costs rise due to scarcity.

Cost-benefit analysis of the LMFBR has been used to demonstrate the discounted present value of the net costs and benefits achieved in the successful development of a commercial LMFBR. Another espoused benefit is that the development of commercial breeder reactors keeps up the country's technological sophistication. Cost-benefit analysis presents as a rather straightforward and simple matter, the benefits of the cost efficiency of the LMFBR compared to the LWR.

Cost-benefit analysis of this comparison is dependent on five factors. First, the discount rate must be chosen. Second, capital costs for the construction of the LMFBR must be compared to those for the LWR. Third, research and development costs for the LMFBR are computed. Fourth, the demand for electricity in the long term is developed. And, fifth, the supply of and the cost of uranium must be ascertained.

Each of these factors are essentially economic in nature. Thus, all that cost-benefit analysis must do is to ascertain the quantitative economic benefits of choosing between an LMFBR and an LWR. Even if analysis of the breeder-reactor program is narrowed to these five elements we will find that we have significant technical problems without cost-benefit methodology.

Each of these factors is controversial. It is very difficult for economists to predict with any great accuracy the proper discount rate to apply to a long-term project such as an LMFBR plant, which may take up to a decade or more to construct and have a useful life of at least thirty to forty years.

The capital-cost differential between the LMFBR and the LWR likewise poses problems insofar as inflation rates make costs difficult to predict. Further, the learning curve, that is, the supposed reduction in capital costs because of experience with the plants, for the development of the LMFBR can be adjusted to affect the date that the LMFBR will be introduced. This means that a comparison with the LWR can be made depending on a particular desired outcome. Moreover the role of nuclear power in national energy policy is constantly undergoing revision. Nuclear power as recently as the early and mid-1970s was the hope for a return to cheaper energy. In the aftermath of the Three Mile Island incident in 1979 the political, social, and financial fallout has been so great that private-sector investors have virtually refused to finance the construction of a nuclear plant. The role of nuclear power in the national energy picture is thus greatly reduced. One question appears then as to the use and wisdom of comparing these two reactors in an energy scenario that is in such a state of flux. LMFBR research and development costs for most cost-benefit analyses have been estimated at $10 billion, and many commentators feel that that prediction is low by half.

Finally, two elements that are crucial to ascertaining the demand for the LMFBR—the demand for electricity and the supply of uranium—are tremendously speculative. Most of the major cost-benefit analyses for the breeder-reactor program were conducted prior to 1975. At that point the demand for electricity was computed using an oil price set at $7 and $11 a barrel. Then, projections in the demand for overall energy use were made, and a translation was made for demand in electricity. Assuming that those conversions can be made reliably, the fact is that oil prices in 1981 ranged from $35 to $42 per barrel. In concert with that price increase, conservation has reduced the demand for energy on a large scale, trimming the demand for electricity drastically.

Finally, the availability and cost of uranium is speculative. At the time of the cost-benefit analysis long-term supply contracts were made for uranium at approximately $7 a pound. The price of uranium increased to over $42 a pound shortly thereafter. This should have a positive effect on the cost-benefit analysis (that is, make the case more favorable toward the LMFBR).

The argument against blind reliance on cost-benefit analysis is simple: Even limiting analysis to hard economic data we run into significant controversy in the technical aspects of the cost-benefit methodology.[6]

One cost that has not been put into the mix is the cost of decommissioning a plant. At the time of the major LMFBR cost-benefit analysis in 1974, it was estimated that the cost to decommission a plant at the end of its useful life would be between $2 million and $45 million. In 1981 that figure has not substantially appreciated in the cost-benefit analysis. However, the cost for premature decommissioning and cleanup at Three Mile Island are estimated to be $2.5 billion.[7] The cost of plant decommissioning is a hard economic cost as opposed to some of the softer health and safety factors to be discussed. Also, some cost-benefit analyses of the LMFBR ignore transportation-safety costs by nonquantification, despite the fact that these are direct economic costs to the development of such a project. Further, the public-health impact of plutonium with its high toxicity is not known yet. Safeguards against sabotage for plutonium also must be taken into account and are quite expensive. Reactor safety and nuclear-waste disposal are other negative impacts regarding the environment that cannot be ignored.

Finally, a questionable fundamental assumption is present in comparing LMFBRs with LWRs. This comparison assumes a nuclear alternative by creating scenarios in which we are using either breeders or light-water reactors. For cost-benefit analysis to mean something to decision makers it is vital to be aware of the usefulness of an LMFBR in a nonnuclear scenario as well.

Given the far-reaching criticisms of it, we seek to discover the usefulness of cost-benefit analysis. We come not to bury it nor to praise it as a proper methodology. However, care should be taken that cost-benefit analysis is not used as the sole determinant, particularly when large-scale projects such as the LMFBR are concerned. The method inherently cannot be used as the sole tool of a decision maker on health, safety, or other societal and less-quantifiable grounds.

LMFBRs, in fact all major power plants, from the date of their inception until decommissioning are planned to last over a generation. Consequently, decisions made today are projected fifty and sixty years into the future. In view of the long-term consequences of those decisions and of their speculative nature, decision makers must be cautious in the extreme as to where the perceived or unperceived costs will lie. Beneficial use in the short and middle terms of nuclear and other plants to achieve identified cost savings may pass on a massive bill to future generations. The bill may be paid not only in our descendants dollars but in their health, safety, and environment in ways and amounts presently unpredicted. We thus embark on a sea of questions about the shape of future energy policy. We have discussed but a few of the questions dealing with the demand for electricity and supply of that demand by a form of nuclear power.[8] Other questions, equally deep and complex, remain for the energy decision maker.

The Place of Cost-Benefit Analysis in Law

Although the cost-benefit methodology has been used for years, it has been legally required only on a selected basis.[9] Curiously it has become a dominant methodology for the application of legal standards with the passage of the National Environmental Policy Act (NEPA).[10] NEPA itself does not call for a cost-benefit analysis.[11] The point at which cost-benefit analysis fits into the legal system presents issues separate from the basic question of the efficacy and wisdom of its use. The legal permissibility of the method is the initial question for a real decision maker. To which decision maker do we refer? If the decision maker is an agency official, then the question revolves around statutory authority that exists regarding the use of the cost-benefit methodology. Is its use discretionary or mandatory? If the decision maker is a judge a different question pertains—

how to apply the proper balancing equation. If the judge is reviewing an agency decision, what is the proper scope of review in overseeing the way in which a cost-benefit analysis is applied at the agency level? This section addresses these questions.

Cost-Benefit Analysis and Administrative Agencies

As a general matter of administrative law, agency officials must comply with the enabling legislation that creates their office and with the rules and regulations that further define their functions. If legislation requires the application of cost-benefit analysis, they must use it. NEPA does not require, but it does permit, cost-benefit analysis. Other statutes such as the Clean Air Act[12] and the Toxic Substances Control Act[13] set general standards for determining controls such as "will endanger the public health," or "present an unreasonable risk of injury to health," respectively. Within these general standards the administrator may employ cost-benefit analysis. As long as the administrator's decision is not arbitrary, capricious, or unreasonable, and as long as the decision is based on substantial evidence when reviewing the whole record, the decision will stand.[14]

The Occupational Safety and Health Act of 1970 (OSHA) has given the Supreme Court two recent occasions to speak on the subject of cost-benefit analysis.[15] OSHA requires the secretary of Labor to set standards so that no employee would suffer a "material impairment of health or functional capacity." In *Industrial Union Department AFL-CIO* v. *American Petroleum Institute,* the secretary set a standard exposure level for benzene, a toxic and carcinogenic substance, at 1 part per million (ppm) after an analysis of costs.[16] The standard exposure level was set without an adequate discussion of benefit, based on a policy determination that when a carcinogen is involved there is no safe exposure level. The Department of Labor further relied on a belief that OSHA requires the secretary to set an exposure limit at the lowest technologically feasible level not impairing the viability of the industries regulated. The lower court held that OSHA required the secretary to determine whether the benefit of the standard regarding benzene was reasonably related to its costs, and it invalidated the secretary's ruling.[17]

Although the Supreme Court reached a consensus on the outcome of the case by affirming the lower court, there was no consensus on the issue of whether a cost-benefit analysis was required. Justice Stevens, writing for the plurality, avoided the issue, and Justice Powell's concurrence stated that the statute required the agency to weigh costs and benefits. Justice Marshall's dissent said that, because the issue was "on the frontiers of scientific knowledge,'' no better estimate of benefits was likely so any imposition of cost-benefit analysis would not be fruitful.

The cost-benefit issue was presented more clearly in *American Textile Manufacturers Institute, Inc.* v. *Donovan.*[18] Representatives of the cotton industry challenged the cotton-dust standard, arguing that OSHA required that the standard reflect a reasonable relationship between costs and benefits. The government and two labor organizations said that OSHA mandated that the secretary set the most protective standard feasible to eliminate a significant risk of material health impairment. The majority opinion, relying on Justice Marshall's dissent in *Industrial Union,* said that cost-benefit analysis was not required, because Congress, when it promulgated OSHA, defined the basic relationship between costs and benefits by placing the benefit of worker health above all other considerations. Further, the Court said that any standard based on a balancing of costs and benefits that strikes a different balance than that struck by Congress is inconsistent with OSHA.

The Court reasoned that if Congress intends an agency to engage in cost-benefit analysis the statute will state so.[19] In the case of OSHA the Court held that a ''feasibility analysis'' was required, that is, the standard must be set that is not necessarily the product of a cost-benefit balancing. Rather, the only limit imposed was that the standard be set to the extent it is ''capable of being done.'' The Court did not expressly state that cost-benefit analysis could not be used. The cost-benefit analysis could not be used, however, to override the language and standard in the statute.

American Textile starts to answer the question of when cost-benefit analysis is required. We know it is required when there is an express direction in the statute. And, although *American Textile* does not preclude the use of cost-benefit analysis in other instances, it does prohibit cost-benefit analysis that subverts the requirements of a law.

One factor deeply affecting how cost-benefit analysis is applied is the question of who is applying the standard and under what policies? Another equally important question is who has the burden of proof? In the OSHA case the agency made a presumption against an industry and invited it to respond. When industry failed to rebut the presumption, higher and more stringent standard was applied, and costs of implementation were passed on to the industry, the major portion of which manufactured petrochemicals.

Executive Orders and Senate Bills

One of President Reagan's first official acts was the promulgation of executive order 12,291 entitled ''Federal Regulation.''[20] The preamble

of the executive order states that its purpose is to ''reduce the burdens
of existing and future regulations, increase agency accountability for
regulatory actions, provide for presidential oversight of the regulatory
process, minimize duplication and conflict of regulations, and insure well
reasoned regulations.'' The president planned to reduce the size of the
bureaucracy via cost-benefit analysis. The order applies to all executive-
branch agencies as opposed to independent regulatory agencies. (The
DOE is an example of an executive-branch agency, and the FERC and
the EPA are independent agencies.) When an agency is promulgating a
new regulation, reviewing existing regulations, or developing a legislative
proposal, it is required to: base the decision on adequate information
concerning the need for and consequences of the proposal; take action
only if the potential benefits to society outweigh the potential costs to
society; choose regulatory objectives to maximize the net benefits to
society; choose the alternative that involves the least net cost to society;
and set regulatory priorities with the aim of maximizing the aggregate
net benefits to society.

Agencies are only required to go through this analysis to the extent
permitted by law. Thus, this order will not affect cases like *American
Textile*.[21] The hard constitutional issue is whether the president may
require executive agencies to be guided by principles of cost-benefits
analysis even when an agency might choose not to do so. A Department
of Justice memorandum in support of the order argues in favor of the
president's use of this power.[22] When a statute does not expressly or
implicitly preclude it, an agency may take into account the costs and
benefits of proposed action. The order assumes such a calculus would
simply represent a logical method of assessing whether regulatory action
authorized by statute would be desirable and, if so, what form that action
should take. Federal courts reviewing such actions would be unlikely to
conclude that an assessment of costs and benefits was an impermissible
tool in making regulatory decisions unless the resultant decision was
arbitrary, capricious, or unreasonable.

Second, the order is predicated on the assumption that the requirement
to use cost-benefit analysis would not exceed the president's powers of
supervision. Such a requirement leaves considerable decision-making
discretion to the agency through the existence of final decision-making
power—the yea or nay of the agency. Under the executive order, although
the agency head is required to calculate potential costs and benefits to
determine whether the benefits justify the costs, the order assumes that
the agency retains considerable latitude in determining whether regulatory
action is justified and what form such action should take. The limited

requirements of the executive order are not regarded as inconsistent with a legislative decision to place the basic authority to implement a statute in a particular agency.

Under the order the agency must file a regulatory impact analysis (RIA) for every major rule. *Major rules* are those that have an annual effect on the economy of $100 million or more, result in a major increase in costs or prices for consumers, individual industries, governments, or geographic regions, or adversely affect competition, employment, investment, productivity, innovation, or the ability of domestic firms to compete with foreign firms. The RIA, furnished to the director of the Office of Management and Budget (OMB), must contain a description of potential benefits and costs, a determination of potential net benefits, and a discussion of alternative approaches. OMB then reviews the RIA and may submit comments to the agency. The purpose behind OMB's review is to identify major rules and to minimize or eliminate duplication, overlap, or conflict between agency and interagency rules.

The order limits judicial review. Since the order is intended only to improve the internal management of the federal government it does not create any right or benefit enforceable at law. However, the cost-benefit analysis performed by the agency and the RIA are to be part of the agency record in the event of judicial review. This provision precludes direct judicial review of an agency's compliance with the order. It makes clear the president's intention not to create private rights. Lower courts have held that an executive order not based on a congressional delegation can limit and in some instances preclude judicial review.[23] The limitation on judicial review presents a delicate interbranch question: Can the executive branch circumscribe the scope of the judiciary in their role of overseeing the workings of administrative agencies? The bar on judicial review of agency compliance with the order does not prohibit a court from hearing a constitutional or statutory attack on the legality of the order itself. A court can also assess whether the agency complied with the order.

Because the RIA required by the order will become part of the agency record for judicial review, courts may consider the RIA in determining whether an agency's action under review is consistent with the governing statutes.

Congress is considering the adoption of an expanded proposal, S. 1080, which would subject independent regulatory agencies to using cost-benefit analysis.[24] The premise behind the bill is that the costs of administrative regulations often exceed the value of the benefits to the public. The bill adopts the language of executive order 12,291 and attempts to make uniform the policies behind the order. The primary policy is to identify trade-offs that occur in regulation between economic efficiency and other less easily quantifiable social goals.

Using Cost-Benefit Analysis

Cost-benefit analysis can be a useful tool in circumstances that recognize its inherent limitations. It is capable of pointing out and highlighting positive and empirical data that are useful for formulating policy and making decisions. However, the method is also capable of distortion, particularly the distortion of noneconomic issues. Hence the method cannot be the sole decision-making method. Far-reaching, long-term public-policy decisions demand consideration of broad issues whose variables may be difficult to identify, analyze, and quantify. The *American Textile* case wisely recognizes that there are standards for decision making other than asking the question: Do benefits exceed costs, or, more simply, is $B > C$? The narrow approach of executive order 12,291 makes the answer to this question paramount. Cost-benefit analysis requires the identification of risks and their translation into costs. Why should not a decision be made on the basis that as a matter of agency policy it has been determined that there are certain risks that are unacceptable regardless of whether $B > C$?

Cost-benefit analysis should be a used, not abused, tool. It is a lifesaver in an ocean of uncertainties. Agencies are called on to make more and more complex decisions. The complexity stems from technical problems that include an expanding but inconclusive data base, disagreement among experts on methods for using data, lack of consensus regarding findings, and interpretations that are simply unquantifiable. Regulators must also compute low probabilities and high-cost events while assessing diverse and changing values in a pluralistic society. In energy regulation these problems are often exacerbated by an atmosphere of crisis. All these factors pull agencies toward reliance on the superficially precise cost-benefit analysis.[25] Cost-benefit gives the appearance of having hard, positive data that can yield a so-called answer. It plays down the significance of the nonnumber issues. The danger of its use is the failure to examine the underlying assumptions of cost-benefit analysis. The method can become consequentialist, relativistic, deterministic, and reductionist.[26] It contains within it a technological bias in which society trades off individuality in favor of compromise for the collectivity. It is consequentialist because it favors ends not means. The bottom line of the equation is more important than how the figure was reached. It is deterministic because an assumption has been made that all net quantified benefits are good. There are reasons for making decisions other than B

> C. There may be times when a decision is right when costs are greater than the benefits. The monetization of the worth of life and health is so problematic that a useful equation cannot be developed.

Cost-benefit analysis can ignore distributional issues. In the case of the safety of a power plant, who is in a better position to absorb the costs—industry and hence consumers or the workers?[27] Cost-benefit analysis may also be relativistic. Because of its allegiance to positivism, it argues that societal and value choices are too soft, too difficult to determine and differ from individual to individual and group to group. Cost-benefit analysis may allow decision makers to eschew value choices in favor of an equation on the premise that everyone's value choices are entitled to equal weight. Such relativism assumes too much. It ignores the fact that certain values are better than others. Finally, blind cost-benefit analysis is reductionist by seeking the "grand quantification." By reducing things, even the nonreducible, to dollars and deciding policy on that basis the numbers dominate the people who are affected by them. In E.F. Schumacher's words, money then becomes the "highest of all values."[28] In a cost-benefit methodology the rightness or goodness of a decision is equivalent to its net economic effect or consequence. The search for rightness or goodness is not the purpose of the decision process under strict cost-benefit analysis. The means for decision are sometimes as important as the ends—the means used to decide issues touch on such basic issues as democratic participation, bias and weight of evidence, dignity of the persons affected by the decisions, and myriad other non-dollar issues. We argue not for the elimination of cost-benefit analysis but for its cautious and thoughtful use by responsible, thoughtful decision makers. So used, cost-benefit analysis can marshal facts, help organize a mass of complex and often confusing data, ease the decision making process, and highlight for review the qualitative choices inherent in energy decision making.

Notes

1. E. Mishan, Cost-Benefit Analysis, (rev. ed. 1976). See also, L. Anderson & R. Settee, Benefit-Cost Analysis: A Practical Guide (1977).

2. *See, e.g.,* Kennedy, *Cost-Benefit Analysis of Entitlement Problems: A Critique,* 33 Stan. L. Rev. 387, 389 (1981).

3. *See generally,* Williams, *Benefit-Cost Analysis in Natural Resources Decisionmaking: An Economic and Legal Overview,* 11 Nat. Resources L. 761 (1979) and Rodgers, Benefits, Costs and Risks: Oversight of Health and Environmental Decisionmaking, 4 Harv. Envtl. L. Rev. 191 (1980).

4. The so-called cost per life saved in various federal-government programs range from $35,500 to $624,976,000. Crovitz, *Costs in a Regulated Society,* Wall Street Journal, Aug. 7, 1981, at 14, col. 4.

5. The critique of cost-benefit analysis is taken largely from Lovins, *Cost-Risk-Benefit Assessment in Energy Policy,* 45 Geo. Wash. L. Rev. 911 (1977). See also, J. Tomain, Energy Law in a Nutshell Ch. 12 (1981); Sagoff, *At the Shrine of Our Lady of Fatima or Why Political Questions Are Not all Economic,* 23 Ariz. L. Rev. 1283 (1981).

6. The Fast Breeder Reactor Decision: An Analysis of Limits and The Limits of Analysis, A Study Beyond for the Joint Economic Committee, 94th Cong., 2d Sess. (April 19, 1976). The study lists the weaknesses of cost-benefit analysis with LMFBR as follows:

1. All the major cost-benefit studies of LMFBR are incomplete because they ignore the possibilities that substantial costs in the form of long-lived radio-active wastes will be transferred to future generations. The waste question pushes cost-benefit analysis beyond its capacity and a new analytical method is required.

2. To project the need for LMFBRs on uranium shortages is wrong.

3. Increases in uranium reserve estimates emphasize the uncertainties surrounding this resource.

4. Because it is expensive to prove uranium reserves proven reserves tend to be relatively low to other resources.

5. Uranium reserves are low because prices were declining at the time of the cost-benefit analysis and hence incentives for exploration and development were weak.

6. Uranium resource analysis excluded consideration of major determinants of future uranium resources and hence a pessimistic bias is created against uranium supply.

7. Growth rates of electricity demand are overstated. It appears that electricity growth rate beyond 1980 may be closer to 2% per year hence the historical growth rate of 7%.

8. Electricity prices have significantly increased since the studies.

9. The capital cost differential between LMFBRs and LWRs is significant. Everyone agrees that LMFBR will be more expensive to build however that differential is not accurately known.

10. It is hoped that there will be a learning curve which will help reduce costs of LMFBRs. The current experience however is the opposite in that experimental LMFBRs have met with cost overruns to the power of 10.

11. The choice of discount rate is important. Some studies use a discount rate substantially less than 10% which greatly affects costs of the program.

12. Future scenarios for the use of LMFBRs are often times too narrow. Some studies analyze only one future that assumes a certain breeder commercialization date. Other dates must be used as well as scenarios without nuclear power.

7. Shanahan, TMI: The Financial Impact; Liberman, The Financial Impact of the TMI-2 Accident; Hyman, Three Mile Island, Two Years Later. (These papers discuss the financial implications at Three Mile Island. They were presented May 19, 1981 at the Iowa State University Regulatory Conference, Ames, Iowa.)

8. *See generally,* Fast Breeder Reactor Program: Hearings before the Joint Economic Committee, 94th Cong., 1st Sess. (1975).

9. Williams, *supra* note 3.

10. 42 U.S.C. sec. 4371 *et seq.* (1976).

11. *See* W. Rogers, Environmental Law 745–47 (1977).

12. 42 U.S.C. sec. 7545(c)(1)(A) (Supp. I 1977). *See also* Ethyl Corp. v. EPA, 541 F.2d 1 (D.C. Cir. 1976).

13. 15 U.S.C. sec. 2605(a) (1976).

14. 5 U.S.C. sec. 706 (1976).

15. 29 U.S.C. sec. 651 *et seq.* (1976).

16. 100 S.Ct. 2844 (1980).

17. American Petroleum Institute v. OSHA, 581 F.2d 493 (5th Cir. 1978).

18. 101 S.Ct. 2478 (1981).

19. *See, e.g.,* Flood Control Act of 1936, 33 U.S.C. sec. 710(a) (1976); Outer Continental Shelf Lands Act Amendments of 1978, 43 U.S.C. sec. 1347(b). Energy Policy and Conservation Act of 1975, 42 U.S.C. sec. 6295(c) (1976). Sometimes this appears in regulations, see, e.g., 10 C.F.R. sec. 51.23(c).

20. 46 Fed. Reg. 13193-98 (Feb. 19, 1981).

21. *See also* EPA v. National Crushed Stone Ass'n, 101 S.Ct. 295 (1980).

22. Dept. of Justice, Memorandum Re: Proposed Executive Order entitled "Federal Regulation" (Feb. 13, 1981). This issue is also debated in: Rosenberg, *Beyond the Limits of Executive Power: Presidential Control of Agency Rulemaking under Executive Order,* 80 Mich. L. Rev. 193 (1981); Rosenberg, *Presidential Control of Agency Rulemaking: An Analysis of Constitutional Issues that May Be Raised by Executive Order 12,291,* 23 Ariz. L. Rev. 1199 (1981): Shane, *Presidential Regulatory Oversight and the Separation of Powers: The Legality of Executive Order No. 12,291,* 23 Ariz. L. Rev. 1235 (1981); and, Sunstein, *Cost-Benefit Analysis and the Separation of Powers,* 23 Ariz. L. Rev. 1267 (1981).

23. *See* Independent Meat Packers Ass'n v. Butz, 526 F.2d 228 (8th Cir. 1975), *cert. denied,* 424 U.S. 966 (1976); Legal Aid Society of

Alameda County v. Brennan, 608 F.2d 1319 (9th Cir. 1979); National Renderers Ass'n v. EPA, 541 F.2d 1281 (8th Cir. 1976); and Hiatt Grain Feed Inc. v. Bergland, 446 F. Supp. 457 (D. Kan. 1978).

24. 127 Cong. Rec. 97th Cong. 1st Sess., S4228–S4242 (daily ed. April 30, 1981).

25. Baram, *Cost-Benefit Analysis: An Inadequate Basis for Health, Safety, and Environmental Regulatory Decisionmaking*, 8 Ecology L. Q. 473 (1980).

26. *See generally,* Kelman, *Cost-Benefit Analysis—An Ethical Critique,* 4 Reg. 33 (Jan./Feb. 1981).

27. *Id.,* and Rodgers, *supra* note 3.

28. E.F. Schumacher, Small Is Beautiful: Economics as If People Mattered (1973).

8 Energy Enforcement

Decisive and effective enforcement is crucial to the success of any regulatory program. However, the enforcement of complicated economic regulations whose basic necessity is the subject of heated controversy is archetypal of the special dilemmas of the energy agency and its enforcement arms.

Congress sets the policy agenda for energy agencies by enacting laws to modify the free market's activities. Usually Congress leaves large discretionary areas to be sketched in by the agency through its rule-making, adjudication, and, eventually, enforcement activities. However, even though Congress either deliberately or inadvertently leaves large gaps in difficult areas in the laws it enacts, it must proclaim its dedication and commitment to strict enforcement of the laws it has created. Thus the energy agency's enforcement arm has left on its doorstep the orphaned, ambiguous child of Congress—the complicated energy statute—with a note pinned to it: "enforce me rigorously."

Law makers and agency rule makers have seen some aspect of the free market function imperfectly and have enacted laws or regulations to be implemented, administered, and enforced. Of course, absent the threat of some type of sanction, segments of an industry will fail to voluntarily comply with laws or rules promulgated to improve the marketplace. Energy policymaking and enforcement is highly visible, unsettled, and complex—yet law makers demand rigorous enforcement policies and procedures. Over the past decade, as perceptions of energy scarcity developed in the national consciousness, as the American public angrily waited in gas lines to pay vastly increased costs for energy, the public eye focused on whether oil companies were complying with the law. As a result, the bright lights of the press, the Congress, and the consumer activists shone harshly on the energy agencies, their enforcement programs, and their relationships with the oil and natural-gas industry. Some of the enforcement mechanisms set up to enforce energy regulations have worked, albeit with moderate success, and others have foundered on the shores of lack of consensus about the need to enforce and wildly varying notions of how to enforce. We discuss in this chapter the development of energy-enforcement programs, their flaws, and different approaches to the energy enforcement problem.

133

A Brief History of Energy Enforcement

Only since the 1970s has the issue of energy enforcement been of any widespread concern or interest on the part of the nation's policymakers. No identifiable energy enforcement programs existed until the oil-embargo period of the 1970s. The Federal Power Commission (FPC), for example, during the period of its existence (1920–1977), regulated all interstate aspects of the natural-gas industry as well as wholesale rates for electric energy and certain hydroelectric facilities. Yet, the FPC conducted no independent enforcement program. No division or office of the agency had defined compliance or enforcement responsibilities. Violations of law were generally discovered in the course of ongoing adjudicative proceedings and dealt with through administrative remedies such as paybacks of funds or gas. No punitive measures were imposed. Lack of any centralized enforcement or coordinated compliance effort by the FPC resulted in largely haphazard and random attempts to obtain voluntary compliance. The FPC's unwillingness or inability explicitly to pursue violations other than as an afterthought to the adjudicatory process meant that most misdeeds were probably unaccounted for, uninvestigated, and left to private parties to remedy with whatever devices available.

Early-1970s energy legislation, to control domestic crude-oil and product prices through the Cost of Living Council, at first engendered little enforcement action. The Emergency Petroleum Allocation Act of 1973 proposed a voluntary-allocation program.[1] The failure of that program, evidenced by the withdrawal of Standard Oil of Indiana, one of the nation's eight largest oil companies, from the program six months after its initiation, resulted in the creation by President Nixon of the Federal Energy Administration (FEA). The FEA took over the Cost of Living Council's crude oil and products price-control responsibilities. The vacillation of the administration and Congress regarding the proper regulatory and enforcement role of the federal government created a sort of nonpolicy that effectively stymied any rigorous or even ploddingly consistent energy regulation and enforcement. Unfortunately, in times of uncertainty over the basic validity of a regulatory program and concurrent pressure to enforce the law regardless of its utility to the nation, to please the Congress that enacted the law, the enforcer must enforce. This mentality led to enforcement actions against gas-station owners rather than multinational oil companies. Thus, by 1976, it was clear to most observers that any ostensible enforcement program by FEA was a failure.

There were several ways in which crude-oil resellers, the focus of most recent Department of Energy (DOE) enforcement efforts, could and did violate crude-oil-reseller regulations, among them miscertifying crude oil sold (certifying that crude oil belonged to a category permitted a higher

price under existing regulations); failing to provide historical and traditional services associated with the sale of the product (layering); and
improperly pricing crude oil sold. The dollar effects of switching crude
oil types to obtain higher prices are massive. In an example given by the
staff of the Subcommittee on Oversight and Investigations of the Committee on Energy and Commerce, a modest-sized refinery could obtain
the benefits of $3.6 million per month by miscertifying lower-tier old oil
to a price-exempt category.[2] Total overcharges resulting from pricing
violations have been estimated at $12 billion.

As a result of public and congressional concern over the ability of
crude-oil refiners or resellers to make vast sums through violations of the
FEA regulations, political pressure engendered a review of the enforcement process. In May 1977 at the request of the newly elected and eager-
to-enforce Carter administration, the Federal Energy Administration Task
Force on Compliance and Enforcement was created. The Task Force's
product, known as the "Sporkin report" (so called after the chairman of
the Task Force, Stanley Sporkin, director of the Securities and Exchange
Commission's Division of Enforcement) drew the blueprint for recent
crude oil and product regulation and enforcement.[3] In the report, effectiveness of enforcement was judged according to its deterrent effect on
potential malefactors and by public confidence in FEA. The FEA's program was declared a failure in both respects. The report emphasized that
deterrence and respect could be attained only through consistent and well-
executed applications of rules and regulations. Of course, the report
assumed the comprehensibility and basic rightness of the regulatory program itself. Thus, although the Sporkin report provides a useful criticism
of what can go wrong with an enforcement program, it does not question
the underlying, much more troublesome, aspect of enforcement in this
area—whether the enactment and enforcement of energy-price controls
are good ideas for the country or whether the program is at all practicable
to enforce meaningfully.

The report chastised the FEA for reactive rather than active enforcement and concluded that the FEA's haphazard enforcement had inured
to the benefit of the largest oil refiners in the country. Thus, those refiners
were designated as the primary targets of any program directed to allocate
and regulate the price of the nation's petroleum and petroleum products.
The report asserted that the means to attain that regulatory goal was by
monitoring the activities of all major refineries through extensive and
intensive auditings.

The blame for the FEA's ineffectiveness in attaining any effective
level of enforcement comprised the bulk of the report. These complaints
rested primarily on the findings that the enforcement program had not
received the necessary attention and resources to be effective. The report

found that the FEA enforcement program lacked centralization and its staff labored in a system with little accountability and incentive to raise a potential violation that would probably never be litigated. Any agency enforcement was hindered by the requirement that civil as well as criminal cases be referred to the Department of Justice for action. Morale at FEA was extremely low when the Sporkin Task Force analyzed it. Both the public and the oil industry had little confidence in the competence of the agency. The FEA's enforcement efforts were not widely accepted and thus became a handy political whipping boy for a newly elected and consumer-oriented president and Congress. The report's criticisms and call for a stronger national office of compliance demanded an entirely revamped organization with new investigative and litigative expertise and, more importantly, power.

The Development of Enforcement Mechanisms

Congress modified energy regulation radically in the DOE act.[4] Among the programs revamped by that law, the enforcement function was at last given some priority by Congress. The entities within the newly established DOE with enforcement duties were and are the FERC, Economic Regulatory Administration (ERA), and the special counsel's office of DOE. The ERA administered and ensured compliance with all DOE regulatory programs, except those assigned to the FERC and the special counsel's office, whose responsibility centered on compliance by the thirty-five major refiners identified by the Sporkin Task Force. The ERA's functions included regulation, price, and allocation of oil and certain regulated products, administration of programs theoretically designed to ensure price stability and equitable supplies of crude oil, petroleum products, and natural gas among domestic users. The FERC carried on most of the natural-gas and electric-utility regulatory duties previously conducted by the FPC and was given authority to regulate the rates of oil pipelines, which were previously the responsibility of the ICC.

DOE Enforcement Process

The ERA's enforcement program was modeled directly on the recommendations of the Sporkin report. (Although the program still exists as of this writing, it has been significantly cut back from levels reached during 1978–1981. Thus we refer to the program in some instances in the past tense.) The Sporkin report urged creation of a watchdog agency that would constantly oversee and audit the accounts of major refiners.

The ERA Office of Enforcement was responsible for civil audits on all companies other than the thirty-five major refiners assigned to the special counsel's office. A 14 December 1981 ERA reorganization incorporated the Office of Enforcement's auditing activities with the special counsel's office. The ERA's auditing activities and authority to issue subpoenas gave it substantial power lacking under FEA. The audits performed of each company comprised the first step in DOE's preliminary enforcement. In the course of its investigation, the ERA had the power to subpoena production of existing documents and to require presentation of testimony.

If the ERA believed a violation had occurred, was occurring, or would occur, it could issue a notice of probable violation (NOPV). The recipient of a NOPV had thirty days to file a reply with the ERA, and any objections raised at that stage were to be considered in the enforcement proceeding. Somewhat analogous to the FERC's preliminary investigation, to be discussed later, issuance of a NOPV was not a prerequisite to commencement of an enforcement proceeding.

If, after the reply, the ERA determined that the NOPV had merit, it issued a proposed remedial order (PRO), setting forth proposed findings of fact and law and authority for ERA's legal propositions.

The Office of Hearings and Appeals (OHA) conducted the formal enforcement proceeding, to which the ERA was considered a party. The ERA bore the burden of proving the prima facie validity of its findings of fact and conclusions of law asserted in the PRO. The party objecting to the PRO or eliciting new evidence had the burden of going forward with that proof. The proponent of an order, usually the ERA, or the proponent of an order or motion or additional factual representations bore the ultimate burden of persuasion.

Disposition of the matter by the OHA could take several forms, including issuance of the PRO as a final remedial order, modifying the PRO, remanding the PRO to the ERA for further consideration, or modification or rescission of the PRO. If the respondent objected to the remedial order, it could be appealed to the FERC or, if the decision was not appealable to the FERC or if appeal was sought of a FERC order, it would be filed in a federal district court.

Apart from remedial orders, the other enforcement devices available to the DOE were issuance of an interim remedial order for immediate compliance (IROIC) and concurrence in a consent order. The standards for issuance of an IROIC were roughly equivalent to those for a civil injunction: a strong probability that a violation had occurred, was continuing, or was about to occur; irreparable harm would occur unless the violation was remedied immediately; and the public interest required avoidance of such irreparable harm through immediate compliance and waiver of the normal procedures applicable to remedial orders.

The procedure for arriving at a consent order was similar to the FERC's procedure and was designed to achieve the same goals. This informal method of achieving compliance and some restitution became increasingly popular with the DOE.[5] Alleged violators were and are sometimes wary of consent orders because, unless the order explicitly states otherwise, the DOE may seek additional civil penalties or may refer the matter to the Department of Justice (DOJ) for criminal prosecution. Territorial wrangling between DOE and DOJ historically has hampered the efficient usage of consent orders, because the DOJ must concur in all proposed settlements.[6] Oil-price decontrol took effect in January 1981, and that event deemphasized ERA's compliance and enforcement programs. Decontrol, combined with curtailed fundings, put the future of energy regulatory and enforcement programs in question.

The latest administrator of the ERA has announced his hope to settle all enforcement actions and abolish the ERA by the end of fiscal year 1982. The inconsistency between the announced desire to dismantle the ERA and the ERA's pronounced intention to fully litigate all actions against companies that refuse to settle has led to assumption of a wait-and-see position by oil companies with actions pending against them. Under the administration's DOE dismantlement proposal all lingering DOE/ERA enforcement matters would be transferred to the DOJ.

The FERC Enforcement Initiative

If the FEA's enforcement efforts were considered inept, the FPC's could only be considered nonexistent. Viewed as a relatively insignificant ''backwater'' agency until the natural-gas shortages of the 1970s, the FPC quietly went about its utility-type regulation unaware of the need for any active enforcement program. The late 1970s brought the FPC's understated approach to compliance, particularly in the area of natural-gas-producer pricing to the forefront of congressional debate. To respond to that congressional concern, in December 1977, two months after its creation, the FERC, in a companion effort to that of DOE, created an Office of Enforcement. The ambitions of the office were to assume the investigation and compliance functions of the FERC through the independent filing of complaints in federal district court to remedy illegal conduct by regulated companies. In addition the office was to establish working relationships with the Department of Justice and to create new regulations and procedures to govern the conduct of investigations and other compliance and enforcement activities.[7]

Mindful of these goals, the FERC promulgated interim regulations modelled roughly after the approach of the SEC and the Federal Trade

Commission (FTC).[8] The objective of the new procedures was to provide a fair, flexible, and efficient framework for commission investigations.[9]

Investigations are the core duty and responsibility of the FERC Office of Enforcement. The Office of Enforcement was to be assisted in its investigative efforts by the referral of matters by the other offices of the FERC, particularly the Division of Compliance of the Office of Pipeline and Producer Regulation of the FERC was set up to deal with Natural Gas Policy Act (NGPA) matters.

The process of FERC enforcement generally begins with the initiation of a preliminary investigation to determine whether sufficient facts exist on which to base a formal order of investigation. Following the preliminary investigation, the FERC may institute a formal investigation; set the matter for hearing; refer the matter to other authorities; informally dispose of the matter by seeking voluntary compliance; seek an independent audit; terminate the inquiry; or bring an enforcement action in federal district court.

A formal investigation may be instituted only with explicit FERC approval to issue agency subpoenas and take testimony under oath. FERC has the right to inspect all accounts and records of regulated companies and is also empowered to administer oaths, subpoena witnesses, and compel document production.

Upon conclusion of the formal investigation, the commission has several options: (1) institute an administrative proceeding; (2) institute a civil action in federal court; (3) refer the matter to the attorney general for criminal prosecution; (4) refer the matter to other governmental authority; or (5) conduct other appropriate action. Among the factors the commission considers in disposing of the matter are the character, nature, and scope of the alleged violation and the extent of consumer harm. Civil enforcement penalties did not exist under the NGA. However, the NGPA specifically provided civil penalties for knowing violations of it, in addition to again giving FERC power to seek civil injunctive relief in the federal courts. The FERC has made increasing use of this option.

Civil injunctive relief was one of the FERC's newly discovered enforcement options. Although the FPC had the power to use civil injunctive relief under the NGA and the FPA, it rarely used this tool, choosing to rely instead on show-cause proceedings. The Office of Enforcement has sought injunctions against NGA or NGPA violations on several occasions and has brought general cases to successful resolution.

Proceedings to show cause why enforcement action should not be taken were commonly used by the FPC but are generally not used by FERC. Show-cause proceedings, to determine whether a respondent violated a statute or regulation, were publically conducted, usually in an adjudicatory setting. Their use has been largely superceded by reliance on the preliminary and formal investigative procedures used by the Office of Enforcement.

Criminal prosecution particularly of individuals rather than corporations is the most onerous sanction the FERC can seek. Criminal liability results from willful and knowing violations. Violation of a statute may carry a penalty of imprisonment or a fine.

As mentioned before, the NGPA gave the FERC power to impose civil penalties.[10] A civil penalty is assessable only if a knowing violation occurs; such knowledge may be actual or constructive. Criminal penalties available under the NGPA require the same knowing-and-willful standard as under the FPA or NGA.[11]

The FERC has abolished the Office of Enforcement as a separate organizational entity and has incorporated its functions into the general counsel's office. Although a separate section within the general counsel's office has primary responsibility for enforcement actions, the combination of diminished staff and 1985 deregulation of many categories of natural gas make future FERC enforcement actions uncertain, particularly in the gas area. However, staff dedicated to the enforcement function have not been eliminated. At the time of this writing, signals about the future of enforcement efforts at FERC, although stronger than those at ERA, are still shaky.

Institutional and Political Limitations on Energy Enforcement

The enforcement mechanisms in place at the FERC and the DOE were set up to keep constant vigil over large and small members of the oil and gas industry. Some of the randomness of earlier enforcement efforts has been eliminated. Institutional constraints persist, however, and these regulatory bodies cannot discern, investigate, or litigate even the most significant violations. The legal and accounting sophistication of large companies sometimes make it possible for them to obscure their most profitable violations, leaving the ERA and FERC to uncover only large companies' minor or technical infractions or small companies' or individual's major breaches of the law.[12]

Already complex and slow procedures are further mired by the need to obtain approvals from several bureaucratic levels before the institution of formal action and litigation in the federal courts. Enforcers must prove their cases not only in the courts but within the labyrinth of turf and authority fiefdoms in the agency itself. On the other hand, every bureaucratic step may signal the weeding out of less meritorious violations, because the facts are not clear enough or the dollar stakes not high enough to warrant a costly major investigation or enforcement action. Thus, the interaction between and among organizational elements of an agency may screen out some unnecessary or unfounded investigations as well as some that should be pursued.

The complexity and obscurity of purpose of the laws and regulations hamper effective and consistent enforcement as well. The DOE has lost a number of cases because a court found that there was more than one reasonable interpretation of the regulations. When the regulations are kneaded, folded, bundled, and rebundled in any attempt to apply them retroactively as well as prospectively, they become so heavy as to collapse of their own weight. This problem is more critical when the agency attempts to demonstrate a "knowing" or a "willful and knowing violation."

Perhaps a more serious danger lies in the inevitable politicization of the enforcement process. The secretary of DOE, the general counsel of DOE, and the five commissioners and general counsel of the FERC are all political appointees.[13] Thus, they must be responsive to their own political views as well as to those of the administration that appointed them. The encroachment of personal philosophies, although inherent in the performance of any job, is particularly troublesome in the energy enforcement arena. An administration's adherence to the ideology that the market operates and distributes perfectly without any government interference can have a chilling effect, reaching down through regulatory-agency structure to the enforcement program. To a limited degree this politicization is vital, however, because it ensures at least indirectly the responsiveness of an institution through the Congress or the executive to the will of the electorate. Additionally, it cannot be overlooked that oversight by the Congress and the GAO tends to force at least minimal adherence to an enforcement program even with changes in administrations.

The legislative branch and its overall deregulatory mood may be somewhat responsible for waning enforcement as well. The vacillating views of legislators, their staffs, and their constituents may signal imminent alteration of enabling legislation and may even result in dismantlement of the Department of Energy as a whole. When the decontrol of natural gas and crude oil becomes a fait accompli, it is difficult for even the most vigorous enforcer to ignore the lack of confidence and interest afforded their retrospective enforcement efforts.

The extraordinary complexity of energy regulation in theory and practice requires formulation and administration of a central plan by a dedicated and formal core cast of characters. John Kemeny became acutely aware of this need while chairing the presidential commission established to investigate the accident of Three Mile Island. Kemeny, although impressed by the capability of scientists and officials at the Nuclear Regulatory Commission (NRC), was appalled by their narrowness and strict adherence to technocracy rather than policy. He found the plant technicians generally dedicated and competent but ill-prepared to cope with the multitude and seriousness of accidents that might occur in the course of their duties. The Kemeny report concluded that safety issues were the paramount duty of the NRC but that the NRC did not elevate these issues in its hierarchy of values. The Kemeny report, like the Sporkin report found that the central purpose of a regulatory body, and the enforcement of rules established to attain that purpose, had not been properly identified, considered, or administered by the agency. The Kemeny report surmised that the best means to remedy the NRC's situation was formulation of a plan, by a less politicized body than Congress, to centralize and properly administer nuclear power. [14]

Although the Kemeny report was directed specifically to nuclear-power issues, many of the same criticisms enunciated in that report can be applied to the DOE's and FERC's regulatory programs and enforcement plans. Simply put, too many actors, too many scripts, without a producer or director result in chaos. The agencies when viewed either singularly or as a total effort do not have a clear vision of their duties. Until the agency can formulate a plan for enforcement that is supported by the congressional committees having applicable oversight jurisdiction, progress toward a coherent, effective enforcement effort cannot take place.

Philosophy of Regulation and Enforcement: Goals

Goals must create the bedrock for any effective regulatory plan. The quality and importance of the goal must be evaluated prior to determining the degree of rigor of enforcement. Is the goal of energy regulation to be production and development of resources or low prices to consumers? Can the two goals be reconciled? Should individuals as well as corporations be held criminally liable for violations? Once violations are uncovered, what is the best means to effect restitution to those injured? And, tangentially, who is better equippped to attain these goals, the energy agency, the Department of Justice, or the Congress through the exercise of its ovesight functions?

The fundamental question of whether a regulation is worth enforcing can only be answered in the context of the prevailing political and economic climate. The idea of any regulation is abhorrent to a newly appointed executive-level free marketer who believes that the market achieves proper allocation and price when left to compete freely. The other side of that coin is the law maker or consumer advocate who believes that the free-market system may not achieve the proper economic or social goals. The enforcement official is caught in the cross-fire between regulation and nonregulation positions; it is that official's job to ensure compliance with possibly ill-founded or obsolete laws and regulations. If one believes in the goals that statutes and regulations strive to attain, and those laws do effect those goals, enforcement is warranted. It is rare, however, in the energy area to honestly believe that all energy regulations are useful to society. Thus is the water muddied. Much of the controversy surrounding DOE results directly from the incomprehensibility and obscurity of purpose of the regulations. DOE has been the butt of derision from the press, Congress, and the public since its inception, thus making it difficult for those affiliated with it to obtain or retain pride in the agency and in their role in the agency. On the other hand, most people would support the general purpose behind the law: DOE is supposed to administer fairly the allocation of resources and guard against unfair and predatory practices by the regulated companies. The value of regulations and their enforcement can only be judged individually by their purpose and as they conform to a personal or political philosophy. An enforcer must have political support for the particular ideology evidence in the enforcement program from his superiors and congressional quarters.

Liability

Inextricably linked to the goals of enforcement is the policy underlying the target of enforcement actions. The Sporkin report advocated a mixed-targeting approach of general and special deterrence. With a commodity such as oil, where the dollar stakes are so high, the targets of enforcement actions identified as top priority were the largest companies, who have the most to gain from noncompliance. The actions of these companies usually have the most dollar impact on the consumer. The targets for the DOE enforcement have been the major, highly visible refiners who are the major oil companies.

Questions have been raised questioning the political forces guiding selection of targets for enforcement. This was the central issue in *Securities and Exchange Commission* v. *Wheeling-Pittsburgh*.[15] When the SEC took a subpoena against Wheeling-Pittsburgh to the district court for enforcement, the company accused the SEC of bad faith and political motivation. The company alleged that a politically powerful senator had suggested SEC action on the basis of his own political interests. The district court concurred with Wheeling-Pittsburgh's accusations and refused to enforce the SEC subpoena. The Third Circuit reversed and remanded, declaring that it could not reconcile the lower court's refusal to find that the SEC's action was commenced in bad faith, while finding that a third party had improperly influenced the SEC's decision to initiate action. If cause existed to bring an enforcement action, the political motivations of the enforcer or "tipster" are not a first priority. The court's support of the SEC lay in the facts of this particular case. Selecting a case for enforcement or dropping a case may easily be construed as a somewhat political process by the targets or the public.

The role of the individual malefactor in energy enforcement matters is equally controversial. Liability for violation of energy laws has traditionally fallen on corporations rather than the individual. The provisions of the FPA, NGA, and NGPA imposing criminal sanctions on malefactors and the FERC's apparent interest in enforcing those provisions has stirred understandable concern by corporate officers and attorneys. The situation under which an individual should serve a prison sentence or pay a large fine for violations of energy laws done willfully and knowingly is an extraordinarily difficult one. White-collar crime in general has not been punished by imprisonment of individuals at the upper echelons of the decision-making ladder. Similarily in the energy area few individuals have faced such punitive actions by the DOJ.

Refunds and Restitution

The DOE/ERA does not have a distinct or consistent policy governing compensation of those injured by energy-pricing regulations. However, DOE has recently entered into a spate of consent orders involving refunds to consumers. Section 503 of the DOE act[16] authorizes the secretary to issue a remedial order to any person believed to have violated a regulation, rule, or order promulgated under the Emergency Petroleum Act of 1973.[17] The remedial order must be in writing and must describe the alleged violation and cite the rule or regulation violated. Remedial orders become final orders unless contested within thirty days, in which case the issue is decided by the FERC.

Refund procedures are complicated tremendously by the virtual impossibility of identifying with precision the parties damaged. In the instance where victims of overcharge cannot be identified, the DOE special counsel or other DOE official may file with the OHA for the implementation of special refund procedures.[18] The petitioner for this refund authority must explain his inability to identify the victims of overcharges or misallocations and inability to ascertain the precise refund to which each victim is entitled. If the OHA finds the petition meritorious, it issues a proposed decision and order outlining the refund procedure and the criteria the OHA intends to apply in evaluating refund claims. The regulations require that the OHA carefully consider any indirect restitution in light of the desirability of distributing refunds in an efficent, effective, and equitable manner geared toward resolving to the maximum extent possible all outstanding claims.

Implementation of indirect restitution plans has been highly controversial. In a major restitution case, Conoco objected to indirect restitution, because it wanted to ensure that every claim was satisfied out of the fund surrendered to DOE under a consent decree to avoid future liability in private actions and the accompanying litigation expenses. The controversy surrounding restitution is epitomized by an act of frustration of the Carter administration's special counsel for compliance at the DOE, who gave $4 million away to several charitable organizations. Eventually, under the Reagan administration the money was returned to the government for more orderly distribution.

In this final exhibition of frustration with the difficulty of finding the injured consumer and making refund to them, the special counsel did the human thing—gave the dollars to organizations worthy to receive and trustworthy to distribute funds paid as restitution. This act perhaps sums up the quandary of the enforcer—even if one is fortunate enough to obtain the refund from the malfeasors, in the energy area, it is difficult even to know how to get it paid back to those who deserve it.

The FERC faces analogous but more limited problems of disposition of refunds. Under the FPA, NGA, and NGPA the structures of the utility systems the FERC regulates allows a fairly orderly pass-through of refunds to consumers. Of course, some consumers may have moved or died, thus they will be unable to receive the refund dollars.

Energy enforcement, even in its denouement, continues to be the rock on which the statutes and regulations controlling energy prices and allocation crash. Energy regulations not only exasperate regulated entities and individuals but bedevil the regulators/enforcers themselves. Their complexity as well as questions about their necessity make them difficult to enforce. The enforcement functions lack a constituency to support the application of the laws and regulations to energy industries.

Resolution of the shortcomings of energy enforcement must begin with the law makers themselves, who, when a law is passed, must be willing to support enforcement efforts with funding and basic confidence in the enforcer. Then and only then will the public receive effective, fair enforcement. The agencies and their enforcement organizations must identify goals, select targets fairly, and successfully litigate enforcement cases. Finally the enforcers must make a thoughtful effort to make restitution to the public in the best manner possible.

Notes

1. 15 U.S.C. secs. 751–756 (1976).

2. April 19, 1982 Memorandum to Chairman Dingell from Staff of the Subcommittee on Oversight and Investigations of the House Committee on Energy and Commerce.

3. Task Force on Compliance and Enforcement—Final Report, July 13, 1977 (Federal Energy Administration).

4. 42 U.S.C. sec. 7101, *et seq.* (1981). Pub. L. No. 95–91, 91 Stat. 656.

5. 15 U.S.C. sec. 3301, *et seq. See, e.g.,* Memorandum to Members, Subcommittee on Energy and Power from Subcommittee Staff, Oct. 9, 1980 (discussing the Getty, Phillips, Cities, AMOCO, and Conoco settlements through consent orders).

6. Such consent can be slow in forthcoming. Although the DOJ undoubtedly plays a critical role in DOE cases involving potential criminal liability, DOJ's concurrence in civil settlements is a procedural step that can only slow down the compliance efforts of an agency such as DOE. This problem is particularly acute in cases involving extremely complicated technical matters where technical staff are needed to analyze the violations and any proposed resolutions of them.

7. Hollis, The FERC Enforcement Program: Natural Gas, Monograph 4B, Callaghan's Energy Law Service (April 1980); Hollis & Marston, *A Review and Assessment of the FERC Natural Gas Enforcement Program,* 16 Hous. L. Rev. 1105 (1979).

8. 18 C.F.R. sec. 16.1 *et seq.* (1981).

9. *See* Preamble in 43 Fed. Reg. 27174 (June 23, 1978). *See also* 44 Fed. Reg. 21486 (April 10, 1979) Notice of Proposed Rulemaking issued in Docket No. RM78–15 on March 20, 1979.

10. 15 U.S.C. sec. 3414(b) (Supp. IV 1980). The NGPA also reinforced the FERC's investigatory powers. *See* 15 U.S.C. sec. 3418.

11. 15 U.S.C. sec. 3414(c)(1) and (5) (Supp. IV 1980).

12. This problem has been described as being able to catch only "whales doing minnow acts or minnows doing whale acts."

13. Since the reorganization of the Office of Enforcement at FERC in 1981, the office is no longer independent, reporting only to the commission itself. Under present organization, the assistant general counsel for enforcement at FERC must report to a politically appointed general

counsel, and all enforcement activity is monitored and screened by the general counsel before presentation to the commission.

14. Kemeny, Saving American Democracy: The Lesson of Three Mile Island, excerpted from President's Commission on the Accident at Three Mile Island (October 1979).

15. 648 F.2d 118 (3rd Cir. 1981).

16. 42 U.S.C. sec. 7193 (Supp. IV 1980).

17. 15 U.S.C. sec. 751, *et seq.* (1976).

18. 10 C.F.R. 250.280, *et seq.* (1981).

**Part III
The Search for Values**

9

Complexity and Uncertainty in Energy Decision Making

In part III we speculate on the causes of and consequences for the conflicts that we see in the interaction of law and policy. The coalescing of a national energy plan, like a comprehensive social policy, may well be an impossibility in our pluralistic society—a conclusion expressed by many social-choice theorists.[1] In the preceding parts of the book we have argued that a cohesive energy policy was precluded because of the institutional structures and methodologies employed by those structures in decision making. In these final chapters we look deeper. We ask whether there is some inherent characteristic of energy decision making that precludes effective policymaking? Chapter 9 answers affirmatively, that is, the essential complexity and uncertainty of energy decisions made in a legal and scientific culture result in a flawed process.

What will the price of imported crude oil be in 1990? Where and how should nuclear wastes be disposed? What are the health effects of low-level radiation? What are the risks and probabilities of a catastrophic nuclear-reactor accident? When will nuclear fusion be a viable source of power? What are the chances and consequences of an increase in carbon dioxide in the atmosphere as a result of the development of synthetic fuels? What is the optimum scale for solar collectors? What are the long-term effects on the environment of burning coal rather than oil or natural gas in electric-generation facilities? By the year 2000 what is a proper technological mix between conventional and alternative energy sources?

These questions have certain common attributes. They all concern energy, they all present complex technical and scientific issues, and they are all somewhat unanswerable. Asking the questions would be not much more than a nice academic exercise but for another common attribute— decisions regarding these issues must be made. As a society we need to decide where to put the wastes that are currently being generated by nuclear-power reactors, whether to have and where to site major energy installations, how quickly to develop synthetic fuels, and how to assemble an energy plan that provides the country with fuel without seriously damaging the economy or the environment. It is imperative that decisions be made, but scientific and technological complexities and uncertainties and a legal process ill-suited to make these decisions preclude their effective resolution.

In exploration of these problems we use a phrase from C.P. Snow, *two cultures:* energy decision making involves a clash of legal and scientific cultures. To the extent that these two cultures clash and in view of the decision-making imperatives, a dispute-resolution mechanism is required. We will review alternative mechanisms in this chapter.

Two Cultures

Science and law have different methodologies, indeed they have different ends, and consequently they rest on fundamentally different values. This chapter will emphasize these differences. However, law and science do have some analogy in methodologies and values. Law draws on the use of the scientific methods of induction, deduction, and analogy to resolve disputes. The law also contains within it burdens of proof, and the law weighs evidence as does science. Nevertheless, both disciplines have distinctive orientations that color and affect outcomes.

Although both cultures are concerned with truth, science is concerned with truth in a harder, more empirical sense than the law is or can be. The legal system is concerned with truth as shaded by concepts of justice, fairness, or equity, and truth is derived from a dialectical process. Science seeks empirical truth as manifest in the world.[2] The law sets up systems that define truth. The outcome of a trial that declares a driver to be intoxicated, as long as it has been a fair hearing, will be deemed to have reached the truth regardless of whether the driver was drunk in a medical or scientific sense.

Scientists have much to criticize lawyers for in the way legal structures may ignore scientific reality. Likewise, lawyers can rightly view scientists with some skepticism. In a perfect world with a perfect technology of justice, perhaps scientific truths and legal truths will meet and be identical. However, in a world where legal decision-making processes do not have the luxury of unhurried deliberation, legal decision makers find that the strict scientific method is too lengthy, cumbersome, and costly a process. Consequently, lawyers find themselves in the unenviable position of having to make decisions involving scientific disputes before all the evidence is in, before a consensus is reached in the scientific community, and before public awareness of the issues is not distorted and reformulated. The decision to continue research into nuclear fusion, for example, when viewed from the eyes of a scientist may be seen as safe and as a necessary enterprise for the advancement of scientific learning. When viewed from the perspective of a community located close to the research and testing facilities, fears (founded or not) of the effects of radiation or concerns underlying the morality and wisdom of such an endeavor can conflict directly with the scientific community. Sometimes these conflicts are presented for resolution in a legal arena. The issue brought to court is not so starkly presented in the form of the goodness or wisdom of research in the area of fusion as a scientific proposition. Rather the court must decide whether to require a particular community to accept their fears to propagate a scientific endeavor. The court or other legal tribunal is asked not only to assess the empirical and quantifiable data surrounding the safety of the research but also to weigh the very human issue of community fear. These nonquantifiable factors undoubtedly confuse the purely scientific issues. However, not only do they not confuse the legal issues, they are the variables for which the legal system was designed.

To dichotomize science and law can help us understand their different orientations, methods, and objectives. However, to polarize science and law distorts our understanding of where the two meet, how they relate, and how they function together. A strict polarization will result in inefficient and wasteful decisions.[3]

The imperfections of the system are admitted, yet we must recognize those imperfections. A positive view of the interaction between science and law can result. Where science and law meet and where they appear to be incompatible is where human values can be introduced, explored, and weighed in decision-making processes. It would be wrongheaded to characterize the siting of a nuclear-waste-disposal facility as a purely scientific question to be answered by an equation containing only statistical probabilities. It is equally wrongheaded to argue that it is solely a legal issue which turns on the issue of agency jurisdiction to decide where the facility should be placed. The decision involves both of these sets of variables and more. The decision-making forum must also take into account the social, economic, political, and philosophical consequences of the decision.

When, where, and how the scientific method is consistent with the legal method shall be examined in this section. More specifically, when and to what extent should a court, faced with a particular energy problem, rely on scientific information to help reach its decision? Are the scientific method and legal methods of reasoning sufficiently compatible to be used interchangeably or should one be given precedence?

The Scientific Method

The scientific method is an ongoing process that can be analyzed in seven stages: observation, induction, hypothesis, experimentation, calculation, prediction, and control.[4]

Observation can be broken down into simple and controlled types.

Even simple observation requires concentration, training, and the use of instruments so that the senses can be extended. Observation should also be as independent and as objective as possible, devoid of preconceptions and anticipations to the extent achievable. Simple scientific observation is the ability to perceive as innocently as possible the particular object which has been selected for consideration. Controlled observation, by its very nature, does not begin randomly, instead it is carried on pursuant to a careful plan.

Observation is the first step in an attempt to understand science and the scientific method. Concepts in science are formed on the basis of observations and then fitted together into systems. The observations are made at the level of concrete particulars. The concepts are then formed and combined at the level of general propositions. Science is the search for those abstract structures that are suggested by observing material objects. Thus the enterprise of the scientific method is one of weaving the two levels together in a world where uncertainty is always an element and where there is no solid ground that can be said to lie altogether beyond errors of observation and of interpretation and therefore beyond all dispute. Nevertheless, it is a goal of the scientific method to reduce uncertainty as much as possible.

The scientist starts to arrive at the abstract structures through the process of induction. Induction consists in the discovery of a general proposition by means of the comparison of particulars and the identification of their similarity. The construction of general classes occurs by collecting certain selected particulars, rather than in an accumulation of all possible particulars.

After the class or classes are formed, a hypothesis is made that attempts to explain the observed facts. The truth of a hypothesis is assumed tentatively as an explanatory statement sufficient to justify further study. Experiments then are used to verify or disprove hypotheses. They are a means to an end. Techniques used to discover factual evidence for or against hypothesis lie at the heart of the scientific method, since they involve experiments. No hypothesis is acceptable until at least one prediction made from it has been confirmed by an experiment. After a hypothesis has been tested successfully, further verification by mathematical formulation follows. This is used as a test for consistency. Prediction is another method used to test the hypothesis. Scientists deduce from the hypothesis events they can expect to occur. The occurrence of those events constitutes another confirmation. Control in the scientific method is a corollary to prediction. It means the ability to bring about changes in phenomena. This type of control is used for the management of events. The last stage is in practical application. The usefulness of a scientific law is its availability as a tool in the real world.

The Legal Method

Although legal reasoning contains elements of induction and deduction, it basically consists of reasoning by example.[5] It involves reasoning from case to case by use of analogy. The standard process involves the doctrine of precedent. A statement is made about case one. This is called a rule of law. That rule is then applied to a subsequent similar situation.

Precedent or stare decisis is seen as an attribute of the legal system that insures fairness, predictability, and a degree of certainty. All these goals would be met handily if the next case were identical to the first case so that the rule of law in case one would be dispositive of the dispute in the subsequent case. In reality the subsequent case, case two, is never identical with its predecessor. The parties are different, the court has changed, time has passed, culture has undergone a transformation, the political and economic climate is different, and so on. Thus the doctrine of precedent as used between cases is only a loose rule by which decision makers are guided.

In addition to cases, other sources of law include constitutions, statutes, and administrative regulations. These are applied to disputes as well, but, because of their generality, they are often insufficient to dispose of a dispute. The application of cases to a dispute (a particular instance applied to a general instance) can be seen as inductive, and the application of a statute to a dispute (a general proposition applied to a particular) can be seen as deductive.

The same parameters that affect how one case is applied to a subsequent case also affects how a statute or constitution is interpreted and applied. Prior cases and other rules of law cannot dispose of disputes with absolute certainty. Consequently, the judge, with the aid of attorneys involved in an adversary system, must interpret and apply the rules of law and tailor them to fit the case. Thus, what the legal system loses in certainty and predictability it gains in flexibility and adaptability. This imbues the law with a dynamic quality.

Similarities and Differences

It should be self-evident that the scientific method is not only more thorough but a great deal more dispassionate than the legal method. The scientific method is colder in that the human element is removed as much as possible. It is the intention of the scientific method to obtain as completely as possible an accurate description of an event or fact for all time.[6] To obtain this accuracy the scientific method relies on its repetitive and self-corrective nature. Scientists' patience and willingness to work a problem again and again allows for the high level of accuracy associated with the scientific method. Additionally, the scientific method is open to manipulation of variables that may affect the outcome of a particular event or fact. Therefore, the control element is another factor that adds to scientific accuracy.

Another distinct aspect of the scientific method is the fact that the direct input of a scientific experiment does not directly affect individuals. Perhaps it will later, indirectly, but unless we are dealing with a significant medical question, scientific experiments will not have the direct personal impact that a legal decision can have. The scientific method also reduces its hypotheses to the unemotional world of numbers rather than words. By reducing hypotheses to numbers and equations the scientist can check and reevaluate the results to make changes and simply to verify the hypotheses.

The legal method on the other hand is by no means as accurate or sterile. The legal process deals with and affects individuals directly. The scientific process deals with facts and elements that can be repeated and controlled with a view toward predicting future events. The legal process deals with individuals and a universe of differing fact situations that, for the most part, have already occurred and that the legal process has no control over. Law, vis-à-vis the legislative process, does make predictive statements. Yet these statements are based on past experience and guesses about future events, which the law hopes to influence but does not aspire to control. Where science is essentially explanative, predictive, and forward looking, law is essentially retrospective and is used to resolve past disputes. The legal method need not and should not be held to the same standard of accuracy or predictability as the scientific method. What makes the legal method functional and equitable is human involvement. People need to and must consider people's problems.

Although science and law have some structural similarities, they are asked to do different things. Even though the methodologies of induction, deduction, and analogy may be used by each they are used for different ends. Consequently, scientific and legal evidence and proofs are used differently.

In science proofs and evidence are required to formulate an hypothesis that is predictive of future events and is capable of being tested by various methods. Often the hypothesis is a small, incremental advance of another postulate, and it is designed to verify a concrete, hopefully long-lasting scientific truth. That is the main goal of the scientist. This is usually only incidental to a lawyer. Rather, the lawyer's primary concern is to obtain a favorable result for his client in a given situation. If that result also helps to establish a long-lasting principle of law, that is an added, but usually not a central, benefit.

Proofs and evidence in a legal context take on various meanings, whereas scientific proofs and evidence seek empirical certainty and uniformity. In the case of criminal activity the proof must be beyond "all reasonable doubt." There is a causative nexus between an event that has happened in the past and a particular individual that must be established before this burden is satisfied. In civil law, the law of torts being the primary example, the general rule is that the plaintiff must establish his or her case by a preponderance of the evidence. That standard sounds less rigorous than what we commonly associate with scientific evidence, but that may or may not be the case depending on the issues involved. If the allegation and nature of the case is one where causation in fact must be proven, for example, the plaintiff is trying to prove that a particular defendant caused the accident, then the proof will approach the rigor of the criminal case. If, however, the case is one in which the rule of law to be applied is designed to assess liability regardless of fault, or liability is to attach to an industry or group of individuals rather than to a more particularized individual, then the evidence and the proofs may be less rigorous than a scientific proof would be. In the administrative context, proofs and evidence take on different connotations. If the issue to be resolved is adjudicatory, then for our purposes the proofs and evidence are similar to those required in the civil case. The rule is that an agency decision must be based on substantial evidence. When the agency is promulgating a regulation for future application the evidentiary requirements are lessened. It is not unlike a congressional enactment. As long as there is a so-called reasonable relationship between the statute or regulation and the end sought to be achieved by the statute or regulation, it will be upheld. Often in administrative law this test is satisfied when the agency shows that its decision is based on more than a mere scintilla of evidence.[7]

Insofar as the sufficiency of the weight of evidence is concerned law and science differ in that the law ascribes different requirements for different purposes. Science treats evidence and proofs with more uniformity. Law and science also differ as to burdens of proof. Scientists carry the burden when they engage in scientific discovery, when they seek to sustain or refute a given proposition. In law, however, the burden can be placed on various parties. The administrative agency could have the burden to justify its rule. Or the party attacking the rule might be required to go forward with a challenge to the rule. Or a shifting burden of proof might be encountered where the proponent of a particular action is required to make a prima facie case. This is known as the burden of going forward. At that point the party being challenged may have the burden of convincing the tribunal of the rightness of its action. This is known as the burden of persuasion.

Thus, as far as energy decision making is concerned, before we can ascertain what the weight of the evidence should be or who has the burden of proof a series of questions must be asked. First, what is the forum? Is it an initial court action, is it an administrative agency, or is it the judicial review of an agency action? Second, what is the nature of the issue involved? Is it civil or criminal? Should the issue be resolved by the adjudicatory or rule-making process? Finally, and closely related to the second question, what is the policy behind the issue presented to the tribunal? An agency, or court, may be viewing a legal issue from a particular perspective.

In the *American Textile* case the rationale behind the legislation was the promotion of worker safety. Therefore an implicit presumption was in effect. Decisions made by the Department of Labor or by reviewing courts would be made to conform to that policy. If the court or agency is guided by a particular view toward an energy policy, for example, conservation, prodomestic development, or reduction of dependence on foreign sources, then burdens of proof and weights of evidence could be implicitly or explicitly adjusted in the decision-making process, thus favoring a particular outcome.[8]

In an environment in which we are faced with a great many energy problems the two cultures of science and law must coexist. Despite the fact that science relies on controlled facts and events from an objective aspect and the law does not, the two systems are not precluded from working together. On the contrary, in today's fast-moving and progressive society where technology creates many legal problems, the two systems must work together. Curiously, the two cultures are moving closer and closer together in the field of energy decision making. The technological and scientific complexities and uncertainties of these issues require a lessening of the rigor of the scientific method because of the gaps created by insufficient information. The science of nuclear-waste disposal or treatment for example is less certain than the basic verities of gravity. As a result scientists must confront more open questions. The law too must change. Because of the broadened scope of administrative actions and an increase in an agency's policymaking functions, particularly in energy matters, the law is less concerned with retrospective dispute resolution and is more concerned with legislating prospective outcomes.

Energy decisions must be forward looking. The decisions have tremendous human implications—decisions made today regarding synthetic-fuels development, nuclear policy, even electric rates affect present and future generations. Science cannot pretend to answer questions with the certitude the discipline might prefer. Nor can law ignore the fact that these decisions are prospective. Science is thus becoming more lawlike because these open-ended issues create more room for the exploration of the human element involved in these decisions. Law, in turn, must become more sciencelike because the issues are forward looking and affect so many people for such a long period of time. Energy law must strive for more accuracy in its predictions. Thus, science and law intersect in the profound issues of energy policy. Science must be held to its high standard of accuracy so that the human element of the law can effectively evaluate and predict the social and normative impacts of energy issues.

Technologies of Justice

Our premise is that energy decision making has certain characteristics that make it particularly worthy of study and reflection. The high degrees of complexity and uncertainty are its two primary attributes. There are others of significance. Professor Wessel of Columbia University Law School has labeled certain types of legal problems socioscientific disputes.[9] Not only are energy decisions technically complex and uncertain they also have an impact that goes beyond the parties to a particular controversy and affects a broader public interest. The decisions sink into complicated social issues. Professor Wessel also argues that the three elements of (1) public interest, (2) technical complexity, and (3) fundamental value issues have a synergistic effect, which calls further attention to the need to be cautious with how socioscientific disputes are resolved.

This chapter has been exploring the issue of complexity and uncertainty. We started with the proposition that, although similar, science (with technology) and law may clash. They have different ends and different ways of achieving those ends. Nevertheless, these two cultures often operate on parallel courses in energy decision making. Sometimes the two courses intersect to form the basis of a well-informed decision, other times the courses miss each other and lead the decision maker to an incorrect or improper decision. In this section we examine whether present dispute-resolution mechanisms are adequate to handle these issues.

Briefly, the structure that exists for most energy decision making is composed of administrative agencies and judicial-review bodies. There are a host of energy matters that are decided in the Congress, by the president, or in a court in the first instance, yet the bulk of the decisions are made first at the agency level and then subjected to judicial review. First, the agency, the specialized body imbued with expertise, not only is given the first opportunity to make a decision, but often makes the rules for decision. Second, as developed in chapter 4, courts defer to agency decision making and generally only overturn an agency decision that is arbitrary, capricious, unreasonable, or not based on substantial evidence. In complex scientific and technological matters, or in socio-scientific disputes, this judicial soft glance is more significant because the decisions have a greater impact on society.

The Adversary System—An Imperfect Process

Although the adversary system has served well as a dispute-resolution mechanism in the private-law arena, it does not function as efficiently for public-law decisions.[10] When legal issues involve the scope and complexity of those inherent in energy decision making, the weaknesses of the adversary system are aggravated. The adversary system works well to solve individual, neat problems. Generally, where the issue to be decided has occurred in the past and is essentially self-contained, that is, the events are determinable and proofs can deduce those events, then the issues can be presented rather crisply. The adversary system is effective in this bipolar atmosphere. Both sides marshall facts and draw inferences most favorable to their side, and the judge or jury then has the responsibility for determining which facts are proven and which are not. Theoretically, given a world of equal access to information and competent legal representation, distortion in fact finding can be minimized. Basic fairness in the adversarial process is usually present because the parties control the litigation, deciding issues to be tried and sufficiency of remedies. The agency consists of the resolution of an individual past dispute involving limited parties. Private-law rules become part of a larger forward-looking fabric only through precedential effect, affecting nonparties only if they become parties to a subsequent similar case.

Public law or socioscientific disputes do not fit in a neatly tied discrete decision package. First, such cases rarely are bipolar, because even if two named parties are involved, one is often a government agency or some other litigant representing the public interest. More important, such cases are decidedly not bipolar in their consequences. Although often only two parties may be involved in the contest of a particular controversy, the consequences of the decision have direct implications for numerous persons not represented. In the event that intervenors are allowed to participate in such a controversy, the ability of consumer-intervenors to participate meaningfully in wildly complex litigation is questionable at best and sometimes nonexistent. The legal issues in these types of disputes are often not historical and retrospective. Rather the broad public-policy decision is usually forward looking and prospective in effect. The facts and proofs to be adduced then are less adjudicative than legislative. When issues involve the types of complexities and uncertainties inherent in energy decisions, there exists a tendency to rely on technical and procedural rather than substantive arguments. As a result, delay is a frequently used strategic device. Discovery, for example, can be prolonged at great cost. These broad far-reaching issues may question the competence of the tribunal to hear and decide the evidence. Courts not infrequently argue that because they lack the requisite technical expertise, deference to the administrative agency must be given. Such instances call the efficacy of the adversary system into question. Because of the number and complexity of issues that involve not only technological uncertainty but uncertainty in values as well—a system that is prone to unequal representation of issues as well as procedural machinations—the merits of the controversy can be distorted, delayed, or simply ignored.

In a traditional private-law case the outcome on the merits of the controversy is usually significant only to the parties involved. In socioscientific disputes the consequences are magnified. The distortion of the merits of a case, such as the construction of a power plant or the continuation of a line of basic energy research, can mean that hundreds of millions of dollars are wasted or millions of people are affected.[11] The avoidance of an issue because of its complexity and novelty may mean that tens of thousands of lives are endangered or that large-scale negative economic effects are felt in our society.

The adversary model was designed for cases with a different composition. The model continues to work well for that for which it was designed, the discrete-issue package. It works less efficiently in deciding energy issues.

The Science-Court Proposal

In recent years, technological and scientific advances have made public decision makers even more reliant on scientific advisors. Controversial scientific issues include the use of nuclear power, the effects of the SST, the safety of food additives, and possible freon damage to the ozone layer. Often scientists have been unable to agree on these issues. To facilitate highly technical decision making, it has been proposed that a science court be established that would deal solely with questions of scientific fact. The science-court proposal most often considered is called the ''Kantrowitz model' after Dr. Arthur Kantrowitz. Dr. Kantrowitz based his proposal on three recommendations:

1. Separation of the scientific from the political and moral components of a *mixed decision,* which is defined as a decision involving both technology and value judgments.

2. Separation of judge and advocate—scientific advocates would sup-
    port their respective positions and would cross-examine the opposing
    advocates before scientific judges, who would be chosen for their
    scientific background and impartiality on the issue being decided.
3. Publication of the scientific judgments to provide the public with a
    statement of scientific facts and a base on which public officials
    could make their decision.[12]

Professor James Martin of the University of Michigan Law School
identifies four reasons for the creation of a science court. First, the need
exists for accurate and dependable scientific and technical information
for policy setting. Second, the proposal serves as a way to limit the power
exercised by scientists by making their input advisory and recommen-
datory. (A more calloused view would be that the science court is a way
to entrench scientists in decision-making processes.) Third, the science
court would eliminate the opportunity for policymakers to hide their
decisions behind so-called scientific conclusions. Instead, normative issues would also be addressed. And, fourth, this proposal can identify and
eliminate spurious issues from public debate.[13]

The Kantrowitz model would be used by Congress or the executive
branch to separate the scientific questions from the policy or political
issues in problems involving science. Under a presidential-task-force proposal, chief adversaries, or case managers, would be appointed by the
science court or collaborating agency. The task force proposes that the
science court take advantage of natural adversaries, such as the Union
of Concerned Scientists or Friends of the Earth, on antinuclear power
issues. The science court would issue requests for proposals for case
managers. Those chosen by the Court would act as chief adversaries for
their respective sides of the issue.[14]

When the advocate selection was completed, the science court would
produce a list of prospective judges to be examined by the case managers
for prejudice. "The requirement for judges . . . is simply that they must
clearly understand the rules of scientific evidence, have no intellectual
or other commitments regarding matters before them, and possess the
mature judgment needed to weigh the evidence presented."[15] After ac-
ceptance by the case managers, a panel of three judges would be formed.

The science court would then select a referee, who would be concerned with procedural matters. The task force proposes that the role of
the referee be undertaken by a chief judge who would be advised by legal
counsel. An alternate proposal is that the referee be separate from the
judges. When the advocates, judges, and referee are chosen, the issue-
formulation process would begin.

The Science-Court Process

The first step in the process suggested for the scientific court's determination process is the formulation of the scientific and factual issues. After these statements of issues have been examined to ensure that they are confined to statement of scientific fact, they are exchanged between case managers. Each side is then invited to accept or challenge each of the opposition's statements. The challenged statements then are first submitted to a mediation procedure, in which attempts are made to narrow the area of disagreement or to negotiate a revised statement of fact that both case managers can accept. If this procedure does not result in an agreed-on statement, the challenge will be the subject of an adversary procedure.[16]

The adversary proceeding would consist of a case manager presenting substantiation of his challenged statement, observing traditional scientific rules of evidence. The task force notes advantages to the written presentation of evidence as well as oral testimony and concludes that much flexibility should be retained in the trial procedure. After the evidence was presented and challenged under cross-examination by opposing advocates, the judges would reach a decision concerning the statement at issue. The published opinion would consist of a series of factual statements including the unchallenged statements of fact made by the case managers and the opinions of the judges regarding statements that were challenged and submitted for trial. The task force emphasizes the stipulation that the judges will stop at a statement of the facts and will not make value judgments.

Critics of the science-court concept argue that it would not work any better than existing mechanisms, and some argue that it would be significantly worse. The findings, they contend, would be authoritarian and elitist, thus hampering free public debate. It is argued that the separation of the scientific from the value-judgment aspects of the case is spurious. The underlying fear expressed by critics of the science-court proposal is that the scientific aspects of the case would be given more attention and value judgments ignored. Finally, by including an adversary element in the proposal with its inherent emphasis on winning, the search for objective scientific truths may be hampered.[17]

A Hybrid Solution

The call for regulatory reform has been a recurring theme over the last decade. The agency growth of the 1960s and the policymaking demands made on them spurred the call originally. In more recent demands for reform of the regulatory process the cries for elimination of waste, duplication, and unnecessary regulation have been continuing catalysts. One path reform might tread is one that is specifically tailored to the nature of matters being regulated. The Administrative Procedure Act (APA) was designed to be a unified procedural code applicable to all agency actions. The desire for a unified theory, however, may be impossible if the general process does not fit the needs of a particular agency. A parallel argument can be made for a fundamental rethinking of the judicial-review process. We mentioned earlier that new dispute-resolution modes would be examined from two perspectives: Reforms altering the structure of existing institutions and reforms adjusting internal mechanisms. The hybrid alternative starts with the premise that the structure in place, agencies with comprehensive judicial review, can accomodate the needs of energy decision making with some internal adjustment to the process.

Joel Yellin argues that high-technology issues require a hybrid decision-making solution. Those issues are described as follows: (1) Issues underlying the decision are neither purely technological, nor purely legal; and (2) The complexity and variety of the hybrid questions must be reflected in the structure of the institutions that render decisions. Yellin predicates his proposal on his observations that the adversary system works poorly in this type of decision making because there is: a focus on the rules governing entry to the process at the expense of attention to substantive issues; lack of consideration of complex but realistic arguments not conformable to the parties positions; and the possibility of manipulating the process itself with an eye on a broader agenda.[18]

Yellin's model keeps the institutions of the administrative agency and the judiciary in place in the belief that the political independence of the courts should not be compromised. Rather, he suggests that a body within the judiciary should be created independently and with authority to exercise procedural and substantive oversight over complex agency decisions. Instead of unquestioned deference to an agency decision or a limited look at the procedures followed in the case, this entity would render a *second opinion*. This second-opinion structure exercises a thorough substantive review of energy decisions that are responsive to the delicate nature of the controversies.

This body would not limit its review to the issues brought to it by the litigants if broader societal issues were involved nor would the body be restricted from examining other technological inquiries. The court of second opinion would be comprised of a committee of scientists, engineers, and lawyers to serve as standing masters as permitted by the Federal Rules of Civil Procedure.

The federal appellate court would then refer certain cases or issues to this committee. The committee then would proceed in two stages.

First, the technical questions would be addressed. Second, the masters would address and assess the societal implications of the proposed program. At this stage the masters would confront scientific and technological uncertainty without having the significance of that uncertainty distorted by the adversarial process. The master could consult with members of the scientific community if they found a need to do so in the hope of creating an atmosphere for dialogue between the scientific community and the courts. Through an ongoing discourse, courts should become more familiar with the methods and traditions of science and scientists in turn could become more aware of policymaking issues and processes.

This differs markedly from a science court or other specialized court because it is part of the already existing judicial structure. It would act as a screener and advisor to federal judges responsible for hearing and deciding cases. The chance for bias would more likely be minimized because of the advisory nature of the committee. Also, the issues that we have denominated as energy issues could easily be labelled environmental or natural-resources issues. Complexity is not confined to energy-production matters. The committee would be called on to handle an array of complex issues and thus further minimize the biases hypothesized to develop in specialized tribunals.

Scientific Consensus Finding

There is no shortage of critics on the subject of the adequacy of dispute-resolution mechanisms. The energy controversies we have been discussing are not adequately served by the adversary system. Lawsuits are at the least long and costly, and issues of major significance are often not adequately addressed by the litigants. More troublesome is the fact that answers to vastly complicated questions often do not exist. There are holes in the technical data, varying and contradictory interpretations of the data, and controversies abounding about the consequences of certain types of decisions. To further complicate matters, in a pluralistic society it is difficult if not impossible to formulate a consensus on values. M. Wessel suggests an interim measure to establish at least a consensus on the scientific and technological issues before attempting to form a consensus on value or policy issues.[19] In this manner some of the gaps in scientific and technical information can be narrowed. The thrust behind this procedural-reform model is a quest for basic fairness in how these issues are presented and in accommodating divergent views. The mechanism suggested would strive for broad public participation as well as wide participation by the legal and scientific communities so that a consensus can be reached by logic, reason, and an understanding of the scientific method rather than through the game-playing atmosphere of the adversary process. This process would occur in a public forum where scientists, businessmen, lawyers, and others could present a variety of viewpoints on complex socioscientific issues for the purpose of developing a consensus to be used by policymakers. At the conlcusion of the forum a white paper would be presented stating the points of consensus and disagreement and identifying the value issues left for resolution. The most apparent weakness of the consensus proposal is its lack of ability to form the basis of implementation. Yet the idea encourages debate with fewer opportunities for distortion and a view toward cooperation and collabortion among widely varying interests.

Toward a Perfect Technology of Justice

There are aspects of the previous proposals that have gone undiscussed. In a sense, the three models analyze the front end of the decision-making process. They are concerned about input. Who makes the decision, what decision is being made, and how that decision is made are the topics with which these models are concerned. A perfect technology of justice must also address the practical difficulties in implementation, administrative and other costs, and the consequences that result from the decision-making process chosen.[20] A deeper issue is what are the ideological or philosophical aspects of choosing a particular process. Naturally a perfect technology would be costless. Settling for second best, we must look for a process that is either least costly or serves some other interest. A process such as Yellin's second-opinion structure, for example, may be more costly than a structure of heavy judicial deference, but the benefits of a second opinion might easily outweigh the costs involved in sending issues to special masters. Wessel's scientific consensus-finding panels may not be as costly to operate as Yellin's, but by limiting the issues to scientific ones and by limiting the benefits to a public-education function, the panel process may be less beneficial.

The process chosen should at a minimum be capable of discussing issues in a comprehensive and orderly way. Issues should be clearly presented, normative as well as positive issues must be identified, and the process should ensure fair participation. Each of the proposals addressed here have administrative costs. The science court would be an entirely new institution. The downside of the science court is the fear that a specialized body will narrowly define cases that are currently troublesome because they contain a host of issues out of reach of the certainty required for a sound scientific judgment. If the science court develops biases (as seems most likely if one examines the life cycle of most institutions), participation might be restricted either because issues have been narrowed or the participants with less simpatico with the court will simply not be heard as clearly. Thus, the method chosen will have imbedded within it certain ideological tendencies. The consequence of the institutional biases is that society may have less respect for the decisions of such a tribunal. Citizen disaffection may well hamper the effective implementation of urgent decisions emanating from that court.

The adoption of Yellin's special-masters concept obviously imposes the most administrative costs and could cause the most delay. Perhaps costs could be borne by the litigants, or the government could defray some costs as Yellin suggests. These costs should be considered against the benefits of the creation of a system designed to educate the judiciary on the intricacies of scientific and technological issues and values. Because the committee's role would be essentially advisory, performing an educative function, it would be given a variety of matters to consider (that is, not just environmental or energy cases) and its bias would be reduced. The committee's mandate compels it to separate and address the positive and normative issues, thereby reducing any compulsion to narrow issues to technical areas. Since an existing structure would be called on, the special master, the rules for the conduct of the body and for the implementation of its recommendations already exist and pose no unusual problems.

Finally, Wessel's policy-forum suggestion is simply an interim solution, designed to begin formulation of complex issues into understandable ones. A public forum to educate the public about the scientific issues involved in particular cases would incur administrative costs. Although the costs could be spread out over the participants in the process, the real problem with the proposal, however, is that it has no immediate impact on a given dispute. There is no decision to implement. The report or findings developed are available for public inspection and review, but there is no requirement to incorporate the work of the forum into any ongoing policy debate. Aside from creating a science seminar, the forum has no practical impact on decision making.

A perfect technology of justice must be sensitive to the processes and the consequences of decision making. A convenient separation of scientific and technological issues from normative and value issues is a start. Then ways must be devised that facilitate the resolution of controversies within each set of issues. We favor an approach that avoids a scientific, elitist bias and fosters collaborative, consensus finding on the scientific and technological issues. Decisions regarding values will be discussed in the next chapter.

A Decisional Rule for Uncertainty

How should remaining uncertainties be handled? After the justice system has taken its course, uncertainties still plague the decision maker. Some decisional rule regarding uncertainty is needed. One way is to assign equal value to all uncertainties in the hope that they will cancel out each other, thus in effect ignoring the problem.[21] Or to state this rule in a more favorable way, the resolution of uncertainty can be left to the discretion of the decision maker. Aside from the pragmatic usefulness of such a rule to help reach a decision, the ostrich view of uncertainties is not palatable, since it goes against the necessity for the exercise of responsibility in making informed decisions.

Professor Rodgers suggests other decisional rules adaptable to the resolution of the uncertainty question.[22] He argues that uncertainty can be addressed by assigning burdens of proof. Burdens are assigned in accordance with an underlying policy choice. If the government favors the free market, then the burdens of proof are assigned to the agency to make a convincing case for the proposed action restricting or regulating marketplace activity. Thus the burden tends to favor industry over government. The more compelling case the agency is required to make, the more the free market will be allowed to operate.

Next he suggests a state-of-the-art model. The burden of production is assigned to the party possessing the information or in the best position to obtain it.[23] Once the agency demonstrates that doubts exist about the safety of a practice or policy then the burden of persuasion shifts to those responsible for the creation of the risk. This model favors a free market yet recognizes that government intervention will be necessary in some instances. It is a midpoint on the spectrum between the least-restrictive free-market model and a most-restrictive model that presumes market failure.

The burdens of proof are to reside with proponents of activities that the government decides are unhealthy or unsafe and are thus prohibited unless these presumptions can be overcome. Rodgers's model could be used concurrently; the free-market model could be used for economic regulation, and the regulatory model could be used for health and safety issues. This dichotomy requires some meta-decisional rule to determine which issues or parts of issues are economic and which are health-safety issues.

The advantage of a decisional rule for uncertainty is that parties know who has the burden to close the gaps in data. The problematic part is developing criteria for assigning the burden in a particular way. The assignment of burdens of proof belie particular policy choices and ideologies. Should these policies be consistent through all the agencies? Or should each agency develop their own? Or should certain types of cases— for example, all energy cases, all food and drug cases, or, more narrowly, all nuclear-power cases—use a particular model?

Prelude to Finding Values

This section addresses two intractable and overlapping problems that are central to energy policy and decision making. Science and law in a real sense have separate cultures. This causes some friction and slippage in decision making. We might put law and science on opposing ends of a continuum:

Science	Law
hard	soft
precise	vague
uniform burden of proof	varying burdens
empirical evidence	vague evidence
rules	standards
quantitative	qualitative

Perhaps the interaction of science and law as it evolves into energy policy or energy decisions may finally be considered a political question. Science purists are given no greater share or input into decision-making processes that deal with scientific issues than legal purists have in attempting to fashion a neat and more elegant rule of law regardless of the scientific data. As lawyers we stand in awe of the exactitude of science and of the luxuriousness of the scientific method, but these are technologies for fact finding and empirical truths. Lawyers, using various formulations of an adversary system, have a fact-finding system that is imprecise, that has been accused of disregarding truth, and that most likely has disregarded truth. We as lawyers have attempted to justify our methods by a jurisprudence known as legal positivism.

Legal method and scientific method are different. Whereas, the strength of the scientific method lies in its ability to find empirical truths, after rigorous testing, the strength of the legal system lies in its ability to find human values such as reason and intent. Where one system is deficient, the other is strong. Law plays loosely with the facts, which are bent and shaped by the litigants and the lawyers. Science meanwhile gives far less credence to the nontechnical human and social values inherent in scientific pursuit.

Recognizing these differences we argue that lack of certainty is not fatal. Rather, lack of certainty is both necessary and desirable in a legal decision-making system. Further, the lacunae of certainty provides us, society and legal decision-making institutions, with a place to inject human values. The idea that subjective values can enter the decision-making processes in not without serious problems in a democratic society. How we go about ascertaining those values is the subject of the next chapter.

Our modest claim in this chapter is that normative values are part of the energy decision-making process and should be welcomed as such explicitly. Clear thinking about technological and scientific decisions and a search for positive answers yield important information and point up sensitive questions on nontechnical issues. The bureaucratic mentality, the overreliance on cost-benefit analysis, the complexities of science and technology, the uncertainties surrounding many energy decisions, and our pluralistic society require hard choices. The choices that must be made are based not only on positive data but on human values as well. Both rationales for a decision, the positive scientific and normative human, should be articulated by the decision maker.

Notes

1. *See, e.g.,* Arrow, *Introduction: The Social Choice Perspective,* 9 Hofstra L. Rev. 1373 (1981); Watson, *Society's Choice and Legal Change,* 9 Hofstra L. Rev. 1473 (1981); and Gibbard, *Social Choice Theory and the Imperfectability of a Legal Order,* 10 Hofstra L. Rev. 401 (1982).

2. *See, e.g.,* Loevinger, *Law and Science as Rival Systems,* 1966 Jurimetrics J. 63.

3. *See, e.g.,* B. Ackerman & W. Hassler, Clean Air/Dirty Coal at 116, where the authors argue that certain Clean Air Act provisions were wasteful: "Yet the proud legislative affirmation of the symbol of technology-forcing only serves to raise doubts about the extent to which technology can answer our ecological predicament."

4. J. Feibleman, Scientific Method (1972). This book forms the basis for this section.

5. E. Levi, An Introduction to Legal Reasoning (1949).

6. At least until a scientific revolution. *See* T. Kuhn, The Structure of Scientific Revolutions (2d ed. 1970).

7. Gelpe & Tarlock, *The Uses of Scientific Information in Envi-*

ronmental Decisionmaking, 48 S. Cal. L. Rev. 371 (1974); E. Cleary et al. (eds.), McCormick on Evidence (2d ed. 1972).

    8. *See generally*, Gelpe & Tarlock *supra* note 7.

    9. M. Wessel, Science and Conscience (1980), and Yellin, *High Technology and the Courts: Nuclear Power and the Need for Institutional Reform*, 94 Harv. L. Rev. 489 (1981). Lon Fuller calls such decisions "polycentric":

> We may visualize this kind of situation by thinking of a spider web. A pull on one strand will distribute tensions after a complicated pattern throughout the web as a whole. Doubling the original pull will, in all likelihood, not simply double each of the resulting tensions but will rather create a different complicated pattern of tensions.

Fuller, *The Forms and Limits of Adjudication*, 94 Harv. L. Rev. 353, 395 (1978).

    10. *See* Chayes, *The Role of the Judge in Public Law Litigation*, 89 Harv. L. Rev. 1281 (1976).

    11. The following quote is from B. Ackerman and W. Hassler, Clean Coal/Dirty Air 24–25 (1981):

> [W]e cannot rely on the courts to make up for the failures of the administrative process. Not only did the EPA readily evade the court of appeals' effort to prompt policy reconsideration, but the flow of litigation only directed attention away from the need for long-range planning. Nor was this distortion an unhappy accident. Environmental litigation is typically generated by actions in the here and now that catalyze environmental anxieties—the building of a new plant, the refusal to clean up an old one. No less important, a successful lawsuit against a particular plant will (ultimately) yield a palpable sense of victory for both the environmental lawyer and his clients. In contrast, a lawsuit to compel the agency to engage in sophisticated long-range planning is a daunting prospect. Not only is it harder to sustain public interest in a complex and esoteric debate, but there is a danger that the lawsuit will never end—with the lawyers sinking without a trace in an endless series of remands and reconsiderations. While environmental lawyers deserve great praise for taking on a surprising number of these unrewarding lawsuits, the cases discussed here—and many others— suggest that litigation obscures as much as it instructs. There is no substitute for creating *bureaucratic* incentives that will reward officials themselves for informed decisions. (footnote omitted).

    12. Kantrowitz, *Controlling Technology Democratically*, 63 Am. Scientist 505, 506–7 (1975); and *see* Kantrowitz, *The Science Court Experiment: Criticism and Responses*, 33 Bull. Atom. Sci. 44 (1977).

    13. Martin, *The Proposed "Science Court,"* 75 Mich. L. Rev. 1058, 1059 (1977).

14. Task Force of the Presidential Advisory Group on Anticipated Advances in Science and Technology, *The Science Court Experiment: An Interim Report,* 193 Science 653–59 (1976).

15. Kantrowitz, *supra* note 12, 63 Am. Scientist at 507.

16. Task Force, *supra* note 14, at 654–55.

17. *Science Court: High Officials Back Test of Controversial Concept,* 194 Science 167, 169 (1976); *see also,* Casper, *Technology Policy and Democracy: Is the Proposed Science Court What We Need?* 194 Science 29 (1976).

18. Yellin, *supra* note 9, at 551–53. A related and substantial problem for judicial decision-making occurs when one questions the efficacy of a jury trial. Should juries hear complex cases? The constitutional guarantee to a jury trial can be used to distort and obfuscate complex technical issues or it can be used to present the more open-ended, human-value types of questions. Yet that in itself may be a distortion of complex issues by a process of simplification. *See, e.g., In re* Japanese Electronic Products Antitrust Litigation, 631 F.2d 1069 (3rd Cir. 1980); and, Note, *The Right to a Jury Trial in Complex Civil Litigation,* 92 Harv. L. Rev. 898 (1979).

19. Wessel, *supra* note 9, at 173–93.

20. B. Ackerman, Social Justice in the Liberal State 21–23 (1980). We borrow the phrase "perfect technology of justice" and the concept of the externalities of decision-making processes from Ackerman. We do not argue that these concepts necessarily have imbedded in them the philosophical attributes of the liberalism that is discussed in Ackerman's book. Although we are sympathetic to Ackerman's analysis it is tangential to this work.

21. *See* Farago, *Intractable Cases: The Role of Uncertainty in the Concept of Law,* 55 N.Y.U.L. Rev. 195 (1980).

22. Rodgers, *Benefits, Costs and Risks: Oversight of Health and Environmental Decisionmaking,* 4 Harv. Envtl. L. Rev. 191 (1980).

23. *See* R. Posner, The Economics of Justice, 8–9 (1981). Posner defines uncertainty as "risk and as ignorance." A decisional rule then would place the burden on the person or persons best able to cover the risk or ascertain the information.

10 Methods of Decision Making

Energy decision making does not and cannot take place solely within the vacuum of a sequestered scientific and technologial empirical inquiry. Science and technology are necessary and vital to energy decision makers, but they do not go far enough. Society's assimilation of scientific and technological advances is as much a part of the decision-making continuum as is the scientific material itself. The organic response of the law to the society in which it grows must include not only the statistics, but also the reasons for their existence. Assuming, in energy decision making, the need not only for scientific analysis but also for value reflection and judgments, the questions of the best forum and the best method for weaving the two systems together must be answered.

Decision Makers

Four distinct bodies of energy decision makers have been noted: the president, the Congress, the judiciary, and the administrative agencies. Given a fairly workable system of checks and balances and judicial review, no one decision maker can become an "energy czar" or "energy despot." However, each individual or collegial body shares the responsibility to make not only correct but good choices for society. No decision maker can ignore the value judgments inherent in a major energy decision. Thus, whoever is charged with the duty to make an energy decision weighs not only the scientific and technical data placed before him but the fears and aspirations of the people as well. The weight the subjective-value-judgment aspect carries will differ from decision maker to decision maker and from decision to decision. The basis of this variation depends on such factors as general applicability of the decision, availability and quality of review, and the degree of political accountability of the decision maker. A presidential executive order to promote nuclear energy rather than conservation of existing energy resources would be an example of a decision carrying profound, sensitive ethical implications. Such a policy agenda sets out a general initiative not requiring nor capable of quantitative precision. Although review of the president's statement is rarely undertaken by the judicial system, a president's energy initiatives are subject to the will of Congress in implementing the policy. Congress is

173

subject to the constraints of the electoral system. Even the most obvious energy decision maker—the president—is not omnipotent or even pivotal in our system of government.

The variables affecting the weight of qualitative issues in energy decision making are appraised in this chapter, drawing from the scholarly literature surrounding the U.S. Supreme Court's use of value inquiry in its decision making. This analysis reveals methods that preeminent legal decision makers use in their search for values. Although the analogy to the energy decision-making process is imprecise, it can guide decision makers in all sectors. The narrow model of judicial decision making may be used in the larger spectrum if the necessary adjustments are made.

The Rule of Law and Value Choices

The energy decision making discussed in this book is bounded by the legal framework of governance. One continuing doctrine is that of stare decisis, a rule developed during the period of the elaboration of the common law. The doctrine simply requires that subsequent cases adhere to decided cases. Today, particularly in administrative law, case law is only one source of law. Other sources include statutes and agency decisions, rules and regulations. The different branches of government, and a fortiori, the decision makers within those branches, are required to follow the law. Thus, decisions must be made within previously established rules of law. The only cases with which we are concerned are those that cannot be answered by positive law. Value issues arise most often when there are gaps in the prevailing case law or in statutes or regulations and the decision maker is required to fill those gaps. It is in these interstices as well as in areas of uncertainty that value choices assume significance.

This chapter discusses the articulation of values by legal decision makers when the value choices are not directed by an existing legal structure or by existing laws. If the decision maker makes a value choice clearly outside established parameters, the decision is illegitimate and void. More often the decision maker must interpret and apply general substantive and procedural rules to a specific case; and, in the absence of a perfect fit to the issues, the decision maker must fashion a decision to fit the case. That fashioning process requires value judgments expanding to the limits of the decision maker's discretionary authority. Value choices must also be made: (1) if the decision involves uncertainties, either positive and technical or normative and subjective; (2) if there are ties among alternative policy or value choices; or (3) if the alternatives present paradoxes, posing conflicting choices.[1]

To account for the nuances in decision making created by the limitations of the role of the decision maker would require another book. An executive order based on the president's constitutional authority, for example, differs from an executive order made pursuant to a grant of authority from Congress. Likewise, the enactment of a statute carries with it certain legal presumptions that do not pertain to a proposed regulation of an administrative agency or to an initial decision by a trial court. The executive and the legislative branches are politically directly accountable, whereas administrative-agency officials and judges are not. All this speaks to the scope and range of discretion available to decision makers in making choices. It is given that although the role of the decision maker affects the range of choices available, it does not affect the nature of that choice. Another decision-making variable not dwelt on here is the structural configuration that the decision may take, the subject of part I. Some decisions involve public institutional choices such as the choice of federal agency to be responsible for a particular decision. Should the Environmental Protection Agency (EPA) make decisions affecting coal production, the departments of Energy or Interior, or a combination of agencies? Another significant public institutional issue is whether the states, the federal government, or both should be involved in dealing with a particular controversy. All these are public-policy choices writ large. Another configuration affecting the outcome of a decision is the identity of the parties. Some parties to a controversy may be individuals, private groups, private institutions, or governmental bodies. The individual or private claimant might be involved in a controversy with the government or involved with another individual. The government-versus-individual confrontation is a particularly delicate one. At its essence it deals with the possible suppression by the majority of legitimate minority or individual will, hope, and aspiration. It may pit one decision-making body, the legislature, against another, the court. In a suit between private groups and individuals, private-law devices and rules most often are adequate to handle disputes. In the case of private-party disputes, individual and private value choices are sufficient. Energy decisions rarely can be based on private-law rules, capable of settling the dispute only between private parties. The magnitude, complexity, sophistication, and subtlety of energy issues involve interest beyond those of the individual disputants.[2] These deeper structural issues are intimately connected with the search for values but will not be elaborated further. Although the issues affect the range and depth of the value inquiry, they do not displace its necessity.

Methods for Finding Values

Constitutional scholarship provides themes useful by analogy to the energy decision-making process. Because of the necessity to bridge gaps left in the law and to arrive at conclusions in the face of uncertainty, the Supreme Court's search for values in its decision has provided a study in the use of power that is of use in energy decision making. The role of the judiciary in general and the role of the justices of the Supreme Court in our political system are curious ones if credence is given to the contention that the judicial branch is either the least democratic or simply an antimajoritarian branch of government.[3] Taking that view of the Court to heart, a good amount of the scholarship, indeed the jurisprudence as written by the Court itself, seeks to limit the range of functions performed by the Court.[4]

When the Court speaks on constitutional issues, methods of reviewing those decisions are limited. The Court can exercise a self-imposed, prudential restraint, a constitutional amendment can undo what the Court has done, or the executive branch through the president may refuse to enforce a Supreme Court decision. The first method does not avoid a Court pronouncement but merely limits it. The second method is cumbersome, there being only four constitutional amendments so directed in nearly two centuries. The third method of review precipitates a constitutional crisis. Thus, because of the stature of the Supreme Court, the literature regarding its methodology for value inquiry is cautious at best.

The analogy from the Supreme Court to energy decision making is appropriate, because the Supreme Court is often called on to fill in gaps in the law caused by either general open-ended constitutional provisions, novel initial interpretations of statutes, changing political tempers, or technological innovations that present new controversies. The various methods we will review, of which we choose eight, not only are models for constitutional decision making but also serve the types of multifaceted disputes we have concentrated on as well. Most energy decisions are made within the framework of administrative agencies with the availability of judicial review. Thus, not unlike administrative-law judges and federal-court judges, Supreme Court justices are relatively isolated from the electorate and are thus less politically accountable. Also, like constitutional adjudication in the Supreme Court, energy issues have implications for society at large, going beyond the narrow interests of the parties in the traditional bipolar private-law suit. A decision made by an agency, although it usually does not have the notoriety of a Supreme Court decision, may have a greater and more direct impact on society because of the magnitude and sensitivity of the issues involved. Energy decision making then, when viewed only from the perspective of administrative agencies with available judicial review, could be considered antidemocratic. Yet when put into a broader framework, combined with executive- and legislative-branch decision making on energy issues, this antidemocratic element is less noticeable. Indeed if the system is viewed as a whole, instead of examining a particular branch in isolation, its process works fairly democratically.[5]

With that caveat, we will discuss various methods ascribed to judges (which, in turn, can be ascribed to all energy decision makers) to be used for purposes of examining the normative issues and values involved in complex energy decisions. One more point must be made about these methods. They are diverse on the surface. Below that surface they conflict at deeper levels and present contrary views of our democratic polity. The contrariety of position is so extreme that one scholar has called the controversy over judicial review ''essentially incoherent and unresolvable.''[6] To enter the fray of this debate, indeed to extend it into another realm, has serious consequences. The method or methods chosen by decision makers for value inquiry are not contentless and ideologically free, hence the method chosen directly affects democratic processes.

A Guiding Hypothetical

To make the discussion of these various methods of value inquiry more intelligible we will refer to a concrete example. The Atomic Energy Act has substantially granted to the federal government almost exclusive control over nuclear-power production to the exclusion of the states.[7] Yet the federal government does not have complete jurisdiction. How should a decision maker such as a federal-district-court judge decide the ambiguous case, such as whether a state might impose a bonding requirement on the operator of a nuclear-power plant? In the event of mishap, some degree of protection to workers and the public would thus be available. The effect of the decision to invalidate the state requirement for purposes of this hypothetical will be construed as pro-nuclear power and centrist. A decision sustaining the bonding requirement on the other hand will be considered anti-nuclear power and favoring decentralization. First, the decision maker must examine applicable law, the statutes and regulations and cases interpreting them. In this hypothesis they are inconclusive. What then should the decision maker do? Positive and empirical findings of fact must be made. Then the subjective, value issues must become an integral part of the decision-making process. In this case, the value issue is whether the states should be given a role in nuclear-energy policy-making.

The Decision Maker's Own Values

At least a theoretical case can be made out for letting decisionmakers utilize their own values.[8] The theory would posit that the system of selection or appointment of decision makers is based on a meritocracy within which the best and brightest are chosen. Under this theory in administrative agencies, administrative law judges and commissioners would be the most qualified to exercise the expertise required by the agency. In the court system, a system designed to define and assign rights and values, judges would be the guardians of those rights and values, therefore people would be selected and appointed who would best fulfill these important roles. This meritocratic selection system, coupled with judicial and appellate review and combined with the checks and balances of the other branches of government, helps allay the fears that decision makers would become despotic and antidemocratic. Arguably, such a system compliments our tripartite political heritage by allowing judges to fill gaps in the law, thus fulfilling their law-creative as well as their law-determinative function. Decision making in this manner allows for substantive adaptation and flexibility as well as procedural certainty, that is, decisions are certain to be made. This flexibility is extremely important, the argument continues, for the law must maintain its dynamic quality, reflecting human values. These values can be infused into the cases by human judges, who deal with the normative aspects of uncertain cases by recourse to their intuition and discretion rather than refusing to consider areas of uncertainty or to allow for random selection.[9]

Theory and practice often do not coincide. Anyone involved with the selection process for judges knows that it is politicized. Anyone who has appeared before any number of judges realizes how varied their judicial styles, competence, and temperaments are.

Admittedly, the decision maker's own value standard is the least likely candidate for normative discourse in our technology of justice. Aside from the question of the varying degree of competence and the political nature of the selection process, the standard relying only on the decision makers personal values is too uneven and quixotic. Inherent in the use of such a standard are severe, perhaps intractable, psychological and empirical problems as well as philosophical ones. The selection or appointment of decision maker X, for example, may be based on the selector's understanding of what decision maker X's psychological, philosophical, and political makeup is. Attempting to make that assessment for someone other than ourselves is hazardous business. Even if we are accurate in describing the character of the person selected (psychologically, philosophically, and politically), there is no guarantee that that character will not change.

It is highly unlikely that we can accurately assess our own character let alone that of someone else. How many of us can articulate a philosophy of law and then say with confidence that we plan to adhere to it throughout our career? Further can we articulate and adhere to a philosophy of life on which we can always draw to make value choices? Are we always utilitarians, or do we sometimes believe in categorical statements? Do we base our value judgments on empirical data and observation or intuition? Do we use both? If so do we use both consistently? Are certain decisions, for example, economic ones, always empirical, and others, for example, emotional decisions, always intuitive? Which mode do we employ when the decision has elements of both, such as the decision to take a lower paying job because it promises more satisfaction? Thus, decision makers, indeed all of us, are not as programmable as the theoretical selector of the so-called perfect decision maker would like. If we then allow the selector to say "Yes, decision makers can change, and one variable that I will grant them is that change is acceptable and desirable," this argument at the same time proves too much and too little. It proves too much if the variable we call "change" goes undefined (otherwise changes would be programmed). If this variable goes undefined then value inquiry subjects itself to becoming totally arbitrary, that is, the decision maker could change at will. The question to put to the selector would be "Do you want an arbitrary decision maker?" If the answer is no, then some programmable decision maker is required. If the answer is yes, then we do not need decision makers at all. Random choices can be made. The argument allowing for change proves too little because the selection process that allows for change in judicial character would be that decisionmaker X will only change within a rather narrow and acceptable spectrum, thus reflecting the attitudes of the selectors.

That is the heart of the argument against letting judges use only their own values in a democratic society. Judges usually rise through the ranks of the prestigious and economically, socially, educationally, or politically elite. The selectors are also drawn from an elite corps; thus for selectors to say that change is permissible and desirable means that changes are limited to the narrow range of the selectors' (usually elitist) values.

Natural Law

For purposes of our analogy from Supreme Court decision making to energy decision making, we adopt a working definition of *natural law* as that which refers to theories providing for rules and principles of law that are determined outside of, or antecedently to, the legal system.[10] No fully satisfactory definition of true natural law can be developed here if one could be developed at all. However, we discuss natural-law principles because they can be referred to when the decision maker is faced with uncertainty and the positive law does not give an answer. The natural law can come from so-called conventional morality,[11] or the collective psychology, or sense of society, or God.

If a decision maker then saw it as her function to apply conventional morality (society's widely shared standard of conduct), it would not reflect the decision maker's or the institution's morality. Rather the choice would reflect society's moral principles. The problem in such a choice is that it is, in a pluralistic society, devilishly subjective and controversial. What are these principles? Where do we find them? Will George Gallup or Daniel Yankelovich or the Bible guide us? Should the decision maker read opinion polls conducted by the *New York Times* or the *National Enquirer* to divine society's values? How many of the readers of this book blanche at the thought of having a *People Magazine* survey set the tone for our value discourse? How many readers read or have read *People Magazine?* How many of you on reflection are struck by the hubris of your reaction to *People Magazine?* Might not *People Magazine* reflect a more accurate picture of what's going on in society outside the walls of university buildings? Would we rather be governed by the values of entrenched elites or, as William F. Buckley once said, by the first two hundred people in the Boston telephone directory?

Clearly, it is the discernment of what constitutes conventional morality that creates the difficulty. And as we write from the academe we must recognize the risk of losing our prestigious perch if we follow conventional mores. Assume we accept that risk of disentrenchment, standards and values must still be found to follow and apply natural law. It has been written that "to discern a society's conventional morality one must live in the society become sensitive to it, experience widely, read extensively, and ruminate, reflect, and analyze situations that seem to call moral obligations into play."[12] That being the case then playwrights or poets probably have decision-making training superior to that of lawyers. (Aside from its political practicality, given the unknowability of the right answers, particularly in the energy context, poets may not be such a bad choice!)

How natural law is defined decides where and to whom decision makers look for guidance in ascertaining what the natural or higher-law principles are. Should judges look to moralists, pollsters, psychologists, or priests for sustenance? If natural law is divinely inspired rather than the product of conventional morality then to which god do we look—the god of the New Testament, the Old Testament, the Koran, the teachings of Buddha, or the sayings of Reverend Moon? The difficulty in defining natural law is the integral problem in its application. As Professor Ely says: the advantage in using natural law is that you can invoke natural law to support anything you want—the disadvantage is that everybody understands that.[13]

The content of natural law then suffers from the ability to ingest too much. At the same time natural law can swallow proposition *A* and proposition *not A*. In our hypothetical "the federal government then should make nuclear policy rather than the states," and "the states should make nuclear policy rather than the federal government," are two contradictory propositions that can be sustained by a broader proposition that says "cooperative federalism is an important value." Natural law, depending on which decision-makers view of it we adopt, can be used to support all three conclusions.

Even if contradictions were disallowed, the content of natural law can be so general as to be incapable of meaningful practical application. The admonition to "do good" or to "see that justice is served" does not give sufficient guidance for the resolution of hard cases. Perhaps the decision maker should look for more content-specific natural laws such as "you shouldn't fool mother nature." Thus, a decision might be upheld by the maxim underlying the regulation or the principle that society should be slow to implement nuclear policy. What if the chosen natural law was "technology is good?" Then the regulation would be overturned in favor of moving ahead. The problem should be obvious. Even if we reject, which we do, subjectivism or ethical relativism, at least those brands that say all value judgments are of equal stature, leaving one value no better than another, the description of the content of natural law remains difficult. In fact, to define the content of natural law another set of principles must be used.[14]

Neutral Principles

The concept of *neutral principles* in the judicial process was developed in a seminal article by Herbert Wechsler of Columbia Law School: "I put it to you that the main constituent of the judicial process is precisely that it must be genuinely principled, resting with respect to every step that is involved in reaching judgment on analysis and reasons quite transcending the immediate result that is achieved."[15]

The neutral-principles method faces an immediate content problem. On their face neutral principles appear contentless and aspire to achieve that state. However, procedural rules and processes are not devoid of values.[16] So-called neutral principles can be applied in such a way or indeed chosen or defined so as to reach a particular outcome. Below the surface of this definition an argument can easily be made that neutral principles are essentially conservative because they pay tribute to the status quo.

Wechsler's essay, written in 1959 in response to a lecture the year before by Judge Learned Hand, was critical of some of the segregation decisions of the early Warren court. Nevertheless, the cogency of Wechsler's argument endures.[17] Using Wechsler's definition we can look at the elements of the method of decision making by neutral principles. First, reasons for every issue should be given. Second, the decision should not be result oriented, another way of saying that principled reasoning gives way to rationalization, rather the opinion must transcend the outcome of the given case. Third, the reasons for the decisions should be neutral. Fourth, reasons for the decision must be general.

In our hypothetical, the decision maker is asked to validate or nullify a bonding requirement. This case may deal with a variety of issues, including whether legitimate authority for imposing or implementing a bonding requirement exists. Most issues in most cases should be dispensed with through the application of the positive law. An obvious first neutral principle would be to decide cases on existing law. But those cases concern neither Wechsler nor us. Precedent is an ingrained element of our legal system. The troublesome points are the hard cases that cannot be decided on the basis of extant law alone. Assuming resolution of all of the positive issues in the hypothetical, a point that allows either choice is reached—the regulation will be upheld or invalidated. The first element requires that reasons for this issue be given. But which set of reasons?

Whichever reasons are chosen they should not work backward from the result. As a matter of psychology and intellectual integrity it is difficult, if not impossible, to disassociate the end result from the means and to place outcome and reasons in separate compartments. Yet the premise is that reasoning should precede, as best as possible, the result, that logic should be utilized and that the use of reason and logic in this manner reduces the amount of capriciousness in decision making. Decision makers should suspend judgment until all the evidence is in, it has been examined, arguments have been made, and all pertinent matters have been analyzed. In this way it is hoped that better opinions will result, that they will be perceived as appropriate, and that such a process promotes the development of law.[18]

The next two elements set out in the principles of decision making espoused by Wechsler are the crucial ones—neutrality and generality. According to Greenwalt, "A person gives a neutral reason, in Wechsler's sense, if he states a basis for a decision that he would be willing to follow in other situations to which it applies."[19] If the decision maker would uphold a bonding requirement on the basis that the states should have a say in setting electric-energy policy and related health and safety issues, would the decision maker reach the same result when the state proposes a bonding requirement on the owner of a solar-energy company? If so, then the decision is consistent with the neutrality principle. If however, the decision maker upholds the bonding requirement in the case of nuclear power and invalidates it pertaining to the solar-energy company, then the reasons for these two results must be consistent according to the neutrality principle. The espoused reason given is that states should have some say in setting electric-energy and related health and safety policy. Following that, however, the requirement should be upheld in both cases. But, the reason for the decision maker's different outcomes are anti-nuclear and pro-alternative energy biases. The reasoning behind the two decisions is inconsistent. The neutrality principle has been violated, and the divergent opinion in the cases can be rightly criticized.

It is relatively simple for the decision maker to satisfy the neutrality element in both cases. The decision maker need only say that the state discourages the development of nuclear energy and promotes solar energy. Then there is no violation of the neutrality principle. This requirement has the virtue of calling on decision makers to think out the actual basis for their ruling and explicitly state those reasons.

The last element of the neutral-principle process requires that the opinion be general. Assume our decision maker says that the bonding regulations should be upheld because states should have a say in electric-power and health and safety policymaking. The generality test will be satisfied if that reason for the decision will be applied in the next case. Suppose the next case is a rate-regulation case in which the issue is whether to allow $100 million of construction work in progress (CWIP) costs for a nuclear generator in the rate base. Assume further that if states handle the problem differently than the federal government that distortions in the interstate market would result. Assume further that existing law does not resolve the issue. Using the rationale developed in the bonding-requirement case, that states should have a say in making electric-power policy, should the decision maker disallow the CWIP (which would be consistent with the principle) or allow CWIP to create a unified market? This latter alternative violates the generality test. One difficulty with the theory of the neutral-principles test is that decision makers are not pre-scient, nor should they be. Nevertheless, decision makers can develop a rule that they would not be fearful to apply in the next case. Generality requires that the reason articulated give guidance as to how related situations should be treated.

The reasons advanced for neutral principles of decision making are that better opinions, which are understood as such, will result, and therefore the law will develop in a more desirable manner for society as a whole. Should all opinions be written with such a pattern or would such an opinion conflict with other goals? In *Duke Power,* for example, what if the Court's reasons for sustaining the Price-Anderson Act were that nuclear power is a good policy, that the legislative history of the Atomic Energy Act demanded sustaining the act, and that North Carolina's bureaucracy for developing nuclear energy was inadequate to deal with the sophistication required to administer a nuclear program?[20] Can or should the decision maker reach a result without addressing all the issues or by obscuring the issues, thus giving false reasons? Is the opinion made on policy, history, positive law, personal morals, or psychological fear? The neutral principles ask decision makers to state what the balance of these factors is. Arguably, if the decision maker has either obscure or spurious reasons for the opinion then such reasons should be kept out of the decisions, allowing the law to evolve, letting its dynamic operate as the opinion takes hold in society, receives scholarly attention, and is applied to subsequent cases. This type of spurious decision making clearly violates the neutral-principles-theory demand for an honest rationale for every branch of the opinion. It violates the point of this book. Admittedly, decision making is difficult. It is complex, and it deals with uncertainties in values as well as in technology and law. However, if society is to have some basis for understanding how the decision-making system operates, the underlying rationale for the decisions that come from it must be articulated. Decision makers who attempt to hide behind spurious reasons of obfuscation for their actions must be called to task—forced by those affected by the decision to clarify, to lay out before them their thought process. Decision making within our legal system will retain its vitality only if it is made on an open record and not behind closed doors or smoke screens.

Reason

The methods of decision making discussed previously are obviously not discrete. They often overlap and incorporate elements of each other. The use of reason is not exception. At some point in each of these methods the powers of reason must be invoked. Even if we were to argue persuasively that hard choices could be made by a process of random selection, we would give a supporting reason for that statement such as "randomness gives every viewpoint an equal chance at being expressed" or "equality of opportunity is fair and just." In this section we seek to carry reason to an extreme position by making it the paramount method for value discourse. Reason then will be explored in its unadulterated and dispassionate form. It will be shown to be a point at which the decision maker can achieve objectivity and disinterestedness so that decisions are devoid of the biases and prejudices of the decider. The process of reasoning simply means that right conclusions are drawn from right premises. Herein lies the hidden issue. Who formulates the premises and how are they formulated? In chapter 9 we described the process of law, arguing that the legal process, in contradistinction to the scientific process, was more open and sensitive to the human element of a controversy. The character, feeling, tone, context, and passions of the parties invariably affect the way a case is shaped. Can we expect less from a decision maker, even one using so-called reason? Without swearing allegiance to a legal realist credo, decision makers cannot help but be affected by the drama in which they are principal actors. To remove the passion of the play would be to return to an era of mechanical jurisprudence, or to update it, justice by computer. That lawsuits cannot be programmed is a strength of the system, not a weakness. It gives our legal institution its resilience and meaning.

An extreme use of reason *qua* reason presents a problem of inclusion and exclusion. Will a ''reasonable decision'' incorporate emotional elements in the decision-making matrix? A reasonable decision is not solely based on cold logic but includes emotion, passion, thoughts, conjectures, attitudes, feelings, beliefs, and so on. The problem here is the ''and so on.'' Where does it end? By defining reason so broadly we run the risk of having the concept collapse under its own weight. The definition expands to the point that everything is included, even seemingly contradictory things such as intuition.

Finally, legal reasoning is not truly precise. ''The finding of similarity or difference is the key step in the legal process.''[21] Our legal system is premised on the existence of gaps in the fabric of the law and suggests how best to fill the gaps. The system should not seek merely to complete the grand equation in which all the variables are known. Thus, legal reasoning is neither an exclusively inductive nor deductive process. It is reasoning by example, and the examples are drawn from real life, actual controversies. This brings into the legal decision-making process the active, perhaps ill-formed ideas of society, ideas in need of resolution. Mechanical formulae do not fit such a process.

Tradition

The use of tradition as a method of finding values is more appropriate, to the extent that it is appropriate at all, in constitutional adjudication.[22] For purposes of energy decision making our tradition is a limited one, and instead of recourse to the Constitution, the debates surrounding it and other U.S. state papers—the ''sacred texts'' examined—are the legislative histories of statutes bearing on the problem under consideration. In our decision-making hypothetical the tradition consists of about twenty-five years of experience with commercial nuclear power, the Atomic Energy Act, the Price-Anderson Act, and some related statutes. The situation has been narrowed as one not answerable by a review of the statutes, regulations, or relevant cases. These normally would be the contolling sources of law. Extracurricular reading is necessary. The congressional debate surrounding the passage of the statutes, internal governmental reports such as Nuclear Regulatory Commission docu-ments, as well as an understanding of other relevant bills introduced in Congress and industry studies can all provide valuable information bearing on the problem to be resolved. This latter set of data is not controlling law.

Again, our decision maker is faced with the basic issue of whether the states or the federal government should control or have an input into nuclear-power policy. Clearly the positive law favors federal preemption of state authority. History shows that the centralization of the commercial development of nuclear power was felt necessary during the mid-1950s when the country was adapting commercial nuclear-reactor capability from military usage. At that time, nuclear power was completely con-trolled by the federal government. The government was needed to finance, subsidize, and oversee the transition. The consensus was that nuclear power could be a cheap and safe way to generate electricity.

What happens, though, when the tradition is ill founded? Today a case can be made that the good-faith beliefs in the economy and safety of nuclear power were misplaced. In the 1950s it was assumed that the risks from catastrophic accidents could be minimized. Dangers surrounding waste disposal, it was hoped, would be eliminated as would transportation and storage issues over time as technology progressed. And, in the 1950s the country's sensitivity to environmental problems had not reached the consciousness of the late 1960s and 1970s. All these matters are reflected in litigation and public protests, documentation of which is available to the decision maker. This history is reflected in various pieces of legislation introduced in Congress to give the states some say in this area.

So, if the decision maker chooses to rely on tradition we must rec-ognize that there are many traditions from which to choose. If a particular time frame is selected, for example, the 1950s or 1970s, does the decision maker attempt to re-create the moral climate of a previous era or use a contemporary viewpoint or some mixture of both?

As lawyers we are not unfamiliar with the argument that there is history and there is lawyer's history.[23] As far as nuclear power is con-cerned, the decision maker can describe a tradition that owes its allegiance to the thought that led to *Northern States Power Co.*—a tradition of maximum federal preemption. Or the decision maker might employ a more revisionist posture and argue that the development of tradition since the 1950s shows that emphasis on federal government preemption to the maximum extent feasible is misplaced, that the industry has not developed as predicted, and that social consciousness of these events dictates another countervailing tradition. We lawyers are a clever lot, why else would the Bard wish us hanged? The point is that, if the rewriting of history depends on the clever exegesis and the selective use of historical texts and documents, then this is a less-than-solid methodology for finding values.

Even assuming that a tradition could be found, it is hard to accept the proposition that yesterday's majority should control today's.[24] Indeed, what will be found will not be some categorical imperative. Rather, the found values will be those of the searcher—a point that has been repeatedly made through this chapter. That being the case, perhaps we delude ourselves into thinking anything else can result. Perhaps we should be satisfied with the recognition that the values of the decision makers will ultimately find their way into the decision. It is better to assume that as a given, recognize it as such, and be explicit about it. That is a grand conclusion, but it needs to go a step further, accepting the point that these methods, to a greater or lesser extent, force the decision maker to evaluate and reevaluate what his values are. Often this evaluation is tested against some standard, elusive though it may be. Here we view tradition. In all likelihood the decision maker's values will be influenced by the search for that tradition.

Consensus

This methodology views the decision maker as the conduit of public opinion—or views the decision maker as pollster. The attractiveness of such a method is that it is an attempt to create a more broad-based constituency for what are the least-democratic branches of government. The decision maker can thus hide the flaws of the process under a mantle of societal representation. The consensus method is also attractive because not only does it attempt to reduce bias on the part of the decision maker but also it gives the law the fluidity to which it aspires. The lacunae in the law are filled with popular values as ascertained by a decision maker. But how is that ascertainment accomplished? Assessing public opinion is a specialized profession. Policymakers are not trained as social scientists. Access is another determinative factor in this method's use. Who has access to decision makers? In suits between private individuals, the adversary system itself, when it functions smoothly, ensures that each side has equal access to the decision maker. Any distortion that is created can be remedied by the parties to the litigation. But that is not true with socioscientific disputes of the magnitude present in energy matters. The access problem has two facets to it, both of which question the nature of the consensus theory as a fundamentally democratic one. If unequal representation is a reality and all interests are not adequately represented in suits before decision makers, then the information they use as the basis for decision is skewed and incomplete. Consequently, by force of unequal weight of these data, the decision must be inadequate. The data-collection mechanisms to determine consensus that do exist are grossly imperfect. Congress itself makes decisions in response to uneven pressure exerted by various interest groups. This situation may be aggravated in agencies and courts.

Even if equality of access is assumed, there is no guarantee that a consensus exists to be found. The consensus that is discovered most likely reflects the domination of one interest group over another.[25]

Thus the consensus might be controlled by the so-called center or by a plurality, dominating all other groups. A more likely scenario than group domination is fractionated public opinion. Pluralistic interest groups form on so many fronts that coalition or consensus building has become an impossibility and has created a crisis of authority.[26] The arguments against finding tradition because the search is too distorted by temporal, spatial, and interpretive considerations and the arguments against finding natural law because there is too much to find or it is too general, also apply to finding consensus. There are too many consensuses, and if we attempt to agree on a general principle, for example, ''a strong economy is good,'' we find that it is a principle of limited useful application. Finally, consensus is what the consensus maker sees.[27]

Again this discussion is more appropriately placed in the context of which decision maker or decision-making institution is best suited to use which method. This consensus-finding approach clearly has more vitality in a legislative arena or is better exercised by a president who is elected with a certain proposition as part of his or her platform than by a judge energy decision maker.

Predicting Progress

In a sense the prediction of progress is an amalgam of the use of reason, tradition, and consensus. If one views the judiciary as a mirror rather than a vehicle for social change, one could argue that instead of reflecting and reporting on what has happened the court should be somewhat predictive and forward looking. Thus, through the use of reason, extrapolating tradition in the way the decision maker believes the future will be formed, the decision maker can make a statement about the future through its decision. Because this method is comprised of parts of others, it is subject to the faults of those methodologies as well as its own. The primary fault of the method is simply that prognostication is a most imprecise combination of art and science. No one could have predicted with precision the curious chain of events eventually causing the Three Mile Island incident. Even after the nuclear fallout from that incident had mostly settled, the financial consequences of the mishap surprised everyone, including the owners of the Three Mile Island plant. How plant cleanup and premature-decommissioning costs were to be carried on the utilities books and allocated among ratepayers, shareholders, and government is a wildly controversial issue. The financial impact of that event could be the death knell for the private financing of the nuclear-power industry as well as other high-technology capital-intensive energy projects. The immediate resolution and impact of these issues are unclear even as we deal with them. Predicting their full effects is close to impossible. Thus, the decision maker, in an attempt to conform a decision with some sense of the idea of progress, might aim at placing the decision in the realm of future values. In the instance of nuclear power the crystal ball is extremely murky. The financial community's fears seem to have abated ever so slightly. This may be a temporary reaction to administration pronuclear statements. Yet Reagonomics vis-à-vis government support of industry appear now to be clearly against federal subsidization of the energy industry—a mixed message if there ever was one.

Also, a solely future-oriented method can be critized as antidemocratic on its face:

> No explanation is given—and I can't see how one could be—why controlling today's generation by the values of its grandchildren is any more acceptable than controlling it by the values of its grandparents: a "liberal accelerator" is neither less nor more consistent with democratic theory than a "conservative brake."[28]

Finally, the subjectivity of the values found in the future will be heavily influenced by the values of the social fortune teller if not identical with those values.

Representation Reinforcing

The representation-reinforcing methodology is one proffered by John Hart Ely and is based on an expansive interpretation of a famous footnote in *United States* v. *Carolene Products Co.*[29]

It is unnecessary to consider now whether legislation which restricts those political processes which can ordinarily be expected to bring about repeal of undesirable legislation, is to be subjected to more exacting judicial scrutiny under the general prohibitions of the Fourteenth Amendment than are most other types of legislation.

Nor need we enquire whether similar considerations enter into the review of statutes directed at particular religious, or national, or racial minorities. Whether prejudice against discrete and insular minorities may be a special condition, which tends seriously to curtail the operation of those political processes ordinarily to be relied upon to protect minorities, and which may call for a correspondingly more searching judicial inquiry. (Citations omitted.)

Ely questions when it is legitimate for the Supreme Court to overturn an action of another branch of government, namely the legislature. The balance of choice between the decision-making authority of a democratic and less-democratic branch when issues are of sufficient magnitude, in Ely's view, should tend toward the more democratic branch.[30]

Primarily concerned with the U.S. Supreme Court functioning as a protector of minorities and as preserver of individual rights, Ely's rule is not calculated to find substantive values, but rather it is a structural one.[31] He asserts that decision makers should seek to protect isolated rights by protecting groups and individuals from being eliminated or diluted by the majority. This goal is to be accomplished by protecting participation in decision-making processes, not necessarily equal participation in benefits. Access to political processes and access to the end products of those processes should not be unfairly hampered:

I have suggested that both *Carolene Products* themes are concerned with participation: they ask us to focus not on whether this or that substantive value is unusually important or fundamental, but rather on whether the opportunity to participate either in the political processes by which values are appropriately identified and accommodated, or in the accommodation those processes have reached, has been unduly constricted.[32]

Participation-oriented representation-reinforcing approaches to judicial review aspire to avoid the imposition of subjective values by judges onto legal schemata. Theoretically, it is process oriented and structural, thus attempting to preserve fundamental political processes so that as different coalitions and constituencies emerge their voices will be heard. Before this scenario is triggered two interrelated events must occur.

First, the decision maker must recognize a malfunctioning in the political process—a political "market failure." This is a decisionmaker-as-referee analogy in which the judge intervenes when one group (the majority) gains an unfair advantage over another group (the minority):

Malfunction occurs when the *process* is undeserving of trust, when (1) the ins are choking off the channels of political change to ensure that they will stay in and the outs will stay out, or (2) though no one is actually denied a voice or a vote, representatives beholden to an effective majority are systematically disadvantaging some minority out of simple hostility or a prejudiced refusal to recognize commonalities of interest, and thereby denying that minority the protection afforded other groups by a representative system.[33]

The second event that must occur is the recognition and definition of the contours of the groups. These events bring back the subjective element of the decision makers themselves as reflected by the affirmative actions necessary to set this methodology in motion. Both of these events call on the decision maker to make a value judgment. The method simply is not value-free or value-neutral. Just below the surface of the participation-protection device lie the inescapable value choices.

Is there a market failure in the case of nuclear energy? Has the game changed so significantly since the 1950s that all bets are off? Which group or groups qualify for protection in the participation-protection plan? Federal centrists? States' rightists? No-nukes activists? Nuclear engineers? Citizens for a Better Tomorrow? The decision maker must decide whose voice is to be heard and the decibel level that voice should achieve.

The Ely model is quite similar to the neutral-principles method. Both are structural, both eschew a substantive-values approach, and both, when applied, call on the decision maker to make significant value choices early on in their application.

Eventually some method is needed to understand which values are being applied and why. Values of the people making choices on behalf of society are permanent features of the energy decision-making structure as well as the broader judicial structure. We wish to underscore their place and make a few suggestions to deal with realities of decision making by human beings for human beings. A decision-making hierarchy should be established. Use of either the participation-protection or neutral principles should come first. Then, when value choices are required, a choice of parts of tradition, consensus, prediction, or natural-law reliance may be necessary. To decide which of the four or combination thereof would be used or in which order, the decision makers own values must be relied upon. This whole hierarchy of method must be tested against some set of values. One that goes through the winnowing of the press, oversight, and public opinion.

It has been suggested that the decision-making problem is essentially incoherent and unresolvable. And a scholar of no less stature than Alexander Bickel was unable to come up with a satisfactory resolution of it.[34] To catalogue the various methods that exist to fill gaps in the law is an exercise serving to reinforce our desire to find solutions to the energy decision-making maze. Clearly no one method is sufficient to solve the political, procedural, and substantive hurdles placed before the motivated energy decision maker. The gaps exist—and we as a society have done a poor job of explaining how they have been patched over and why. Far-reaching social and ethical issues have been sidestepped, smoke-screened, or ignored when they should have been explicitly addressed. To ignore these issues is an abdication of the decision maker's duty, disserving the law and society. Various ways exist to define and apply values. The decision maker must be aware of the methods or processes used, thinking through the consequences and implications of the process selected, and articulate the values relied on and the reasons for the decision.

Notes

1. John Farago, in two articles that examine the nature of legal systems, makes distinctions between discretion, uncertainty, controversy, incompleteness, ties, and paradoxes; for our purposes each poses a gap between positive law and the application of positive law to a particular case for decision. Thus, although we draw on the articles, we do not adopt these distinctions for our analysis. *See* Farago, *Judicial Cybernetics: The Effects of Self-Reference in Dworkin's Rights Thesis,* 14 Val. U.L. Rev. 371 (1980), and Farago, *Intractable Cases: The Role of Uncertainty in the Concept of Law,* 55 N.Y.U. L. Rev. 195 (1980).

2. Jesse Choper, for example, makes a distinction between normative decision making when individual rights as opposed to institutional rights are involved. *See* Judicial Review and the National Political Process Ch. 2 (1980). We argue that such a distinction is unnecessary. Indeed a viable distinction between public and private value choices may be an illusion, *see, e.g.,* Hampshire, *Public and Private Morality,* in Public and Private Morality (S. Hampshire ed. 1978).

3. Choper, *supra* note 2, at Ch. 1. See also, A. Bickel, The Supreme Court and the Idea of Progress (1970); and A. Bickel, The Least Dangerous Branch (1962).

4. *See* A. Cox, The Role of the Supreme Court in American Government (1976); and Ashwander v. T.V.A., 297 U.S. 288 (1936) (Brandeis, J. concurring).

5. Choper, *supra* note 2, at Ch. 1; D. Hofstadter, Godel, Escher & Bach Ch. 10 (1979); Brest, *The Fundamental Rights Controversy: The Essential Contradictions of Normative Constitutional Scholarship,* 90 Yale L.J. 1063 (1981).

6. Brest, *supra* note 5.

7. *See* Northern States Power Co. v. Minnesota, 447 F.2d 1143 (8th Cir. 1971), *aff'd mem.* 405 U.S. 1035 (1972); State Dept. of Environmental Protection v. Jersey Central Power & Light Co., 69 N.J. 102, 351 A.2d 337 (1976); Pacific Legal Foundation v. State Energy Resources Conservation & Dev. Comm'n., 472 F. Supp. 191 (S.D. Cal. 1979); Washington State Building & Construction Trades Council v. Spellman, No. C-81-154 RJM and No. C-81-190 RJM (E.D. Wash. June 26, 1981). *See also,* Woychik, *State Opportunities to Regulate Nuclear Power and Provide Alternative Energy Supplies: Part I,* 15 U.S.F. L. Rev. 129 (1981).

8. The taxonomy is taken from Ely, *Forward: On Discovering Fundamental Values,* 92 Harv. L. Rev. 5 (1978), which is elaborated on in J. Ely, Democracy and Distrust (1980). The discussion of methods is derived from these sources, the authors' views, as well as cited sources.

9. Farago, *supra* note 1, 55 N.Y.U.L.Rev. 195, 238 (1980).

10. *Id.* at 195, n.1.

11. Choper, *supra* note 2, at 4; Brest, *supra* note 5.

12. Brest, *supra* note 5 (quoting Wellington, *Common Law Rules and Constitutional Double Standards,* 83 Yale L.J. 221, 248 (1973)).

13. Ely *supra* note 8, 92 Harv. L. Rev. at 28 (1978).

14. See D. Hofstadter, *supra* note 5, for a thorough description of this recursive function in various contexts.

15. Wechsler, *Toward Neutral Principles of Constitutional Law,* 73 Harv. L. Rev. 1, 15 (1959). Also at 19–20: "A principled decision, in the sense I have in mind, is one that rests on reasons with respect to all the issues in the case, reasons that in their generality and their neutrality transcend any immediate result that is involved."

16. Brest, *The Substance of Process* 42 Ohio St. L.J. 131 (1981).

17. Greenwalt, *The Enduring Significance of Neutral Principles,* 78 Colum. L. Rev. 982 (1978).

18. *Id.* at 994.

19.. *Id.* at 985.

20. Duke Power Co. v. Carolina Environmental Study Group, Inc., 438 U.S. 59 (1978).

21. E. Levi, An Introduction to Legal Reasoning (1949).

22. Sandalow, *Constitutional Interpretation,* 49 Mich. L. Rev. 1033 (1981).

23. W. Harbaugh, Lawyer's Lawyer 508–512 (1973).

24. Ely, *supra* note 8, 92 Harv. L. Rev. at 42.

25. As gracefully demonstrated by Robert Nozick in his discussion of the redistribution of wealth, the middle 2 percent can control a question:

[W]hy don't the least well-off 51 percent of the voters vote for redistributive policies that would greatly improve their position at the expense of the best-off 49 percent? The fact will seem puzzling until one notices that the bottom 51 percent is not the only possible (continuous) voting majority; there is also, for example, the top 51 percent. Which of these two majorities will form depends on how the middle 2 percent votes. It will be in the interests of the top 49 percent to support and devise programs to gain the middle 2 percent as allies. It is cheaper for the top 49 percent to buy the support of the middle 2 percent than to be (partially) expropriated by the bottom 51 percent. The bottom 49 percent cannot offer more than the top 49 percent can to the middle 2 percent in order to gain them as allies. For what the bottom 49 percent offers the middle 2 percent will come (after the policies are instituted) from the top 49 percent; and in addition the bottom 49 percent also will take something for themselves from the top 49 percent. The top 49 percent always can save by offering the middle 2 percent slightly more than the bottom group would, for that way they avoid also having to pay to the remainder of the possible coalition of the bottom 51 percent, namely the bottom 49 percent. The top group will be able always to buy the support of the swing middle 2 percent to combat measures which would more seriously violate its rights.

R. Nozick, Anarchy, State and Utopia 274–75 (1974).

26. T. Lowi, The End of Liberalism (2d ed. 1979).

27. Ely, *supra* note 8, 92 Harv. L. Rev. at 49.

28. *Id*. at 53.

29. 304 U.S. 152 n.4 (1938).

30. Ronald Dworkin has put the matter somewhat differently. The legislature is the proper body for policy arguments, and the judiciary is the proper body for arguments of principle, which he defines as: ''Arguments of policy justify a political decision by showing that the decision advances or protects some collective goal of the community as a whole. . . . Arguments of principle justify a political decision by showing that the decision respects or secures some individual or group right.'' R. Dworkin, Taking Rights Seriously, 82 (1978). This distinction is a neat one, but it does not fit our class of cases. Nor does it seem to comport with what judges are called on to do these days, Chayes, *The Role of the Judge in Public Law Litigation,* 89 Harv. L. Rev. 1281 (1976).

We mention Dworkin to highlight the point we make about Ely in the text. Energy decision making is not the traditional bipolar model. Thus elegant arguments that ignore this assumption are misplaced when it comes to the class of cases we are discussing. Nevertheless, the models that Ely and Dworkin set up help place our discussion in a broader context.

31. Choper also makes this claim. J. Choper, *supra* note 2.

32. Ely *supra* note 8, Democracy and Distrust at 77.

33. *Id.* at 103.

34. See generally, Purcell, *Alexander Bickel and the Post-Realist Constitution,* 11 Harv. C.R.-C.L. L. Rev. 521 (1976).

Conclusion

When we started this book our aim was to examine descriptively some of the law and processes that the federal government uses when decisions are made relative to natural resources used for the production, transportation, and distribution of energy. As our work progressed several themes became apparent. First, even though so-called energy law is a rapidly changing field, the changes take place within a narrow range of options. President Carter's attempt to construct a monolithic bureaucracy was no more successful than will be President Reagan's rhetorical attempt to dismantle his predecessor's creation. Within narrower lines Carter did centralize some decision-making functions and Reagan has already undone, at least de facto, some of that work. In either case an energy decision-making institutional structure is in place, with a recognizable set of parameters. This structure of administrative agencies with judicial review of final agency actions existed and will exist independently of the policy preferences of either president. Both Carter and Reagan, like Nixon and Ford before them, espoused different energy policies. Both can suggest alterations in the system. Both can propose legislation that eventually brings about changes in the substantive rules and regulations that govern decision makers. But neither can dramatically affect the institutional and structural environment within which such decisions are made. The energy agencies contain, by their very bureaucratic nature, forces and an ideology of their own. This is less a political ideology than it is a predisposition to seek and maintain decision-making power. Once energy decisions are made they will continue to be made, absent a congressional mandate that halts the process, because these decisions are supposed to be made—it is in the nature of things.

Second, energy decisions are made by methodologies that are grounded in an economics of scarcity. Ratemaking, cost-benefit analysis, and the more heavy hand of enforcement are designed to maximize economic efficiency in a world of recognizably limited resources. This attitude is of relatively recent origins. The economic prosperity that our nation enjoyed after World War II, which allowed us to indulge in and experiment with social-welfare programs, is luxurious in comparison with the high inflation, high unemployment, and declining growth we have witnessed over the last decade. At the same time we cannot, nor should we abandon the ideals, principles, and aspirations contained in the social-reform efforts that prevailed in the 1960s and early 1970s. The clash of these two world views, that is, the world as a place of scarce resources versus the world as a place capable of satisfying all basic human needs, inevitably produces conflicts and hard choices. Recent energy legislation such as the National Energy Act and the Energy Security Act has imbedded in it both world views. Such a situation presents conflicting choices. These conflicts are aggravated by the fact that the methodologies employed by agencies are economic-efficiency oriented and the governing legislation is less committed to that single goal.

Third, because of the existing institutional structure, which remains largely impervious to the political climate, and because of the clash of goals reflected in the methodologies used by these institutions and in the legislation that guides the institutions, substantive energy law does not form a consistent whole. No uniform, comprehensive national energy policy emerges from the decision-making process. Perhaps this is inevitable in a society that espouses and often encourages pluralism. Perhaps it is inevitable because of the complexities and uncertainties contained in essentially polycentric decisions. At the same time the failure of a comprehensive national energy policy seems odd given the following: a president whose single term was largely devoted to constructing such a policy; an economy that depends on energy production for its very health; a society that developed a reliance and life-style based on an overabundance of cheap energy; and, a legal system that has become, in part by design, more comfortable with, if not desirous of, a greater policymaking role. We argue that the absence of a comprehensive policy is also attributable to the fundamental inability of a legal system that is predominantly procedural to adopt a consistent uniform policy. The reasons for the lack of a national energy policy stem directly from the very sources that made energy decisions possible. Energy decisions are possible because a relatively stable institutional structure exists and because policy-neutral methodologies for decision making are available (even if they are not consistently utilized). Yet these structures and methods generate conflicts in substantive law the result of which is a failure to develop a national policy.

Finally, each of these three points raises questions about the central values of our energy decision-making system. Basic assumptions about law and policy, their interaction, and their institutions and methodologies cannot go unexamined. Is society satisfied with the lack of a national energy policy? Is the institutional structure, which is fairly nonresponsive to exploring value-laden issues and is perhaps incapable of doing so, satisfactory? Are the methods employed by the bureaucracy too positivistic, empirical, scientific, and ecnomic? Should the decision-making apparatus reflect these concerns? We posit that value issues are at the heart of energy decisions and that too often the current decision-making apparatus submerges this aspect of these decisions. We argue that decision makers at all levels cannot and should not escape responsibility for stating, as explicitly as possible, what those value choices are. Further, decisions should be made within a framework that allows an airing of those more-subtle value issues. This is a hard task, but it presents our policy and legal regime with a grand opportunity to reach for a greater understanding of energy questions.

Index

About the Authors

Sheila S. Hollis has practiced law in the energy regulatory field since 1974. She established the first Office of Enforcement at the Federal Energy Regulatory Commission. She is now a partner in the Washington office of the Houston law firm, Butler, Binion, Rice, Cook & Knapp. Since 1979, she has been a professorial lecturer on the subject of energy law at George Washington University National Law Center. A graduate of the University of Colorado with the B.S. in journalism and the J.D. from the University of Denver, Mrs. Hollis has published a variety of articles on the subject of energy law and policy and has lectured extensively on the subject.

Joseph P. Tomain is a professor of law at Drake University Law School. He is a graduate of the University of Notre Dame, where he received the A.B. in government, and he is an honors graduate of the George Washington University National Law Center, where he recieved the J.D. in 1974. After two years of private practice Tomain began teaching, designing one of the first energy-law courses in the country, which he has taught since 1977. He has compiled and edited two editions of class materials and has published *Energy Law in a Nutshell* (1981). He has also published articles on energy law, land use, and the legal profession.